17.99

D1498717

Women Managers Moving On

There has been much speculation about whether women are leaving senior management jobs in significant numbers. *Women Managers Moving On* explores this phenomenon through a qualitative study of sixteen women who have reached middle or senior management levels and paused to review their careers. By telling their stories in detail, Marshall explores experiences of working in male-dominated cultures, of being change agents, decisions to leave, next steps and alternative career patterns. The book invites the reader to reflect on their own assumptions and sense-making as they read, and adopts an open form of presentation to facilitate this.

A true second generation study, this challenging book raises real questions about traditional models of career development.

Judi Marshall is Professor of Organizational Behaviour at the Centre for Action Research in Professional Practice, the School of Management, University of Bath.

Women Managers
Moving On

Exploring Career and Life Choices

Judi Marshall

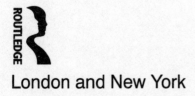

London and New York

First published 1995
by Routledge
11 New Fetter Lane, London EC4P 4EE

Simultaneously published in the USA and Canada
by Routledge
29 West 35th Street, New York, NY 10001

© 1995 Judi Marshall

Typeset in Palatino by
Ponting–Green Publishing Services, Chesham, Bucks
Printed and bound in Great Britain by
Clays Ltd, St. Ives PLC

All rights reserved. No part of this book may be
reprinted or reproduced or utilized in any form or by
any electronic, mechanical, or other means, now known
or hereafter invented, including photocopying and
recording, or in any information storage or retrieval
system, without permission in writing from the
publishers.

British Library Cataloguing in Publication Data
A catalogue record for this book is available from the
British Library

Library of Congress Cataloging in Publication Data
A catalogue record for this book has been requested

ISBN   0–415–09738–X (hbk)
ISBN   0–415–09739–8 (pbk)

Contents

Acknowledgements

I would like to thank:

Rich – for the many forms of support you have given me during this longer than expected project.

Peter – for discussing the inquiry as it went along and helping me clear space to write by taking over some joint jobs.

The research participants – for your openness, commitment, time and energy.

The many people – too numerous to mention – who have encouraged me along the way.

David and Peter – for reading a first-draft text.

Mum and Dad, Eileen and Geoff – for being supportive presences in my life.

My children, Richard and Katie – for tolerating the times when I have been preoccupied or absent because of this research.

Setting the scene

Introduction

INTENTIONS

This book presents stories from sixteen women's lives. The people involved had reached middle or senior level management positions and been successful in career terms. Some then decided to leave employment, some were forced to leave, and some contemplated leaving but eventually stayed.

Their accounts provide detailed grounded data about the possible phenomenon of women leaving management which is now receiving some media and academic attention. The possibility that women are leaving is sometimes used to doubt their commitment to employment, to question whether they are really tough enough to be senior managers, and to justify lukewarm interest in taking equal opportunities thinking further. This book therefore enters contentious territory, but seeks to do so with an attitude of curiosity rather than combat.

Increasing numbers of women are now aspiring to have careers. This development is one of various forms of potentially radical change which are affecting organizations simultaneously. Other changes promise drastically to reduce the numbers of management jobs available. I see current expressed concerns about gender in organizations as reflecting a disturbing phase in social development. In this turbulent context, the stories are, then, offered as glimpses of issues which are in process and provisional 'truths' which are continually in flux. They are historically and culturally located, as I am. (I speak as a white woman living in the west and north of the world geographically.)

I, the women involved, and many other people to whom I have spoken believe that these stories should be told. They express experiences of organizational life that many women – and probably some men – will recognize. They may reflect a particular stage in development, as women pioneers reach senior levels and assess what they find there, and as senior men face working with women as colleagues for the first time.

From this selective perspective the book contributes to current debates that want to ascertain what is happening to women in management. The titles of two recent contributions, from the United States and Australia respectively, give some flavour of the sense of fundamental questioning which often pervades these explorations: *Prisoners of Men's Dreams* (Gordon, 1991) and *Where to From Here? The managerial woman in transition* (Still, 1993).

The accounts in this book are very personal in some ways, showing how these people have lived in what until recently has been relatively unexplored territory for women. But they are also shaped by social, political and organizational contexts. In these, issues of gender and potential gender inequality are pervasive and often implicit (although also increasingly better understood and addressed). For example, many women still face limited life options, have meanings attributed to their behaviour (based on gender stereotypes) which devalue them, and have power in various forms (often unwittingly) used against them. As these stories reveal the effects of these and other similar (overt and covert power) processes they are also, fundamentally, political.

And women are creators of themselves and of their identities and can reject, ignore, challenge and reform expectations and ranges of available options. This book shows some of these processes in action.

The stories as a collection bring into contention aspects of organization, employment, management and career, and make them available for review. This is especially fitting, since commentators such as Handy (1989) suggest that they are already in debate. This book represents some women's contributions to these debates. If significant review of employment is truly under way, women's voices and issues of gender must be incorporated at fundamental rather than superficial levels of understanding and valuing.

WHEN IS CHANGE, CHANGE?

Much gender-associated research has an overt or covert interest in change. I believe that this preoccupation is both appropriate –

I want to live in a society in which people are diverse and equally valued – and sometimes a conceptual and practical trap. Often proposed changes are not implemented because they are unimaginable or unacceptable in the system researched. Sometimes change is attempted but seems to have only superficial effects. Change suggestions are often difficult to formulate conceptually because they must be addressed to powerholders within current systems, using rhetoric they will find acceptable and persuasive. This inevitably risks reinforcing prevailing cultural values and basic assumptions (Schein, 1985).

Here I try to take a different approach. I seek to understand what *is* rather than what should or could be (Marshall and McLean, 1985). I am interested in how current patterns are sustained. My approach is therefore primarily that of inquiry and questioning.

Gregory Bateson (1973) said of learning: 'The word "learning" undoubtably denotes a change of some kind. To say what kind of change is a delicate matter' (p. 253). (He went on to develop an influential model of four 'logical categories of learning and communication'.) In my view much change is not really change but rather a rearrangement or development of what was happening before. Watzlawick, Weakland and Fisch (1974) distinguish between first- and second-order change. First-order change is within an established pattern. Basic assumptions remain the same. A change of fundamental pattern is second-order change. It often seems to require a reinforcing (or prompting) change in the context as well as a readiness of the organism in question.

I can best illustrate this distinction between levels by giving my favourite example of the stereotypically stressed executive (taken from my previous incarnation as a stress researcher and sometimes trainer). I exaggerate a little and speak of a 'typical case' to make my points clearly. The stressed executive begins to worry about their health and looks for advice they can follow. They decide to take up jogging to become fitter and protect themselves from potential heart disease. They jog regularly, forcing themselves to do so however unfit they feel. They battle to fit jogging into an already busy schedule. They find it motivating to time themselves and to do a little more each day. Sometimes they find that they are pushing themselves to jog faster than is comfortable as they compete with someone younger or fitter who appears on the scene or they are aware of being watched.

This executive has taken their established attitudes of control, competition and time pressure into the activity which was meant to make a difference to their lives. They may well feel more stressed rather than less as a result. This is first-order change, the basic assumptions of the system (person) have remained the same and have even become reinforced in the change attempt. I am greatly in favour of exercise, but not as an additional form of pressure. Second-order change in this instance would mean challenging the established attitudes, seeking alternatives or more balance in their application which could be applied to all life activities.

Much equal opportunities change in organizations has been first order. It has taken the route of reform, winning women equality against ideal characteristics of men, defining equality as similarity. It has not significantly challenged the relative devaluing of many characteristics and activities labelled 'female' or the associated polarizing of gender ideals, and so is within the frame of pre-vailing cultural assumptions. (Although more radical revision has taken place in many individual people's lives and in some organizations and institutions.)

There is now some dissatisfaction with the reform approach, particularly as it leaves many norms of organizations largely unchanged (Hewlett, 1986; Gordon, 1991). One result is that equality for difference or diversity is being advocated. But this too could bring familiar patterns in new guises. For example, there has recently been a feminization of some images of manage-ment, espousing values such as teamwork, partnership, employee development and intuition. (There has also been a hardening of some images; managers are portrayed as needing to be tougher, better able to handle stress and to stand alone.) Some people think appreciation of previously stereotyped 'female' qualities will entitle women to credibility and acceptance. It may do. But it may also prove a new rationale for restricting them in certain kinds of down-graded management jobs in flatter organizational structures, whilst power shifts to strategic posts (Calas and Smircich, 1993).

Researching gender issues can also be a matter of first-order change. Many theoretical explorations in the area have a sense of circularity, of being trapped within frame. For example, organ-izational forms may be critiqued, but using current concepts, such as hierarchic 'success' as a way of judging people's lives and careers, which are potentially gender-biased as reference points. Martin (1994) calls them 'language traps', and this is certainly their surface structure. I am not claiming that I can easily escape.

In this book I explore issues of change and invite you to join me. This involves questioning assumptions, paying attention to patterns in the phenomena discussed and reflecting on how we keep things the same. It could also mean imagining what might constitute second-order change. For me this would inevitably involve examining the importance we attach to organizations relative to other areas of community, family and individual life. Second-order change may well not be beyond current belief and practice, but may be only a shift of the light away (Marshall, 1994).

IMAGES OF EXPLORATION

This book is also about inquiry, because trying to make sense of women's lives requires an approach of exploration. In it I attempt to play with sense-making lightly, but not evasively. I want both to convince you of injustices and difficulties in the stories reported and to advocate that women's lives are appreciated from different perspectives simultaneously. In this I am acknowledging multiple perspectives but not willing ultimately to take a relativist view that all perspectives are equally valid in given circumstances. Neither, however, do I argue for one interpretation as 'the truth'. Sense-making is a creative, active process we live by. It will often be appropriate to entertain more than one possibility, and we shall often need to choose one 'truth' temporarily (and with openness to review) to guide our action.

One of the key images which emerged early on and has since shaped this study has been related to the kind of sense-making just described. My image is that I have been turning things – stories and interpretations – in the light, revealing different facets as I do so. The 'things' appear as crystals or prisms, reflecting and refracting light, always offering new impressions.

Two broad choices of interpretation I have not wanted to make affect the tone of the book. I have been suspicious of taking either a committed pessimistic or optimistic stance. Whilst many of the stories contain accounts of difficult experiences, I have not wanted to write a despondent positioning for the study as a whole of hardship, forces beyond people's control and despair. This would not be a valid portrayal. Nor have I wanted to tell a euphoric tale of wonderful tomorrows: such tales invoke a certain kind of energy, which can easily be misplaced. This book is, nonetheless, written with a sense of hope.

Making sense of women managers' lives

In this chapter I outline the book's core intentions, explore issues encountered in trying to realize them and explain how I have organized the remaining text.

FROM CHALLENGING QUESTIONS TO GROWING CURIOSITIES

I had been thinking about doing this research for several years. The idea came partly from a question I was sometimes asked when giving public talks about women in management. Typically a male manager would say that a woman who had reached a senior level in their organization had then left. People were confused afterwards about why she had gone. I was asked to offer explanations. This question often seemed like a challenge. I heard: 'Explain *that*, if you are advocating opportunities for women!' Sometimes the tone was more puzzled than combative, from a man who had sponsored women's development but then felt let down. The questioners thought women were ambivalent about the senior positions to which they had ostensibly been aspiring.

I also heard stories of women leaving from women directly and through networks, but with a very different gloss. Typically, after being outwardly successful, but also struggling to achieve an identity she valued and feeling under pressure, the woman would decide to leave. Doing so was a celebration of personal power, a positive step rather than the result of confusion, an inability to cope or running away. The person concerned would often describe the move as taking control of her life.

The woman who left – in both sets of stories – was usually either the sole woman at her organizational level or one of a small number. They were therefore highly visible and represented a potential change in the composition of management. When such women leave, people seeking role models or advocating equality can feel disappointed, even betrayed. The leavers would sometimes admit that they felt under pressure to stay, not to benefit themselves, but to demonstrate – or not cast doubt on – women's abilities. Women can become symbols to themselves as well as to others.

I wanted to know what was happening to these women, how *they* saw their situations. So I formulated this study. I set out to tell some of their stories, from their perspectives. This book is based on detailed research with sixteen women and on informal discussions with others. The sixteen were chosen because they had reached middle or senior management posts and then either left employment for a while (the majority) or considered doing so. Their stories map a range of possible decision processes, dynamics and next steps. This is not an exhaustive range or a uniform set of experiences. Rather it reveals some of the diversity of women's lives.

This book has three core intentions. It is, first and foremost, an exploration in sense-making, which I invite you, the reader, to join. The stories which form the heart of the book are offered with explicit commentary on the interpretive and presentational processes which created them. They can be read with different assumptions and values in mind. Questions about potential choices of sense-making are asked throughout the text. Secondly, this book seeks to tell relatively full stories about the women's experiences, taking risks – it seems – by revealing more difficult or stressful aspects of lives which are also successful and satisfying in many ways. Thirdly, currently contentious aspects of organizational life – such as the nature of careers, managerial identity, and organizational cultures – are brought into the light and explored, drawing on the experiences of these women.

I would now like to set the scene for the rest of the book, by reviewing some of the issues raised by having these intentions.

FRAMEWORKS FOR SENSE-MAKING

In working on this research I have been preoccupied with the processes of interpretation or sense-making. These have been significant in several ways. I have wanted to voice each woman's view, to be authentic both to their experience and to their self-reflection as they reviewed their story. I have also been aware of my own sense-making and questioning, and have woven this into the accounts as a further voice.

There are many ways of making sense of what the women say. I have not written with the purpose of proving particular interpretations. I have been turning things in the light (see Introduction, p. 7) seeing different impressions as I do so, sometimes glimpsing many layers underpinning one surface representation. No one image is the only truth or the only plausible account, although some may feel more authentic, consistent with the person's values and being, more chosen than imposed.

This kind of open engagement with the book's data involves, I think, a questioning or suspension of initial reactions and assumptions. In gender-related areas this can seem particularly challenging. Notions of gender, employment, career and organization are currently said to be in flux; they are certainly being challenged and reformulated from various directions. I notice, however, how readily sense-making frameworks which seem to me to be very traditional are used to judge the experiences women managers currently report. I met some of these in people's reactions to the study.

Many people enthusiastically encouraged me to do the research, but I was also frequently asked two questions which implied that this is really a dubious project, built on shaky foundations because my topic is insignificant or gender-biased. I shall address these questions to explore some of the sense-making dilemmas involved.

One line of challenge ran:

'Surely there are not enough women leaving to make this important?'

I cannot prove that large numbers of women managers are leaving employment. Perhaps trying to do so would miss the point. I have no idea what would constitute a 'significant' number. However, there is now growing attention to women managers' 'turnover rates', especially in North America. A survey reported by Taylor (1986), for example, suggested that women and men Masters in Business Administration (MBA) graduates in the United States had differential career development rates. Ten years after graduating, more females than males had left employment. Taylor concluded that most had done so to become parents and raise families. These findings have become a classic reference point, particularly as they seemed to affirm stereotypes of women's life priorities.

More recent studies do provide evidence that female managers leave organizations (this is not necessarily equated with leaving employment), at higher rates than men in similar positions (Trost, 1990). For example, Brett and Stroh (1994) found a 12 per cent difference in turnover rates between female and male managers in a survey in twenty *Fortune* 500 corporations in the USA. From this literature it seems to be an emotive topic and one full of mythologies, most of which can be refuted (Korabik and Rosin, 1992). Researchers are now emphasizing that women are likely to leave because of dissatisfactions with career opportunities and organizational cultures, reasons they share with men who move jobs (Korabik and Rosin, 1992; Brett and Stroh, 1994).

In May 1994 there was a flurry of media interest in the United Kingdom because an Institute of Management press release announced 'Fewer women managers: the number of women managers in Britain's top organizations is falling' (Institute of Management, 1994). The latest National Management Salary Survey of Britain's 'largest organizations' had shown a decline in the proportion of women in posts designated 'section leader' to 'director', from 10.2 per cent in 1993 to 9.5 per cent in 1994. (The proportion of directors who were women was 2.8 per cent in both years.) Women were said to be 'twice as likely to resign their positions as men' (p. 2) – rates were 4.5 per cent and 1.7 per cent respectively. Women under 40 years old were more likely to leave voluntarily (6 per cent) than were women aged over 50 (2.8 per cent).

There ensued much media conjecture about why women might be leaving management. This was partly attributed to disillusion with 'male management cultures'. The nature of this debate was fascinating, if somewhat disappointing. At one extreme I heard women called 'wimps' for being unable to stand up to the challenges of corporate life. More moderately they were said to be just not ambitious enough, and too preoccupied with other aspects of their lives to succeed. For the most part stereotypes of what it takes to be a senior manager – toughness, political skill, total commitment – went unchallenged or were reinforced in the debates. Women were in question, not organizations. Women who say life in senior jobs is tough were depicted as an elite and privileged group, who are now complaining.

I wondered why there was so much interest, and why at this time. Some seemed genuine curiosity and concern about the pressures women might experience. But I suspect that women's supposed ambivalence about senior jobs could be used as the next in a long line of justifications for not taking them wholly seriously as potential managers (Marshall, 1984). The argument would read that as women will not stay, even if you give them a chance, there is no point in further reshaping organizational cultures to accommodate them. This could be a subtle form of backlash, in response to signs of significant change in the composition of management, a warning to women to align with, rather than challenge, prevailing employment norms. Some of this book's material could be interpreted as showing that women are ambivalent about or unsuitable for management, if you want to draw such conclusions. I hope you will consider other possibilities.

Through various networks I now hear of enough organizationally successful women deciding to leave to believe this is a phenomenon worth exploring. Recently such cases do seem to be on the increase. But I would not argue the significance of this research on the basis of numbers. Stories of women managers who leave speak from an important realm of women's experience. They can help us understand more about women's lives in organizations and their career and life choices. They offer some insights into women's still poor representation at senior management levels, and into what life can be like for those who do reach them.

These stories are also important *precisely* because they are contentious in terms of meaning. There are plenty of ready-made explanations waiting to be applied, as shown above. Few, I suspect, will interpret the women's decisions positively. So these stories invite us to question the criteria by which we judge, and challenge us to relate these to the present and future of management rather than to its past.

A second common challenge to the intent of this book ran as follows:

'But men are leaving employment too. It is therefore inappropriate to study only women.'

Some male managers are certainly leaving organizations, for many diverse reasons, and with more or less sense of initiative. It seems from anecdotal evidence, however, that men who choose to redirect their lives often do so by moving from one employed identity to another which they feel has more inherent value – the oil-executive-to-schoolteacher style of transition – rather than by challenging the assumptions of employment.

I am not claiming that only women leave. I am certainly not claiming that all the experiences described in this book are exclusive to women. I think that many men could tell similar stories. Rosin and Korabik's (1995) recent work shows, for example, that male and female managers in their Canadian samples had very similar reasons for dissatisfaction with organizations. They argue that 'because women are in a minority and vulnerable to stereotyping, their behaviour is noticed and used to maintain the belief that they are different' (p. 13). The potential similarities make the material more interesting rather than less. Perhaps they will provide a shared base for questioning notions of career and what it means to be a senior manager, and create more potential for change.

It does seem, however, that some of the factors involved are gender-related, and so may affect men and women differently. I do then think it worth examining women's experiences in depth, especially as so few women have so far reached middle and senior management. Now is an exciting time to study women, because what they, in all their diversity, want from employment, is developing and changing. This research is therefore with and about women, but I do not believe or claim that their lives are wholly different from those of men.

Making sense of women managers' experiences does seem especially contentious at the moment. In gender-related debates, adversarial explanations present themselves all too readily. It seems difficult to reflect on the nature of management, organization and career as these notions are potentially in the process of radical transformation *and* hold simultaneously in mind gender and power issues.

AVAILABLE PERSPECTIVES

As I have been working on this research I have been aware of the many different perspectives, with their diverse foundational assumptions, from which the material can be viewed. I shall now briefly sketch some of the main choices, to invoke a range of possible reference points in sense-making.

'Male' models of management

Many social and employment norms have been based on *idealized* male sex role stereotypes – idealized notions of what men are like and do – and so are often called 'male models'. Many men as well as women feel under pressure to satisfy these norms. Schein's (1976) blunt article title – 'Think manager–think male' – still captures much of the imagery of management. These norms may not be as rigid as they appear to organizational newcomers and marginals. But traditional models still strongly influence our valuing, still offer standards against which to judge ourselves and others. Interpreted against these, women often seem inadequate, unpredictable or pushy. Their presence threatens to disturb deep-seated, often unconscious, cultural assumptions. If women speak in 'a different voice' (Gilligan, 1982), affirm alternative values to the supposed mainstream, have different notions of career and commitment to those considered 'desirable' in senior managers (Marshall, 1989), they could be judged unacceptable. If this happens, it may be that conformity and fear of difference are as much at issue as gender.

In this organizational world, women are placed differently from men. Much research data shows women as adapting to prevailing cultural norms and stereotypes, by one strategy or another (Marshall, 1984, 1993c; Loden, 1985; Sheppard, 1989). It is important to remember, however, that many men too are excluded and marginalized by power dynamics through which hierarchic structures and elite social groups are maintained (Kanter, 1977).

'Female management styles'

Recent developments of theory have argued that women may bring alternative qualities to management which are of equal value to traditional 'male' norms (Marshall, 1984; Statham, 1987; Rosener, 1990). Rosener's work has been particularly influential because she aligned the 'interactive' style of management she found amongst women with 'transformational' leadership, an approach heralded as a valuable model for the future. This line of theorizing seemed to affirm women's suitability for management (although Rosener cautioned that organizations may automatically resist any style perceived as 'feminine'). It runs the risk, however, of recreating old stereotypes of women as caring and relational, and as fitted to jobs in new female ghettoes. Calas and Smircich (1993) forthrightly point to the dangers of this approach. Women may become identified with revised management roles in de-layered organization structures. These are likely to be characterized by lower pay and status and demand humanistic styles of management to reconcile diverse staff motivations. Simultaneously, they argue, strategic, international management posts retain associations with traditional 'male' qualities and may therefore be considered the province of men.

This literature shows the difficulties of trying to affirm alternative models of behaviour. They can too easily be pulled back into polarized gender stereotypes.

Feminist and pro-feminist voices

There is a wealth of feminist and pro-feminist contributions to theory which have relevance to this book. I cannot review them adequately here, but shall mention a few key themes.

Some writers argue that it is fallacious to treat mainstream theories of organization as if they are gender-neutral, given their selective foundations (Pringle, 1989; Calas and Smircich, 1992; Martin, 1994). Any assumptions about organizational life must therefore be scrutinized for potential gender bias. Various researchers point to the potential workings of gender and power dynamics in everyday workplace interactions. Mills (1991) provides an exploration of communication as 'gendered acts', for example. Martin (1994) examines the several processes of exclusion and marginalization which can affect female academics. Such analyses alert us to the possibilities that gender inequalities are created, and can be resisted, in interaction and may covertly shape behaviour (West and Zimmerman, 1991).

Another strand of writing criticizes the model of equality for similarity to men on which much equal opportunities change has been based. Gordon (1991), for example, contends that many 'successful' women have aligned with prevailing organizational values and become 'prisoners of men's dreams'. They are, therefore, unlikely to transform employment towards being more

humanistic and caring, and instead, are contributing to a toughen-
ing of organizational cultures, which makes the latter more hostile
environments for women and men. Such critiques raise questions
about how much power individuals have to challenge dominant
cultural rules.

Most feminist analyses are inherently and fundamentally about
power. One of their predominant themes is who has the power to
name and assign meaning. Spender (1982), for example, in her
history of 'women of ideas', details how women's attempts to
contribute their definitions of reality to the pool of socially
accepted knowledge have repeatedly been undermined: 'All
human beings are constantly engaged in the process of describing
and explaining, and ordering the social world, but only a few have
been, or are, in a position to have their version treated as serious,
and accepted' (p. 9). In male-dominated societies, women have not
been accepted as legitimate meaning-makers if their interpretations of reality have differed significantly from established notions
of truth. This has limited their power to name and interpret their
own experiences (Marshall, 1993a). Offering the stories in this
book feels risky, in case they are automatically assessed from
dominant, gender-biased, frameworks of meaning, or the women's
rights to make sense of their own experiences are denied.

Much feminist work is about overcoming silencing. In the
evocative words of Marge Piercy (1973), poet and novelist, it is
about 'unlearning to not speak' (p. 38). The influential black
writer, bell hooks, uses the notion of taking the right to 'talk back'
as an equal to people who are supposedly placed in authority as
an image for her work (1989, 1984). Also, Goldberger *et al.* (1987)
have identified a central theme of many women's individual
development as 'gaining a voice'. These issues are relevant within
individual women's stories and to this book as a project.

Changing formulations of career

Another available set of perspectives are the alternative ideas
about careers which are gaining some currency. Will women
managers' decisions be assessed against notions of portfolio lives
(Handy, 1989) and the likelihood that people may soon need to
have 'three careers in one life-time' (Still, 1993)? Or will more
traditional ideals be invoked? Will part-time working and pauses
seem suspect, judged against accepted standards of a 'good'

curriculum vitae? Or will these concerns be less important because women's careers are being considered rather than men's? Are there still gender differences in expectations?

Emphasizing personal or political explanations

Of particular concern in this study is how to appreciate the interplay of individual and organizational factors. Much research on women managers focuses on the individual, both in generating explanations of their situation and in proposing potential remedies (Gutek, 1993). But often women cope individually with conflictual aspects of their environment that they are managing on others' or the organization's behalf (Sheppard, 1989; Marshall, 1993b). Because of the individual story form of the data in this study we may lose sight of the organizational, structural and political backcloths against which the women's stories are set. Organizations are, nonetheless, implicitly at issue.

In offering this book's stories I am, then, aware of a background clamour of available sense-making frameworks, some of which may be potentially hostile, unsympathetic or uncomprehending. Any which are prefigured to interpret women's behaviour and experiences negatively deserve to be treated with suspicion, and challenged.

It is not that I want to disarm you before you read, to deter all critical thought and comment. Rather I would like this book to become an exploration in interpretation. I invite you to join in as you read – to notice your reactions, reflect on why you like and dislike what you do, catch your assumptions in action, trace their sources, and explore alternative possibilities. I hope that you can enjoy questioning yourself in these ways, and that you may also sometimes feel sufficiently unsettled that new impressions will arise for you.

The issues addressed in this research seem to me to defy clear interpretation. They need to be viewed from multiple perspectives. But a multiplicity of facets will sometimes be difficult to maintain. My hope is to make sense which is open, in process and self-reflexive rather than narrowed and pinned down. I also want entertaining different possible interpretations to become a form of play, rather than a compulsive, over-serious, process of seeking to 'get it right'.

SEEKING APPROPRIATE TERMS

How we demarcate phenomena and name them is a taking of power, an attempt to define the world (Spender, 1984). In writing about women managers I am working in territory which is already largely defined, where boundaries, norms and valued goals are established and labels assigned. For example, much of the language in this area of research affirms employment as a major life activity, and moving upwards as a standard of progress. By talking about women managers as 'leaving', I create employment as the reference point. Articles using 'quit' (Trost, 1990), 'bailing out' (Taylor, 1986), and 'flight' (Korabik and Rosin, 1991) in their titles have similar effects.

I have considered at length how to describe the moves the women managers have made, but many of the available terms – such as 'escaping' – seem loaded in ways that feel inappropriate. A sense of moving away from an identifiable reference point does feel true to many of the research participants' experiences. In this way 'leaving' is an appropriate label. They are extricating themselves from a meaning system. In doing so, most are *moving on* to formulations of their lives over which they feel they have more power. They also expect change and movement to continue. Most are taking into account concerns and life considerations other than employment. This territory is much less clearly defined and valued in management and career-based perspectives. Language use mirrors this patterning. Still (1993), for example, refers to time spent out of employment as 'dysfunctional', because career viability is her concern.

I have, then, settled on the terms 'leaving' and 'moving on' for use in this study. I am aware of the potential power of employment and career 'success' as reference points, but shall seek to escape some of their glamour and affirm other possibilities when appropriate.

CHALLENGING SILENCE, RISKING VULNERABILITY

As I noted above, I have been encouraged to write this book by many people, mostly women but also men. They believe that the stories of women who feel at odds with employment or decide to leave management jobs need to be told, that the issues they raise about organizational life need exploring. This encouragement has sometimes seemed to entrust an important and timely task into my care. I feel I am being invited, pushed, to find ways to speak through some of the silences which are maintained by women in management, to tell some of the less palatable 'truths' of their experiences. I must be careful, however, not to make these seem the only truths. What now need voicing, sharing and exploring are further dimensions of experience. Doing this is another stage in an evolving process of social change. It links with increasing public and academic interest in whether women sometimes collude in disempowering themselves, and whether they can do more to create, resist and change social meanings.

This breaching of silence will not suit everyone. Some women ask not to be told the problems but the keys to success in the organizational world as it is. Others feel that women should protect each other. Others do not believe women managers face difficulties, and do not want to be undermined by people who suggest they might.

Speaking through previous silences feels exciting and also risky. However much I seek to pay attention to the complex processes through which meanings are made, I know that I, as writer and as woman, have no control over what sense anyone makes. I am concerned about rendering this group of women vulnerable through the research, or being so revealing that women generally are made more vulnerable. And yet I believe that women need now to speak more openly about their lives. I think that some women want to hear each other speak in this way; some want to be understood; and some feel a sense of duty to disclose their experiences, despite their pain or embarrassment, as warnings or comforts to others. Speaking out is partly to break through the isolation that many women managers feel. But it is also done in a spirit of exploration, wanting to create a different world, to encourage new ways of managing, organizing and being by opening to critique current organizational practices revealed through some women's eyes.

Spender (1982) claims that she will not make women vulnerable through her work: 'Because women have no control over the knowledge we produce, I think it unwise, if not plain destructive, to produce knowledge that can be used against us' (p. 18). I do not think she can have complete control over what she says. If people want to devalue women's experiences they will find something to criticize in even the most sanitized account.

Spender intends to protect women in a social world she perceives as dominated by elite groups of male power-holders, who are in charge of the social processes of defining meaning. In this portrayal women are largely defined by men. I appreciate her reasoning and believe that many situations still display this dynamic. But I also believe that more women are now defining their lives for themselves, and influencing organizational and social contexts to take their meanings seriously. (And some men resist these dominating dynamics.) Women can act with power by speaking to each other and to men who are willing to dialogue. I also believe that this is a precarious process. People with altern-ative values can be attacked, experience backlash and be ejected from organizations. They can encounter many challenging dif-ferences of life circumstances and views amongst themselves. Any dialogue must be conducted with some appropriate sense of protection.

So, whilst vulnerability and confidentiality are concerns, I and the participants in this research have decided to take potential risks. I want to tell these stories as fully as possible, and yet realize that they could be used against women.

FINDING FORM

I sought a form for this book which is compatible with my aspirations for it. I wanted to set the stories at its heart, and to make my processes of working with them explicit. I hoped to encourage you, as reader, to join me in exploration.

I read several books which looked at women's lives, both for their content and to see how the authors had organized the text (including Bateson, 1989; Dix, 1990; Freeman, 1990; Gallese, 1985; Gordon, 1991). Some told lots of individual stories, one after the other. Others organized their material around themes or issues, including short vignettes of people's lives as illustrations. I decided that I wanted to tell each story in some fullness, and that I wanted to incorporate some general commentary on the themes and issues raised. But I did not want the latter to become a summary, as this seemed likely to be tedious. Nor did I want to tell the stories one after another in a long string, as I thought their details and flavours would blur. I have therefore grouped the stories into like kinds, and interspersed them with strands of commentary, sense-making and questioning which I hope will provide another level of reflection on the text. I want to invite you out of the data occasionally to reflect.

In the next chapter I explain how I conducted the research study. I then move on to the interwoven stories and commentaries, after a little more detail on what you can expect.

Inquiring in practice

In this chapter I shall describe the various phases of the study. I do this in detail for two reasons. Knowing how the stories and other sections came to be as they are provides an essential grounding for reading them. Also, the dilemmas facing any inquirer often reflect the topic studied, thus providing valuable insights into the latter. But you may be impatient to move on to the stories themselves, which you are obviously free to do!

RESEARCHING I *HAD* TO DO

A few years ago I had some time off work to become a parent. Following this experience of leaving – and returning – I became excited about researching women's experiences of leaving management jobs. I wanted to tell the women's stories from their perspectives.

I encouraged myself to start the project at a busy time in my life by applying for a research prize from Routledge, the publishing company. I found myself giving the research proposal priority over other, supposedly more urgent, tasks. This seemed like research I personally *had* to do. Talking to other people confirmed the topic's wider interest and significance; I was encouraged to take it on. I was awarded the research money and so became committed to conducting the inquiry.

I realized from the outset that not all women managers leave organizations; that most stay. So I am dealing with a small subgroup. Nonetheless they are interesting as test cases of what happens to some women who are organizationally successful.

The project has happened in phases. I wanted to do it in a way which did not erode my life too much, so there were some times of intense activity and then lulls as other work and life areas needed attention. When I was making the initial contacts it was as if people came to me to make it happen, rather than that I had to push to find them. This sense of synchronicity contributed to a feeling of rightness and timeliness about the research. Later on I did not feel so favoured, especially when national railway strikes repeatedly undid my plans to hold feedback workshops with research participants. I also had to be more ruthless about committing my life to the research in order to complete this book.

MY PERSPECTIVE

My style of research can be broadly labelled 'constructivist'. I do not believe that there is objective knowledge that we discover, or that the researcher should maintain a distance from the issues they study and the participants involved (Reason and Rowan, 1981; Lincoln and Guba, 1985). Rather I believe in research which is experiential, action-related and collaborative in intent. Any ideas generated are constructed through the process of research, and historically situated.

Such research is often linked with the researcher's life process, as they pursue topics of personal relevance and hope to achieve life development as well as intellectual insight (Marshall and Reason, 1987; Marshall, 1992). This is certainly true of this inquiry. I have wanted to leave employment at some times. I am a working parent managing a range of demands in my life. How to operate, survive and possibly thrive as a woman in organizations is a continual question, and sometimes a challenge. The research themes were therefore directly relevant to me (Marshall, 1992), and working awarely with this connection was a major aspect of the inquiry.

Research is also a political process, both as inquirers seek to make a difference in the world and as the 'knowledges' they offer frame meanings (Kitzinger, 1987; Denzin, 1992). My commitment to articulating women's experiences and my puzzles about how to develop more diverse societies have influenced the study. Because of these interests I identify with some feminist analyses, particularly as they illuminate how gender and power dynamics are often intertwined and highly resistant to change. I regret that feminisms are disparaged or treated warily in many organizational and academic communities these days (Marshall, 1995).

They offer a set of evolving possible perspectives, with much richness, diversity and vitality. I value them and am challenged by them. It would require an extended essay to place myself as a feminist: it is a selective allegiance I hold amongst other identities, rather than an exclusive ideology. Such an essay seems out of place here, and might become overly defensive and paranoid as I sought to deflect unwarranted attributions. I do not want to be drawn into such an exercise. I will let this book stand for me.

I see research as 'a distinctively human process through which researchers *make* knowledge' (Morgan, 1983, p. 7). But this does not mean that it is 'subjective' in the disparaged sense of that term. Rather, working with aware subjectivity is a complex but engrossing aspect of being a researcher and attempting rigorous practice (Hollway, 1989; Denzin, 1992; Stanley and Wise, 1993 and many others). I seek to be critically aware of my own perspective (which may well change), and how that affects my sense-making and action. I seek to develop 'critical subjectivity' (Reason and Rowan, 1981, Chapter 10), partly by pursuing awareness skills such as those described by Torbert (1991) as 'action inquiry'. I engage very fully in this process, as I describe below. I shall share some of these explorations in this book to make this particular constructing of sense-making explicit (I do not believe that it could ever be 'transparent' to me or to you). These accounts of inquiry in action are selected from a more extensive self-reflexive process, conducted alone, with 'friends willing to act as enemies' (Torbert, 1976) and 'friends willing to act as friends' (Marshall and Reason, 1993).

MAKING CONTACTS AND DEVELOPING IDEAS

I wanted this to be a qualitatively rich study, telling the stories of about a dozen women in some depth. I started out by drafting an invitation to possible participants or intermediaries (see Appendix, p. 333). I explained that I was primarily interested in women who had reached middle to senior level organizational positions (and so had shown considerable commitment to career development), and who had then decided to leave jobs for reasons other than to pursue their careers. I noted that this categorization was somewhat ill-defined, but that I wanted to let what did happen to women emerge through the research process rather than set out with narrow preconceptions. I also wanted to include 'others who have left for a mix of motives, have been forced to leave, want to leave but have not yet decided to'. I wanted to cover a range of employment sectors.

I mailed copies of the invitation to a wide range of people who might know suitable candidates or had access to particular networks. I also talked about my research to friends and contacts. The topic seemed to strike a chord with a lot of people and I soon had many relevant conversations. I received plenty of recommendations of suitable people to talk to. My contacts then tried to help me track them down. As they had left organizations some were not easy to trace; a few we never did find. In two instances I sent my invitation to network contact points asking whether they knew anyone suitable, but my message was initially misinterpreted. Both women had recently left organizations in circumstances which made them suitable participants – they wondered how my letter could be so appropriately timed. I also published an article describing the planned research in a journal which reaches practitioners as well as academics (Marshall, 1991), and asked for volunteers.

I vaguely assumed that people might spend time 'at home' after leaving, as this had happened to several I had previously met, and was what I had done. I soon realized that this assumption could be a thinly disguised version of 'a woman's place is in the home'. I decided to relax any ideas of what women do 'after leaving', only holding to the interest in people who felt that they *had* to leave. In this way I let the sampling process inform me of what people did, and help me map the territory, which seemed full of variety and open to continuing change.

Letting the inquiry process inform me about the topic is rather different from many forms of traditional social science research, in which the topic area has to be defined in advance. Had I controlled the sampling more, however, I would have learnt much less. And my sampling is still obviously selective. It does not include any black women, for example, although I initially tried to do so.

INTERVIEWING

The study as a whole was conducted between the early and mid-1990s. In the initial phase of fieldwork, I interviewed seventeen people individually. I went beyond my original target figure of twelve because I could not resist some of the further opportunities which presented themselves. Two people, for example, came from relatively male-dominated employment sectors which had not previously been represented. I did then come across even more possible candidates, but decided I could not extend the study further. Instead I talked to these people informally, continuing to accrue experiences and ideas for the research. Two participants ('Patricia' and 'Dorothy') were not based in the UK at the time they left their jobs. I decided to include them, despite this inconsistency, because their experiences were similar to others I had heard about.

Some interviewees were in the process of leaving when we met; others had left months, a year or more before. I therefore benefited from freshness in some accounts and retrospection in others. The interviews were guided by four broad topic headings:

a brief review of career and life history;
the job and organizational situation;
the decision to leave and process of leaving;
general views on being a woman in employment and managing
    one's identity as a woman manager.

Within each topic area I had identified a few more specific questions to ask if appropriate. The interviewee and I typically shared the resulting checklist, using it as a prompt if necessary. All interviews were tape-recorded and fully transcribed. The resulting transcripts ranged from 19 pages to 46 pages of single-spaced typing, with many at around 30 pages.

I found interviewing interesting, stimulating and often moving. Most people were reflective about their experiences anyway, and so meetings felt like shared journeys of exploration. The interview helped them articulate their current feelings. Later several people said how much they had appreciated being heard by someone who would not be (they felt) judgmental; as one said: 'it was a safe place to talk'. Some people found telling their stories fully emotionally powerful. One person was surprised and delighted to note her positive tone, and to realize that she had now left much of the pain of the events behind. Another realized how upset she still was: being interviewed helped her address these feelings. Several said explicitly that they were handing their stories over to my care because they could not tell them publicly themselves but thought they should be heard because they are significant for women generally.

RESEARCH THROUGH JOURNALLING
AND CONVERSATION

Throughout the research I kept notes of ideas, my experiences, my reactions, and conversations which seemed relevant. I deliberately set up opportunities to talk about the research with practitioners and academics, for example by giving public talks. I honoured promises to write various academic papers, in which I developed associated ideas. I would usually conduct research in these ways, but they had a refreshed energy in this project. A supplementary aspect of the inquiry was challenging and seeking to develop my own sense-making processes.

On my return to work I had let myself become aware of my persistent niggling concern that much of what I wrote or said about women in management was in some ways partial, idealistic, defended against contrary viewpoints. This concern was linked to uncertainties about saying anything about gender because so much debate is adversarial, or interpreted through firmly held frameworks (be they male-dominated, postmodern, feminist or many others).

My previous book on women managers – *Women Managers: Travellers in a Male World* (Marshall, 1984) – had seemed a risk at the time, but had received much positive comment. It had become a valued reference point for some people, which was really pleasing. I wondered, however, if it could be attributed too much credibility, and whether I wanted to have so much apparent effect on some people's lives. It had also been criticized, for example for seeming to imply that women and men are essentially different, or for unwittingly recreating stereotyped gender categories in my attempts to escape them (Hollway, 1989).

I realized that I was trying to ensure that my ideas were 'right', so that I could be sure when voicing them, and not expose myself to either undue praise or criticism. I despaired of achieving this, especially given some of the thorny, long-running questions in the area (such as whether men and women are *really* the same or different), and the many committed camps of theorists. I envied the makers of films such as *Thelma and Louise*, who seemed to be able to present multi-faceted explorations of gender-related issues without taking the mincing steps of academic debate. Happily I woke one morning with a revelatory insight – that I would never get it right, that seeking to do so was a futile waste of energy, that

I should proceed with this 'truth' in mind and allow myself to be more playful in my explorations. With this 'permission' I could appreciate theory and action in gender-related areas as ever-evolving. They need clear, forceful expressions at their appropriate times, not in order to stand as enduring truths but to become available to be explored and used as bases to move on. This book is offered with this intent.

To facilitate these developments in my own thinking I decided to seek out different, potentially conflicting, views. I explicitly invited feedback and debate. I appreciated the confirmation this produced, of which there was much, and occasionally being told that there were issues I was in danger of missing. I particularly appreciated – as always – discussing my work with colleagues at Bath and with the Postgraduate Research Groups there, whom I can trust to challenge me rigorously as well as be supportive.

I also resolved to become my own travelling research culture. Before my pause from employment I had been very involved in administration and teaching, and had let my research vitality become squeezed to the edges of my life. I wanted to re-place it in the centre. I therefore had phases when I answered casual inquiries about how I was, over coffee at work or during a train conversation with a stranger, by telling people about my research, how it was going and my current puzzles. Some people must have been surprised at my bizarre-seeming behaviour. But I prompted many wonderful discussions this way, and met several more women, and a few men, leavers. I could not maintain this energy all the time.

This book is a further step in this process of exploration. I cannot control what meanings you take from it. There are some possibilities I would like you to hear. But I offer it as a kaleidoscope of potential interpretations, hoping that you will explore different views, reflect on your own processes of seeing, and come to no one fixed conclusion. I do hope that it will make us question habits of thinking about what gender, careers, management and organizational life mean. In it I offer my own current thinking as ideas for the present, explorations in process.

STORY-WRITING

I wrote a draft story for each person based on our conversation. This was a demanding, engaging activity, and somewhat formidable, as I wondered if I could do justice to all the material and its many facets and nuances. To write the first stories I went away from home, to be free of distractions.

I wanted to tell rich stories in some detail, to speak from the perspective of the person concerned. By expressing their meanings, I hoped partly to counter potentially devaluing interpretations of their experiences by other people.

But there is no one true story; there are many possible tellings (Denzin, 1989; Mann, 1992). The stories presented here have been created through an iterative and consultative process. Each was initiated as the person – in specific, but diverse, circumstances, and with their conscious and unconscious purposes – told their story to me. Most participants were actively making sense of what had happened to them, reviewing this in retrospect. Some may have been seeking 'plausible' explanations for events which had significantly jarred and disrupted their lives.

I think that often I was hearing a woman's story as told to another women, who was assumed to be sympathetic and had expressed an interest in understanding. This is a very private contract, and I am seeking to present these stories in a much more public space. When writing, at first I largely suspended concerns about disclosing too much, in order to tell the story fully.

The stories have been shaped by me. It is difficult to capture in writing the many essences and qualities of each story as recounted. Any telling of a biographical account is organized in some way which imposes a structure and covert sense of order (Denzin, 1989). This affects what is said and not said, what potential meanings are made available or excluded. Life stories are often arranged chronologically, implying that there is an evolving meaning to someone's life and/or that later experiences build on earlier experiences. It is tempting to expect consistency. Some element of tension may add excitement, but ragged contradictions and explanations which trail off or will not fit together seem less acceptable. Also, we may expect to be able to understand stories, but some may be beyond the range of our potential identification or empathy.

In telling the stories in this book, I have tried to be aware of the processes of sense-making, naming and valuing involved, and of the personal processes that have been triggered. I shall comment on these as seems appropriate, to explicate my workings.

With each story I started by reading through the interview

transcript several times. Once I had some initial impressions, I started to make notes on it in coloured pen, and to circle key words. This process was descriptive rather than analytic, initially. Engaging with the material required iterative processes, going through and through again. It was dangerous to be in a hurry; if I was I would gain no impression of the whole. I had to be patient. After a while, I would begin to form some sense of shape, identifying key features and how different aspects of the material seemed to relate to each other, deciding which details to include and which to omit. I wanted to tell a reasonably elegant story, but also to incorporate as much detail and illustration as possible. I did not want to reconcile apparent conflicts or disjunctions, and so often wrote these in. I organized each story as a sequence of events through time, but commented if a research participant's account had been shaped by other preoccupations, such as a current dilemma or excitement. After a while I would feel ready to begin writing. It usually seemed as if the overview was 'demanding' to be written first. This readiness gave me a sense that I had sufficient appreciation of the story to move to the next stage of working.

In writing I started with an attitude of 'faithfulness'. This meant that I stuck close to what the person had said, including quotations when possible and elsewhere often using their words. I tried to include all their points, links and explanations. This process had qualities akin to a 'factual transfer', but I was also shaping and creating. It requires a certain kind of dual attention, enabling a relaxed, agile engagement. One facet is like Bakan's (1966) communion and involves accepting, 'beholding' and taking in without apparent coding. I encounter the 'data' as exposed to my way of seeing, as a ground for the next stages. The second facet is more like agency (Bakan, 1966). It involves an active, but light-footed, conceptual sense-making. An essence of meaning is identified, matched and contrasted to other emerging themes, fitted within tentative schemata. If either facet of attention is not working well, the process falters. Communion can become flooded with indigestible impressions; agency can become mechanical categorization of uncomprehended material.

At a later stage of writing I took my draft story, read it to refresh my image and then worked through the interview transcript again to see whether the two were in harmony and whether more detail or qualification needed importing into the story. I would then make amendments if necessary. At some point I would usually sense a change from careful faithfulness to feeling a confidence or 'right' to speak for the person concerned. I would then feel more free to name key features, pose dilemmas and to include my intuitions about connections and possible issues.

As I wrote I was aware of how I was shaping the stories. I noted (in journal entries) the principles I was using to create order. I had to be selective, and therefore had to make decisions about what to exclude. I questioned myself on these decisions. Sometimes I recognized a reluctance to include certain details or quotations. I usually then tried to comment explicitly in the story on the dilemma I had been about to resolve surreptitiously.

Often as I took a break from writing or stepped back from a near-completed story, I became aware of a vague concern, question or sense of incongruity which seemed part of the data. Rather than form my own opinion when there was no warrant for doing so, I often incorporated these questions explicitly into the story. Alternatively, I would choose a potential interpretation and write a question asking the research participant to comment when she reviewed the draft.

When a draft was nearly completed, I found it helpful to read the story aloud, at a slightly quickened pace (pausing to make corrections). This seemed to reveal any jarring or inappropriate phrasing; it helped me remedy these in passing and sometimes prompted additional commentary about the shape of the story or its issues. I developed my story-writing technique and confidence as I went through the study. Drafts of early stories were too long (given the book's word limit) and rambling. I tried two out on colleagues and received helpful feedback. This affirmed my attempt to tell multi-stranded stories, showed how eager people were to place different interpretations on the material (in a way which somewhat alarmed me as I did not feel I could address all possible interpretations in my own writing), and suggested that I did need to keep the stories from becoming over-long if I was to maintain reader concentration. With a few exceptions, it was easier to write later stories of an acceptable length, and with themes, issues and conflicts incorporated more directly.

I considered whether to give brief descriptions of people's appearance, mannerisms and so on, to create a visual impression for the reader. But I found I did not usually like those offered by writers of similar works, and my own early trials were little better.

Any description seemed to rely on ready images of some kind, most of which carried hidden messages about beauty, femininity, masculinity, competence or confidence, and so came potentially loaded. I was particularly uneasy and sometimes outraged in reading Gallese (1985). She described one interviewee as 'wearing a cotton turtleneck that she had pulled haphazardly over corduroy jeans, trying, it seemed, to hide a prominent spare tyre' (p. 41), for example. I wondered whose concerns about physical appearance and acceptable weight I was hearing. So I decided only to include issues of appearance, size and weight when these were mentioned as significant by research participants.

Despite my concerns about reader indigestion, I stubbornly resisted the suggestion (made with helpful intent by several people), that I should include only a selected sample of stories in the book or tell some in précis form. I held the image that the stories mapped a potential territory (although certainly not comprehensively), with some similarities but many individual differences. I did not want to lose any people, because each represented an important reference point: there was insufficient repetition in the data for a few to stand as illustrative types.

This phase of the research went more slowly than I had hoped. This was partly because I had other busy demands on my time from work and home. Writing the stories required concentrated and sustained time, energy and attention which I could not always find. I did later discover that I could work on them at home, enjoying the odd break to talk to people or go for a bike ride, as long as I could keep my unconscious attention with the writing. But sometimes I had to leave a story partly finished and move on to other activities, such as teaching. Doing this was frustrating and painful. And it meant that I started nearly afresh the next time I worked with that story, as I had to repeat the groundwork of engagement before I felt confident to write.

NOTICING PERSONAL PROCESS

While interviewing and writing the stories I would engage with someone's situation in some depth. I sometimes experienced intense mood swings about my own job and organization. At this time the latter was often not a comfortable place to be, and I would sometimes want intensely to leave. I once got to the stage of planning my – very punchy – leaving speech. But by then, ironically, I was the main family income earner and feeling more tied to employment than at most previous phases in my life.

As the research progressed and gathered its own energy it became a substantial reason for staying. But then working on it challenged my lifestyle. I wondered why I work so hard and for so many hours a week and for so many weeks a year. I regretted all the other life activities I do not find time for. I questioned how much choice I have in these matters, and what motivates me. These last few years have been busy and tiring on all life fronts. (They have included the building works which predictably occur in the middle of any major academic project – but we *are* delighted with our new kitchen and functioning central heating.) Some of my lifestyle questions await attention when I finish writing this book.

A high point of irony occurred during one New Year university holiday. I was working on Claire's story (p. 71) in which she powerfully articulated her needs to stop, to rest. I was very tired, I would have loved to stop and to rest. I wrote notes on these feelings as I worked. An extract reads: 'This whole process is playing havoc with my motivation. . . . It's all so wonderful as data, and yet I can hardly bring myself to read it a second time, it's too demanding.' The tension of pushing myself to continue while feeling my actions contradict the decision in the story was intense. Writing was a struggle, jarring, an effort of will. I thought that this would show in the product. To my surprise, I later felt that it read well and gave an evocative account. Perhaps my own mirroring had added a particular form of energy.

(My files contain many notes of the kind glimpsed above, monitoring the sense-making process in various ways. I used them to cultivate my own awareness and as a base for issues to explore with friends acting as enemies or friends – see 'My perspective', p. 24, above.)

NEGOTIATING AND REVISING THE STORIES

The next phase was to offer their story back to each participant for comment and amendment. We had agreed to achieve a telling which satisfied us both. People were identified by code letters at this stage, but I had done little to disguise their identities. I needed to check how open to being identified each participant wished to be. I wanted the stories to be rich and powerful in content, and was willing to fictionalize life details if necessary to give us the freedom to tell a different sort of truth about the nature of the dynamics and experiences involved. This general approach had been agreed at our initial meeting. By this time I was not sure whether some contact addresses still worked. I telephoned or wrote to people to check. A few had moved and I had some unsteady moments thinking I had lost them, but I was able to track them all down in the end. At this stage, one person decided to withdraw from the project.

I sent out the stories for feedback. I asked people to comment fully on the detail and to give their overall impressions. On most drafts I asked direct questions about my interpretations, facts which seemed unclear and apparent contradictions. The women responded speedily, and with interest and commitment. Most were generally happy with the drafts, but wanted minor amend-ments. (Details of this feedback are given at the end of each story.) The interpretations I had offered were largely validated. Many people paid precise attention to wording and tone. Several wanted to be disguised, and suggested how to achieve this. One felt that her views had changed significantly since we met. We discussed how to accommodate these developments.

I had been concerned that the research was progressing more slowly than I would have liked. This did, however, have advan-tages. Some people had developed different perspectives on their stories; some felt less sensitive about telling them fully because they now referred to past selves. Also people could tell me what had happened to them in the two years since we had originally met, adding to their accounts. I revised each story, taking the research participants' comments into account; sometimes I added quotations from their feedback. I blurred or masked identities when necessary. I also reorganized a few stories which by then seemed to me repetitive in style. I found that I could not do this work without entering the story fully and becoming engaged with it again. Except for very simple modifications, if I tried to be more mechanical I lost confidence in the changes I was making. My process was therefore usually very similar to that described above for the original writing. I added two sections to each account, summarizing each person's feedback on the draft and giving a brief next instalment in their life.

At this point the risks and vulnerabilities of the project struck me again. I was slightly shocked at how revealing many stories seemed. I wondered whether I dare or should publish all the detail. I realized that concern could make me tone the book down. I resisted this impulse, hoping that the stories could be read with an appreciation that people can be both vulnerable and strong simultaneously, and that sense-making is multi-faceted and elusive.

I then checked my proposed final version of their story with each person. A few more minor amendments were suggested, mostly to make people less identifiable. But most people were very pleased with the resulting accounts. Some affirmed again how important it was to make their experiences public, even if they still felt slightly at risk. One, for example, said that publishing was 'more important than being cosy'. In letters and telephone conversations people told me updated information, insights, reflections, and recent excitements. Although tempted, I decided that I would not incorporate new material into the stories.

One participant decided that her story now made her feel too identifiable and vulnerable. Her reasons for this reaction are highly relevant to the research because they centre on the difficulties of establishing a positive and accepted identity as a lesbian manager. We agreed that I would write a brief account giving the key features of her experience, but decontextualizing them so that they became a potentially indicative rather than specific case (See 'Ruth' p. 257). At this stage I or the participants generated the pseudonyms by which they are now identified. (A few people had been happy to be identified by their names, but as the majority preferred to be disguised, I decided to adopt this policy generally.)

Throughout the research I have appreciated research participants' involvement, commitment, patience and helpfulness.

MAPPING THE STORIES ALONGSIDE EACH OTHER

During the later stages of research, I also conducted a qualitative content analysis of the stories. I mapped recurring issues, similar and contrasting experiences, and ranges of opinion on to large sheets of analysis paper, building up a sense of themes within the material. I adopted a similar process to that described in Marshall (1981), again using the dual form of attention mentioned in the section on 'Story-writing' above. I was not seeking to summarize the data comprehensively. The experiences of these research participants are highly diverse, especially if the wholeness of each story is appreciated. The mapping was, instead, a necessary intermediate stage to provide a base for the commentary, reflection and questioning which is interspersed through the book.

I had another image which guided this work: it portrays the kind of sense-making I am trying to achieve throughout the book. (The image arose spontaneously in a writing workshop we ran for postgraduate students at Bath.) I felt as if I was working with a multi-coloured, multi-stranded tangle of wool. What this 'tangle' was as a whole did not matter to the image, nor was I close to finding this out. But my task was to free the ends currently available to be worked with. In discussing any strand I can pull it away from the rest just so far and have it still retain its flexibility. If I pull too tightly, if I interpret beyond my warrant, the wool/theme will tense and lose its texture. Sometimes I can follow a strand back to its next apparent root (knot) and disentangle that. But usually this only makes the interconnections more apparent, so I must next move to another area (issue), rather than persisting with the one I have temporarily highlighted. Hence sections which include sense-making in process or questioning are offered during this book as speculative essays. Occasionally summaries of specific aspects of the research material are included as grounding for these debates, and to offer the reader a wider view.

I am not impatient to disentangle this tangle. Working with it is mostly enjoyable, exciting, lustrous. I do not think there is a final goal or realisation to be achieved. I can leave the task, and return if I choose. My preoccupation is with not pulling each strand of wool too tightly, lest it lose its texture. I expect the tangle to continue to change as I work with it. For example, it is quite likely that some ends I thought freed will become entrapped again as I work with other strands.

PARTICIPATIVE WORKSHOPS

I had planned to invite all the research participants to meet for a day to discuss issues which had emerged from the initial phases of research. This was to offer feedback in appreciation of their participation, to check the emerging ideas with them and to involve them in making sense. I later decided to organize more than one workshop, as one date seemed unlikely to suit everyone. Despite their keen interest, national railway strikes frustrated my planning, and attendance was lower than anticipated.

Eventually I held two workshops: one each in Bath and London, attended by four and five people respectively. At each I presented the themes and issues emerging from mapping the stories, and we discussed them. These events were both exciting and demanding. I was aware that these were the people whose lives I was claiming to speak for. I wanted to show that my sense-making warranted their apparently high levels of trust in me, to portray their diversity without alienating people, and to be open and questioning without giving the misleading impression that I needed helping out. The debate was lively, engaged and reflective. It provided confirmation, a few challenges or qualifications, and insights into issues now preoccupying the research participants. I have woven some of this material into my discussions in the text.

LATE STAGES OF WRITING

The research process in this study has been iterative, with multiple interacting strands. I designed it to be this way. I also found that towards the end I was flooded with a myriad of impressions, both received from other people and my own that I had carefully noted, and I became rather bogged down. I took deliberate steps to review and then incorporate or discard this wealth of material.

In the later stages I began to feel like an amalgamated version of the research participants' accounts of tiredness. I was beavering away inside the project, but became concerned that I had lost my sense of perspective. I had set aside all the life activities I could, to give the writing priority. But my life became flat and dull, and this affected my writing. There were times when I seemed to have a very limited vocabulary; words with texture did not come readily. I noticed all this and allowed myself a little more activity, leisure and reading fiction. A new academic term began, and provided some alternative views of the world – and duties, delights and pressures. I took a final break away from home to review the draft book in its entirety, and complete the project.

Who the research participants were

Tables 1 to 5 summarize the personal and organizational characteristics of the sixteen research participants, at the time when they left their jobs. One partially withdrew from the study in its closing stages, not wanting to be identifiable (see Chapter 35). I have therefore mentioned her as 'not classified' on most tables.

Table 1 Occupations

Personnel and Organizational Development	5
General Management	4
Nursing*	2
Public Relations	1
Sales	1
Community Work	1
Training	1
Not classified	1

* Both non-UK at time of leaving job.

Table 2 Employment sectors

Local Government	2
Service Sector	2
Health Care	2
Financial Services	2
Electronics	2
Education	1
Law	1
Chemicals	1
Construction	1
Other/Not classified	2

Table 3 Organizational levels

Chief Executive	1
Director Level	5
Senior Management Team Member/Departmental Head	4
Senior Managers	2
Middle Management or Professional Staff	3

Table 4 Ages

Mid-thirties	1
Late thirties	5
Early forties	0
Mid-forties	3
Late forties	3
Early fifties	3
Not classified	1

Table 5 Life Situation

Single or Divorced	3
Independent Partnership*	1
Married or Partnered+	6
Married or Partnered – with young children	1
Married or Partnered – living with older children	4
Not classified	1

* Long-term relationship.
+ Three people in this category have older children who no longer live with them.

A high proportion of this sample are in relationships and are parents, in contrast to repeated findings that successful women are less likely than male colleagues to be married and to have children. Most of their partners actively supported the research participants in having a career identity. People were not being encouraged to leave employment from this quarter. In some cases the reverse was true.

Signposting for what follows

The sixteen stories are at the heart of the rest of this book. I have grouped them, based on key features they contain, into seven clusters. These are not clear-cut categories, but do provide some sense of the diversity of issues which prompted the women involved to leave or want to leave employment. The clusters are:

Wanting different lifestyles – Kathy, Christina, Claire, Jane
Wanting a more balanced life – Sarah
Leaving change roles which became untenable – Teresa, Judith, Patricia, Dorothy
Blocked promotion prospects – Mercedes, Stevie
No longer wanting to battle – Kim, Margaret
Fighting for legitimacy – Ruth
Being forced or pressured to leave – Pamela, Julia (see also Patricia, Margaret, Ruth)
(The women are identified by pseudonyms.)

Interspersed with the stories are commentaries which invite you to step back and review emerging themes and issues. Some summarize particular issues, although I have not sought to provide a comprehensive overview. Most comment, question and speculate. In these sections I have drawn on my appreciation of the stories as a collection (acquired mainly through mapping their themes), on workshop discussions with participants and on other sources. In this approach to analysis I am favouring divergence over convergence. I am bringing the material of this study together in a form which seems appropriate to its diverse, shifting and often elusive qualities.

The stories and commentaries together provide an incomplete map. There are experiences I have not included, most obviously those of black women. There is relatively little about family–work conflicts and nothing on caring for the elderly. In the comment-aries I have been selective; other researchers would probably have pulled at other threads to identify issues. Also, so many of the themes with which this book deals are changing and trans-forming. We can see this in the women's lives. This sense-making contributes to a wider web of related research, which is necessarily continually in process, and so should be treated tentatively.

To implement the format of moving between stories and commentaries, I have adopted the following convention. When research participants are refered to individually in commentary sections, their names will appear in ordinary type if their stories have already appeared and *in italics* if their stories have yet to appear.

In the stories, statements are often made which represent the research participants' *interpretations* of situations or events. In interviews they usually illustrated these conclusions and some-times debated whether these were appropriate inferences to draw (see 'Assigning responsibility' p. 159ff.). But often the processes could not be 'proven' in any straightforward sense. Much organ-izational experience is of this kind. Understandings are based on subtle processes of inference, which other people may or may not be willing to underwrite from their perspectives. Claims that gender is at issue are especially likely to be contested or denied. Much organizational 'work' goes into constructing gender as irrelevant, for example in treating job characteristics used in recruitment as if they are gender-neutral. (Being unable to have their views of the world affirmed by other people was a major pressure for many research participants, as the data will show throughout.) In writing the stories I chose not to preface state-ments with 'she said' and 'she thought' because this seemed too cumbersome and because the purpose of the book is to tell each woman's account from her perspective. That the stories are interpretations is both implicit and central to the study. I have often indicated when sense-making or speculation is mine, to make this change of voice apparent for the reader.

Wanting different lifestyles

The stories of: Kathy, Christina, Claire and Jane

I grouped these four stories together because they share the pattern of seeking new lifestyles more congruent with the women's developing self-images. Only once I had done so did I notice that all had been in personnel, three leaving director posts. These three felt that they had lost touch with themselves and their needs, partly through being so responsive to other people's and their organizations' demands.

Claire was also partly affected by feeling that time to have children was running out. Wanting to become a parent after achieving success in a career is a theme readers may have expected to appear significantly here. Early studies of women MBA graduates 'bailing out' in the USA developed this impression (especially Taylor, 1986). Perhaps this motivation is not significant amongst this group partly because many of the research participants were already parents. It also seems, from various data sources, that women who reach middle and senior management levels are more likely to continue working if they have children than they are to leave.

Kathy

OVERVIEW

Kathy had spent her early career being personal assistant to chairmen and managing directors of various companies. In her late twenties she decided to give her working life more focus. She moved into personnel. The company she then joined was a start-up in the electronics industry, and expanded rapidly. She grew with it, eventually becoming the director of human resources.

Various factors then contributed to her decision to leave. She began questioning her lifestyle, in what she described later as a 'typical midlife review'. She was becoming disillusioned with the personal costs of being so committed to work, and believed that she was neglecting important aspects of her identity. A change of company ownership then severely affected her. It reduced the scope and satisfaction of her job. The new parent had very different attitudes towards human resource issues, meaning that Kathy's organization could not live up to the promises it had made to employees. Whilst she had all the symbols of success, she was more isolated and less influential than at previous phases of her development. Life was no longer fulfilling.

Kathy left with immediate plans to move into consultancy, do a postgraduate research degree, study with the Open University and engage in various sorts of training and self-development work. She delighted in the freedom of keeping all her options open.

EARLY CAREER HISTORY

'The first thing was that I didn't have a degree, which was because my father told me that he couldn't afford for me to go to university and my brother was at Cambridge. So that sets the scene for me.'

Kathy went to commercial college. For about ten years she worked as a personal assistant to chairmen and managing directors in various industries, in the UK and abroad. Her life emphasis was on 'fun and frivolity and freedom', a typical 'Sixties' profile. She was surrounded by male models of managing (her father was also a managing director), and these have strongly influenced her. She gained a breadth of valuable experience, and managing companies came to hold no mystique. But she grew increasingly frustrated, wanting a chance to manage in her own right and perhaps do things differently. With the backing of a mentor, and by now in her late twenties, she studied for membership of the Institute of Personnel Management. This was her first conscious move to improve her prospects. She chose personnel because she had relevant experience and it was a feasible route to pursue through part-time study.

AN OPPORTUNITY TO PROVE HERSELF

Kathy grew up with a strong need to compete. She was aware of people's low expectations of women, although she had not been socialized at home to fulfil female stereotypes. She also felt angry at her father for not sending her to university.

'One way I dealt with it [her father's behaviour], and I'm now recovering from it, was this incredible drive to prove myself. It was very, very strong, and it's why I got to where I did, I'm sure. That's what I'm now questioning.'

Kathy left the organization which had sponsored her personnel training, seeing few opportunities for women to succeed there. She joined a newly launched electronics company to help set up a personnel function. She soon found another mentor, who was influential throughout her time there. Kathy noticed her ambivalent feelings about this.

'I've always had two very conflicting sides in me in terms of confidence. . . . I'm actually very confident in my own abilities, probably too confident, and on the other side there's always been this feeling, which is something I feel is totally ingrained in me, of being grateful, feeling I'm not really up to it. . . . It's very strange.'

She believed the impulse to feel grateful was fostered by the images society offered her as a woman, and that this affects many women.

The new company was the ideal environment in which the confident, now ambitious, Kathy could thrive. 'The opportunities were really unlimited', and she felt the fervour of being a founder member. The organization was 'a very exciting experiment', developing innovative human resource approaches, which Kathy summarized as 'treating people as adults' compared to standard practices of the time. She drew on her wide-ranging experience and was a significant shaping force. The staff on her site were highly qualified academically, and willing to be passionately involved in work which offered them creative challenges. The company placed minimal constraints on them – for example there were no fixed working hours – but enabled people to devote their time, energy and commitment to work. Open dialogue and trust were encouraged, organizational status marking minimized. 'There was no them and us about it, it was all us.' Later she said: 'In many ways, we were ten years ahead of "Learning Organization" concepts.'

The company was highly successful in its initial growth phase, expanding in employee numbers, financially and internationally. 'There were loads of difficulties, but an extraordinary feeling of family and belonging, and tremendous achievement.' The organization was like 'some little creature that kept coming up against brick walls and managing to get round and over them'. Kathy was promoted rapidly and after a few years became personnel manager. She was given trust and a 'completely free rein'.

COMMITMENT

Kathy became totally devoted to work. She was involved and committed, and thoroughly enjoyed it.

'It was an insidious, gradual, complete absorption into work, and a complete withdrawal from anything to do with me as a person.'

This was only partly because of the 'horrendous' workload. It resulted more from her complete identification with the company, and her sense of contributing fundamentally to its development. She was also motivated by her 'very high standards', a personality characteristic shared with her father. She typically worked very long hours. She travelled abroad extensively, exercising a lot of responsibility. Gradually, she had less and less social life outside her work. This did not trouble her. Because she was single, she was able to be 'totally selfish' in this way. Her life was demanding, but for the most part thoroughly satisfying. There were good reasons for her commitment and 'it was tremendous experience'.

The company attracted attention for its human resource practices, and she became identified publicly as a key architect of its culture and success. She was the only woman in such a position in the industry, and enjoyed being special in this way – 'I do like being individual and different'. Inside the organization she did, however, sometimes have to emphasize her title in dealings with external visitors to avoid being patronized as a woman.

A difficult phase of several years occurred when one of the organization's manufacturing units was established. Kathy would have loved to apply the company principles to this too. But someone with manufacturing experience (which she did not have), and more traditional views, was recruited to develop the facility, and was given a parallel position to hers. The organization made a 'safe' choice for a potentially risky development. Kathy was placed in an ambivalent organizational and power position. There were anomalies of pay and rewards which she took time to redress, acknowledging that 'these trappings did become very important to me'. She and the other personnel manager communicated poorly, and he refused to acknowledge her authority for company-wide systems. She believed he was unable to accept a woman as an equal. A battle of personalities, status and authority ensued, which Kathy found very unpleasant and in some ways undermining. Kathy weathered this period partly because she put company interests before her own, but also by having become 'a very tough person'. Her early career experiences had taught her to be 'very competitive and good at politicking and manipulation.' She was not afraid to use such tactics, although they were not a dominant feature of her own organization's culture.

Another aspect of her toughness was never asking for help or admitting that she had any development needs. She attributed this both to the male models of management she had identified with, and to not wanting to show potential weakness as a woman:

'I was on this achievement track. It was everything that had been modelled around me. . . . I knew I could do it and I wanted to show that I could. I was damned if I was going to say to anybody along the way that I needed any help.'

If she failed she would prove what everyone had always tried to prove to her, 'that women can't do it.'

In the early phases of her career Kathy sometimes had to manage negative reactions to her from other women. Some were jealous or suspicious of her success and would belittle or undermine her. She kept herself somewhat apart from them as self-protection.

'I had a lot of knocks along the way and got very tough. . . as a result, and thick-skinned, and some of that was from women.'

Kathy regrets some people's needs to discount women's successes, although she appreciates that socialization covertly teaches such attitudes. She learnt them too. She described herself as being 'very paranoid' at one time because she wondered if fellow employees might be explaining away her organizational success in some way. For example, they might have thought she had too much influence because she worked closely with her mentor, or that they were having an affair. She learnt not to wonder what impressions people had of her. Within her company few patronized her or made her feel inferior as a woman – 'they wouldn't have dared'. On the contrary, she had plenty of evidence that she was central, respected and powerful. Her occasional doubts about whether her capabilities were recognized by others may, however, have reinforced her already high need to prove herself.

In this phase of her career, Kathy did not reflect much on her lifestyle. She was highly motivated, the pressure was acceptable. Just once in a while she would wonder whether she really wanted to get up in the morning, to keep up the pace. But the vague question was soon suppressed, and the job brought a series of enticing challenges, especially in growth and overseas expansion. Occasionally friends would ask about her quality of life; but she had not reached a stage when she needed to question this for herself.

BECOMING A DIRECTOR

A company reorganization was planned. Her mentor became chief executive. Kathy's strong suggestions that human resources should be represented at the top level were accepted and she was appointed director of human resources. She would have been 'devastated' if she had not been chosen, because she believed herself the best candidate for the job and because she so wholly identified with the company. (The other personnel manager left soon afterwards.)

Thus Kathy gained the highest position she could aspire to in the organization. She had a staff of thirty people, a high salary and smart company car. As her salary was already well above her needs, the material rewards had mainly symbolic significance.

> 'But it was extremely important to me. . . . it showed that I, as a woman, had got to the same level as men. I was still utterly in that system and knew no other.'

STARTING TO QUESTION

An array of factors – personal and organizational – then began to contribute to the questioning which eventually led Kathy to leave.

> 'It's really been a process over the past three years of gradual and increasing concern about things.'

The questioning was partly prompted by ageing. When she turned 40, she said 'I started to realize that I would die one day'. This meant that she did not have unlimited time to do what she wanted with her life. She was also affected by watching her father after retirement. Having devoted his life to his career, he then had no sense of importance, no interests and poor health. She thought 'My God, that's going to be me', and realized that 'all this stuff is immaterial and doesn't do much for the soul'.

As a professional development exercise, Kathy completed the Myers Briggs Type Indicator, a personal-style questionnaire based on the work of Carl Jung. This caused her to inquire in a major way. She explored Jungian frameworks as part of the interpretation; they are particularly relevant to someone reviewing their talents in midlife. Kathy concluded that significant aspects of her job were no longer in line with her core personality preferences, and wondered whether she had been neglecting potential aspects of her identity. She felt that the costs of acting 'out of character' were becoming more evident. For example, she became aware of the 'tremendous tiredness' she lived with, doing nothing but sleep at weekends. She later wondered whether she had been 'on the way to burnout'.

CHANGING ORGANIZATIONAL FORTUNES

Kathy had started to review her life. Where this would have led on its own, she does not know: perhaps to similar conclusions in the end. But then Kathy's organization was sold to a much larger organization. The consequences of this event were key determining factors in her eventual decision to leave. The new parent company had a more interventionist approach than its predecessor and brought with it traditional views on human resource practices. Kathy's role became more limited and lost its innovative mission. She had advocated the change, and later still believed it should be beneficial in the longer term, but the immediate consequences saddened and demotivated her.

Kathy's company had to reduce their workforce. She became aware of the double-edged sword of high commitment cultures, if either party cannot live up to the implicit contract. She was particularly disillusioned because the reduction in staff numbers was beyond the control of her and her colleagues, and had not been a declared intention of the change of ownership. Given the committed ethos her company had lived by, making staff redundant seemed especially likely to do them harm and to break the culture's distinctive bond of trust and mutual fate for those who remained. Kathy described her disillusion with this situation as 'the primary reason' that she eventually left. She had been key in creating the organization's culture, in attracting people away from other companies and in 'getting them to believe that this was not a company but a belief system, an amazing place to be'. Having then to tell people that they had no jobs seemed a 'devastating' thing to do to them.

(There may be links here to the more personal questioning Kathy was doing. She had seen how high investment in career had limited her father's other life interests and was wondering whether this was happening to her.)

Later Kathy emphasized her continuing faith in the kind of culture her organization had developed, with its distinctive attitudes and philosophy towards employees. She would do most of it again if she were setting up a company. Her greatest disillusion was with the system which made it necessary for them to be taken over in the way they were.

Kathy could not establish a power base in the new parent company. She had 'no credence or authority at that level', and found its chief executive 'at the other end of the universe' in his views on human resources. For a couple of years she therefore lived with 'split loyalties'. She felt loyal to her chief executive, whose confidante she was, and to her people. She felt that her company could not survive without her, but later described this as 'an appalling arrogance'. Her strong sense of commitment, the base for her 'contract' with work and the company, made it difficult for her to employ distanced, calculative decision-making about her own situation. She kept hoping that the situation would improve, but also felt an increasing sense of disloyalty to people she had recruited but could no longer protect.

> 'I felt rotten. I felt like a rat leaving a sinking ship, and still do to some extent, although I'm getting used to that.'

By this time Kathy's own job scope had been drastically reduced. She had no remit to generate and implement progressive schemes. She was mainly left with administering routine personnel practices. She felt increasingly unable to do good work because she was not interested, but did not believe this was evident to other people. She was now 'actually bored to tears'. The job obviously held little future for her.

MORE SENIOR: LESS MOTIVATED, LESS POWERFUL

Kathy had lost her sense of personal challenge, of being on the edge of her capabilities. She had become progressively more confident about her abilities as a manager during her time in the company. When she was appointed director she was further affirmed. She had proved herself and largely satisfied her strong needs to achieve. But, she thought largely because of the takeover, she found reaching her ultimate goal a surprising anti-climax.

> 'I got the car and the salary, I was a director. I was bored to tears with my job and thought "So what?"'

And Kathy did not enjoy life as a member of the senior management executive. It was characterized more by hierarchy and separation than by teamwork. She did not feel that the directors had gelled as a group, or that she was amongst peers. The chief executive, her mentor, seemed to pull back from her once she joined the senior group.

'I think he probably went too far the other way, but I absolutely respect why he did it. He was always very conscious of never treating me differently to anyone else, and never treating HR [human resources] differently, because that was his background.'

He took a tough line on people issues in public, and seemed to Kathy sometimes to make a point of putting her down. At the time she thought he was trying both to dispel any possible suggestion that his relationship with her was any different to that with the other (male) directors and to reinforce his own credibility by distancing himself from human resources. In retrospect, she believes that he started to treat her differently to help her 'move up a gear and behave in ways he thought were more fitting for a senior manager'.

Functioning at this top level, Kathy became more aware of herself as a woman in a male group.

'Increasingly I disliked it. I felt isolated. And I didn't always like the way they dealt with issues, aggressively and nastily.'

Whilst the group could be fun to work with, there were times when she did not seem integrated as a team member. She felt discouraged from contributing about matters other than direct human relations, but wondered if this was due to her own lack of confidence. She was not good at hiding her feelings, and felt her style was not accepted 'in a macho, male group'. She noted that the feelings she did not easily disguise were most often those of anger, rather than those of upset with which women are stereotyped. She also felt distanced from her previous peers: 'Some treated me differently when I was elevated'. This 'didn't matter to start with, but increasingly it did'.

Kathy had never looked for support in her work environment, believing that to do so was a sign of weakness. Talking difficulties through with people might, anyway, make her vulnerable, which she did not want to become. This self-sufficiency had not previously bothered her. But later she had no one with whom she could discuss the new challenges she faced.

As her life changed in these several ways and the consequences of the company's change of ownership became more apparent, Kathy's satisfaction with her role decreased.

'So I actually started to feel really quite isolated, which is a really strange feeling, having been such a leading light in setting this thing up.'

(When she reviewed the first draft of this story, Kathy noted that we had not discussed other important aspects of her last few years in the company. She noted, for example, her pride at how other women were then progressing, the majority of them in departments within her broad area of control. She hoped she was a role model for female employees and that they enjoyed having a woman director. This contrasted with any suspicion of her earlier in her career.)

By this stage Kathy was questioning all aspects of her life. A brochure advertising a life choices course caught her attention.

'It all started to crystallize in my mind. I was going to leave and put myself on that course and go off in a completely new direction.'

A conversation with an organizational consultant sowed another seed. It affirmed for Kathy how much she enjoyed finding things out and exploring. The idea of doing some research and other forms of learning gave her things to leave for, directions to move in. Prior to this, her feeling that she was indispensable seemed to be keeping her in place. Kathy's decision was made. She planned to earn an income through consultancy, but also estimated that for the first year or two she could afford to devote a large amount of time to her own development.

LEAVING AND AFTERWARDS

Her experience of leaving was an anti-climax. She expected that people would be upset about her departure, and that there would be some marking of her service and importance. Instead there was a brief ceremony in the canteen, some wine that she had provided, and a few small gifts. In retrospect she realized that she was 'insensitive', too absorbed in her own process. Too many redundancies had recently taken place for her leave-taking to be special.

The next day she was involved in a self-development workshop and felt a sudden, intense sense of loss and grief. To her surprise these feelings were brief, perhaps because she had effectively been preparing to leave for so long.

'So it wasn't quite the shock I was expecting. I was expecting every day to wake up and think "My God, what have I done?" And I haven't at all. Not once.'

I met Kathy six months after she had left. She was doing some consultancy; her clients included her previous employer. She had also opened up many opportunities for learning and exploration. She said: 'I'm doing it all for me at the moment.' She had became involved in a range of self-development activities and training courses, was studying psychology with the Open University, and doing some organizational research for a postgraduate degree. She was 'like a kid with lots of toys', and was thoroughly enjoying herself. Of prime importance were Kathy's sense of freedom, being able to keep all her options open about longer-term developments, and feeling free of being driven. She could not imagine being employed in a company again, ever.

She had not stopped working twelve hours a day. If she did have any space she would 'want to fill it with painting, reading, gardening, something worthwhile'. I asked what would happen if she gave herself more opportunities to do 'nothing', but her only reply was to note how difficult that would be.

She was delighting in the friends she had made and the several support groups which her activities provided. She was developing a new relationship with her sister, who had followed a very different, non-corporate, life path and had also taken new directions lately. Kathy was not worried about money: she was confident that she could earn a living somehow, and said she would sell her house or car if necessary.

KATHY'S FEEDBACK ON THE DRAFT STORY

Kathy commented extensively on the draft story. She said she had 'moved on a lot' from when we met, and some of the impressions in the draft now seemed 'a little misleading'. Also with the benefit of hindsight she attributed different interpretations to her own and other people's behaviour. She sought to reassure me by writing: 'It's no reflection on you – I think you've done an amazing job! I think my main problem is one of time-lag.' We discussed her responses and revised views at length. There were two main themes to these.

Firstly, she wanted to be fair to other people and to herself. For example, the draft seemed to portray a bleak and rather isolated picture. She emphasized how much she had enjoyed her time in the organization, and the many good relationships she had had there. She said that the first best thing she had done in her life was to join the company, the second best thing was to leave when she did, and that the time in between had often been wonderful, a great experience.

Secondly, Kathy was very watchful about the impressions people might take about women. She wanted to make it clear that leaving was a positive choice, prompted by not wanting to belong to a particular sort of world, rather than a failure to cope. She thought that people could interpret what she had said as fulfilling various negative stereotypes of women, perhaps because her comments now seemed out of context. She therefore paid close attention to the tone of several sections.

We discussed these issues and jointly decided how to address them; I revised the draft accordingly.

ADDENDUM

Kathy is still engaged in the activities she was pursuing when we initially met. She is close to the end of her Open University psychology degree and halfway through a Counselling at Work diploma. She has continued to explore and enjoy Jungian theoretical frameworks. Her consultancy work is flourishing.

Christina

OVERVIEW

By the time we met, Christina had left her post as a personnel director in financial services, had thoroughly enjoyed being an independent consultant, and had been head-hunted into the position of chief executive of a national charitable organization. She was full of her new job and her visions for re-energizing the company. She was willing to look back, but doing so mainly held value as a contrast to the enthusiasm she now felt for her work and life. Despite being outwardly successful, her career had lacked full internal commitment until recently.

Christina had left a previous job without immediately having a position to go to. I shall therefore start her story with this experience.

LEAVING: THE FIRST TIME

Christina's early career was in personnel management in various electronics companies. By the late 1970s she was personnel director of the UK subsidiary of an American organization. She enjoyed the creativity and power of this job, which had been a company start-up. She felt particularly proud of recruiting the design team. The industry met difficulties, however, and an American chief executive arrived to sort the UK company out. Christina implemented the resulting redundancy programme.

The organizational changes, and the ruthlessness of her new boss, made Christina clear that she wanted to leave. Before she could find another position, however, her boss's attitude to her became overtly hostile, perhaps because she had questioned some of his demands. She found that he had offered her job to one of her subordinates. Christina challenged the chief executive directly, and threatened to take the case to an industrial tribunal and accuse him of constructive dismissal. In these exchanges she had the upper hand, being well versed in UK legislation. The chief executive was initially belligerent, but moderated his attitude after taking legal advice.

Christina negotiated a significant financial settlement. Her power in this situation was rooted in her anger, about the company's treatment of other people as much as of herself.

'So they paid up every penny and I left. And it was so stupid of them because I was going to leave anyway. But I was very tired and very angry and thought they shouldn't get away with it.'

This episode taught Christina the value of anger if directed appropriately. Had she been less angry she thought she would have done 'negative things' to herself.

As she left she was already in discussions about other jobs, and felt relaxed, sure that something would come up.

'I NEVER REALLY WANTED TO GO THERE'

Christina took on her next post, as personnel director of a major organization, with little enthusiasm and no clear sense that the position would suit her. She applied more at her husband's instigation than her own. When offered the job she felt she 'might as well give it a go'. If it did not work out, which she thought extremely likely, she would have to leave, accepting the 'blip' on her curriculum vitae. She gave herself six months to find out.

Christina eventually stayed with the organization for ten years. During this time there were many peaks and troughs in both her motivation and her sense that she had something to contribute; she nearly left several times. She is stimulated by change and innovation, rather than by maintaining systems. The organization she joined was 'very quiescent'. She believed that the person who recruited her anticipated the major transformations which were to come and wanted her for her ability to manage change, and for her experiences of information technology, which later figured significantly.

The changes Christina encountered were of two kinds: those of senior personnel and those of changed industry circumstances to which the company needed to adapt. Whilst these maintained the challenge and variety of the job, they also created pressures:

> 'Inevitably some really dreadful things happened from time to time, and I got on several occasions to a point where I thought I would leave. But I didn't actually go about it in a particularly determined way.'

She had a 'series of bosses' who were 'difficult people'. With each she had to adjust and find ways to work effectively. She also had to manage her function and promote a sense of organizational coherence despite personality clashes amongst senior personnel. There were several phases of severe conflict or uncertainty, times she described as 'dreadful' and 'appalling'. Her own power-base was threatened early on. Soon after she joined the company, the person who had recruited her left, leaving her 'orphaned' in a highly politicized senior management culture. For some time her reporting relationships were unclear and thought by others to be 'appalling'. But she ignored the situation and carried on, and later thought that had been the most effective strategy. Eventually she reported directly to the chief executive, a more appropriate arrangement.

In the content of her role there were also significant phases of change, which proved stimulating. These caused her less pressure, except when she felt there were limits to the change the company could accommodate, or when activity seemed to have ceased for a while. Christina was part of a major expansion, linked to the introduction of extensive information technology, and later a major contraction, as market conditions changed.

In describing specific changes she introduced, she revealed some of her values about organizations, advocating a person-orientation and environments in which all employees can participate creatively. For example, she articulated a clear, multi-stranded, rationale for introducing a youth training scheme.

> 'I thought it would be healthy for people to see different faces around, it would give us an excuse to give first line supervision training to people who were not yet first line supervisors. . . and it was a way of getting minorities in and people used to them. . . and also it was an all-round good thing because of the school leaver unemployment problem at the time.'

Christina's sense of power to initiate change fluctuated, and was a significant factor influencing her satisfaction. Initially she had a substantial impact:

'I had quite a good time in my early days there because I was different and nobody could figure me out, so I could move faster.'

As new challenges emerged, she benefited from being established and having people's trust. She could lead new initiatives, especially when there was pressure to respond to outside demands. But towards the end Christina was feeling 'bogged down', both because people had become used to her and able to react against her, and because there were organizational limits to change in 'impossibly inappropriate structures that just didn't work any more'.

CREATING POWER

Christina described her core strategy for creating and maintaining power as networking. This involved being in a certain kind of relationship with other people, so that they allowed her to do things and provided support and resources. It was as much about making demands as about providing mutual support: 'It's a lot, also, about bull really.' (By this she meant being 'assertive to the point of cheek, trying it on, being pushy'.) Requests for support should be made clearly and assertively.

'You have to go in and say "This is what I want and you are going to give it to me, and this is why you're going to give it me. And this is what I'm going to do if you don't".'

Christina saw no sense in expecting people to recognize her value and give help voluntarily, believing this approach naive.

Her networking involved building relationships in many directions simultaneously. Diversity in contacts gave her independence, as she was never reliant on single sources of support. It also meant that she could exercise power more subtly.

'Nobody knows where the rest of your power comes from. They only see a bit and they know there's a whole lot more and that's useful.'

Christina believed that some of her power within the organization came from the image she created externally, through business-related public activities. Developing her external credibility was a deliberate strategy which she adopted early on when her political support amongst senior management seemed doubtful.

'Once my first boss left nobody was going to listen to me, internally. I had to find a way to get the buggers to listen, and the way to do that was to become powerful externally.'

Christina also used an explicit networking approach to maintain contacts with a 'super set of friends'. These have been invaluable sources of support, especially during recent times of change and pressure.

BEING A WOMAN

Christina did not feel that her experiences in the company were greatly affected by being a woman. Initially friends asked how she would survive in what was assumed to be a bastion of male chauvinism. In fact she found financial services an easier environment for women than the engineering industry. The former is based very solidly in relationships, is more sociable, and she found that more people were interested in art, literature and theatre. This diversity afforded more points of contact than she had previously had.

It may also be significant that Christina had not carried a prominent sense of herself as a woman at work, either as someone restricted by traditional female stereotypes or as disadvantaged relative to men. She believes women do have 'specific problems' in organizations, but did not see herself as in opposition to men generally. She felt her self-image was not markedly 'feminine', partly because she grew up seeing herself as ugly and unattractive. As a child, she was praised instead for being 'bright', and so has built her identity more on this foundation. This did not mean that she had 'compromised' and adopted male-style clothes. She felt free to wear a range of styles and enjoyed bold colours.

STAGNATION

When we talked, Christina was much more interested in telling me about her new post and its challenges than in dwelling on the past. She felt that she had achieved what she could there.

'I've put it a long way behind me. In many ways it was a very repressive place to be, and I was sick to death of feeling compromised and had had enough of it. I'd put an enormous amount of work into my time there, had done everything I believed it possible for me to do.'

She also had a sense of a past self beyond which she had grown:

'I really didn't feel I could be me, I had to be the person people expected me to be.'

This was equally true for her marriage as it was for her as personnel director. Perhaps the two experiences of feeling 're-pressed' reinforced each other sufficiently for change to arise. It seems that Christina may have stayed longer than was healthy for her in her previous job: she mentioned feeling inevitably 'sapped' by the organization. But there are several reasons why she stayed on. Sooner or later new challenges did arise in the job to refresh her interest. The 'external applause' from her outside activities maintained her sense of self-worth even when her own job lacked stimulation. But most significantly her job provided the sense of worth that she was not then receiving in her marriage.

'It was through my work I existed and through my relationships at work that I felt valued.'

Work became a valuable source of stability as she began to take seriously her general sense of dissatisfaction.

TAKING STRESS SERIOUSLY

Eventually Christina consulted the company doctor because she was feeling 'appallingly stressed', almost to the point of immobilization. She was encouraged to talk about her life history, including her childhood which was 'chaotic, awful'. She sees herself as a survivor, protected by tough strategies of self-defence. Rather than make her doubt this self-evaluation, these con-sultations made her realize how unhappy she was in her marriage. She felt constrained, reinforced in a negative self-image she had developed in childhood, and unable to spend time on activities she liked. Eventually she decided to leave her husband. Until this decision was made she had too little energy to address her job situation clearly; she described herself as 'just surviving'.

At much the same time a new chief executive arrived. He asked Christina whether she wanted to stay, in view of her long time already with the company. After some thought she decided to leave. They negotiated that she would implement a radical change of organizational structure before she did so. Christina welcomed this invitation: it was change she had been advocating for a long time. A financial deal for leaving was agreed.

At this point Christina thought that she might have another position to go to. After protracted months of negotiation, and two months before she was due to leave, this proved not to be the case. One key executive in the new organization declared that he would not work with a woman.

This situation seemed fitting.

> 'So I was in a situation where I was going to leave with nothing to go to. It didn't appal me at all, although people expected it to, because having left my husband three months before, I was in the business of creating a whole new life for myself. And creating a whole new working life was just as achievable and it made sense to be able to do it all at the same time.'

Potential financial insecurity was of especially low significance at the time. She had analysed what was tolerable and not tolerable in her life, and 'being potentially impoverished was not a problem in comparison to other things'.

The next phases in Christina's story show a strengthening sense of self-discovery, an increasing vitality and clarity of judgement.

> 'I have a lovely quote saying "All my life I have wanted to be somebody – now who the hell was it?" And as far as I'm concerned it was me. It's taken me a very long time to have any real sense of me, of what I want, what I stand for. But now it feels really good.'

INVITATIONS TO FIT IN

During the next few months Christina was approached by various head-hunters. She thought that some of this was 'window-dressing', there needed to be a woman on the shortlist, and that there was also a sense in the industry that she should be looked after. She was pleased that the posts discussed were in general management rather than personnel. This reflected her own view of her developing competence and interests.

But the process of being interviewed became irritating, helping her clarify her own motivations. She felt that she was always the 'radical' candidate on the shortlist, not because of being a woman but because she expresses her views openly and was a known personality, with the potential to intimidate. She also noticed that much of the negotiation was about how she would fit into the existing organizational culture.

'It took me a while to realize why I found it so stressful, which was that I didn't want to fit in. And I didn't see why I had to. I was getting cross about the fact that all the things I considered my strengths were being treated as weaknesses. The things that made me different and special. . . were going to be disruptive.'

She later learnt that she had been described as 'idiosyncratic' and 'a harridan' by some of the assessors.

TRAVELLING

Christina was already committed to an extensive trip, to be a keynote speaker at a conference in New Zealand and visit other places *en route*. Timed as it was, this journey offered two important insights in her process of becoming more herself, and signposts for her next steps.

The first insight involved her own sense of personal identity. Christina visited relatives in Australia, where she had lived as a child. In doing so she 'discovered' her mother, who had died when Christina was 10 years old, and about whom no one had been able or willing to talk to her.

'Up until then I hadn't really the foggiest clue where I came from because I'd never seen anything of myself in my father and. . . siblings. I had come to the conclusion that I was self-invented. I learned. . . that I'm very like my mother, not to look at. . . but in things I was interested in, the way I talked. . . . It was very exciting because I realized I did actually come from something, which was a good feeling.'

Her second revelation came through the professional work she did. In addition to her speech, she ran two large-scale workshops, planning them spontaneously and eliciting people's participation. These had an impact on the conference. She had not run such events before on this scale and in an unfamiliar environment. She reasoned that if she could do this away from home, where she was unknown, then she could create her own business, based on her own expertise, when she returned.

'MY BRAND WAS ME'

Christina returned to the UK clear that she should set up her own consultancy, using her skills for achieving change at board level. She saw this motivation as markedly different from becoming a consultant because she had no alternatives: 'it has to be a positive decision'.

The next few months were a highly generative time. With a new sense of her own worth and of her differences from others, she set out to refine her business identity in order to project it as her 'brand'. Rather than fit in, she would build on the reputation she had for doing things in a distinctive way. She wanted every aspect of her business to be congruent. For example, when people picked up her stationery she wanted them to say: 'Yes, that is Christina, that is what she would do.' She was fiercely protective of this professional identity, wanting not to dilute it, deciding what she would not do, who she would and would not work with, in order to maintain its integrity. She was forthright in negotiations.

Within a month of launching her business Christina had signed her first major contract. The immediacy of her new life, the sense that she was using all her professional skills, and being directly responsible for her successes and income made this an exciting and heady time.

She had been ignoring the continuing calls from head-hunters. She was, however, eventually persuaded to put her name forward for the post as chief executive of a national charitable organization. As she had done in the past, she said 'yes' but considered it very unlikely that she would be selected.

> 'So I was quite appalled when they offered it to me, because the implications were quite terrible. Everything I'd been planning got swept away.'

'AN ORGANIZATION THAT WANTS *ME*'

Christina accepted the invitation to become chief executive. She wound up her eight-month-old consultancy. When I first talked to her she had been in the post for only six weeks. She was both elated with her new life and its potential, and regretful for the sense of freedom, individuality and achievement she had briefly tasted and might now lose.

But, initially at least, life in this organization was radically different from any she had experienced previously. She thought she might be able to maintain the strong sense of identity and vitality she had developed.

> 'What's extraordinary, I'm finding, is that I never have to think about how I should say or do something. I do what comes naturally and it works. It's what they want and they love it. . . . All the energy that you normally find that you have to put into fitting in, I don't have to do here. And this organization is a perfect match for me. . . . I feel I haven't lost myself, but I've gained an organization.'

Christina identified with the organization in various ways. Firstly, there were lots of women in it, although not many at senior levels, and she admired their style of self-presentation as 'strongly feminine' rather than androgynous. This contributed to a positive culture, in which women and men were not restricted by stereotypes. Secondly, she saw it as a crusading organization, which fitted her values. Thirdly, she felt that it had the potential to operate both in a businesslike way and to treat people as whole rather than as narrowly defined work-selves.

Repeatedly during our conversation, Christina came back to the actions she was taking, and planned, to develop her new organization. Diversity, flexibility, participation and empowering all employees were her criteria for a good culture. In this job she felt she had the mandate to pursue these values, and a very enthusiastic membership to join her in doing so. This seemed a fitting organization for her passions.

A PROPITIOUS SEQUENCE

Looking back over the last eighteen months Christina was exhilarated. She also felt that the sequencing of changes could not have been better had it been planned. She could only have left her husband when she had a job as a place of support. She could not have left her previous job freely had she still been married, as her husband's anxiety would have undermined her determination.

Only once she had made her discoveries in Australia and New Zealand did she have the image from which to create her consultancy. And only when she had been herself and operated independently could she engage with a new organization in a different way.

> 'Someone who knows me really well and knows this organization said he thought I would not have got this job straight from my previous job because I wasn't the person then that I am now. I think that's right.'

Her sense of being a renewed person is the most striking aspect of this story.

> 'One of the reasons I feel so youthful is that I recognize myself now as the person I was twenty years ago, and not the person I've been in between. The things that amuse me and the way I express myself are much more like they were then.'

Christina was also more open with her feelings. This shift was unlocking not only her self of twenty years ago, but also aspects of herself she had hidden since childhood. Her guardedness was a protective strategy she had developed very early in life. Christina felt that her childhood had profoundly shaped her. She had wondered whether she was permanently damaged by her experiences, despite her strong coping strategies. She concluded, however, that she had developed 'all kinds of skills' and a sense of being strategic.

> 'I actually feel quite sorry nowadays for anyone who takes me on, because the chances of anyone having developed the same set of skills I have is fairly remote. They were painfully acquired. They really are worth having.'

Her recent life changes had provided a challenging test of her resilience. Her delight in her new self and life reflected a greater confidence in her own grounding. Her lifelong sense of independence, for example, was highly appropriate to her current role.

> 'One of the greatest strengths about working here is that I don't need to be here and they know I don't. I'm here because I choose to be, and I'll stay as long as it works for us both and no longer. There's no dependency and it's very useful. It means that people are more likely to deal with you straight, which releases energy.'

Her solid sense of her own power had also affected Christina's presentation of herself as a woman. Earlier in her career she thought she unconsciously presented a 'shield', deterring people from responding to her sexually. When we met she said she was comfortable to be a woman, and to express her sexuality at times.

'Now I will flirt because I feel entirely in control and can turn it any way I like, which suits me, and I can deal with the consequences. I really enjoy getting older. . . . I don't regret the loss of youth one bit.'

IN REFLECTION

Christina's view of her current life was very positive, and it was repeatedly and starkly contrasted with the repression she felt in earlier life phases. I could not help wondering whether her euphoria could be sustained, especially once she became more involved again with a single work organization. Her self-appraisal was also uncompromisingly positive. Her celebration of her own abilities seemed clearly warranted, and delightful in its freshness. And it could also come across as boastful. It certainly contradicts the stereotype that women underplay and undermine their own confidence.

When I wrote the first draft of this story I had a striking experience of synchronicity. I had worked all day on the analysis and writing. I finished late evening and turned on the radio. Within five minutes Christina was being interviewed. She made sound points clearly, but in the flatter tones of her public persona. This was not the celebratory voice I had heard. I felt I was being reminded of the person beyond the euphoria, of the capable experienced professional, with a somewhat guarded exterior.

CHRISTINA'S FEEDBACK ON THE DRAFT STORY

Christina made only minor revisions to the draft story, to aid clarity. She said it was 'incredibly impressive' and 'shook her' by bringing the events which she had put behind her close to home. It felt personal. (Later still, at a workshop, she felt the story might not include enough positives. She said she had had a strong sense of achievement and had gained much worthwhile experience in her financial services post.) She thought that she might have been a little 'naive' in taking up her chief executive role, as subsequent events had shown. Christina supplied a frank, self-reflective account of recent developments, from which I have written the next section.

ADDENDUM

'The task I had undertaken was massively more difficult than I had envisaged.'

Christina was soon sure what needed to be done, but there were severe financial constraints and a well-hidden, but very significant, resistance to change, despite her approach of extensive consultation. She really wanted to believe that she had found an organization matched to her values, and would not have to devote energy to guarding her back. But 'far from "belonging", it turned out to be the loneliest job I had ever had'.

Christina was working 15-hour days, fulfilling a demanding external programme as well as developing the organization internally. She had no time for other life activities, and lost touch with her friends and professional networks. She never felt tired because she was chronically exhausted. She discounted these personal issues, determined to deliver what she had promised.

Eighteen months in, having a company medical check, the doctor warned her that she seemed close to collapse. As the organization was then beginning to show signs of change, she felt able to assert her own needs more. She took steps to regain her health and gain professional support. She talked with the organization's non-executive directors about reorganizing her role. These talks unexpectedly turned sour, and she felt left with no choice but to resign.

'I was furious and upset, but also hugely relieved to be able to live my own life again.'

Christina set up independently again. Work has come to her in a variety of completely fortuitous ways. People seek her out *because* she is different. She holds several non-executive directorships, is a sought-after public speaker, and takes up unpaid roles of her choice.

'In every way, my life is hugely improved. I have more discretionary time than I have ever had in my life. I am also earning at a level which comfortably exceeds my previous salary.'

She is finally learning to accept that a portfolio of activities fits her best. She is 'not remotely tempted' to undertake another full-time executive role.

Her time in the chief executive post was by no means disastrous. She developed additional skills, became much stronger in herself and more realistic about her limitations. She is satisfied that the change processes she introduced were right: they have continued, slowly, and are increasingly producing better results. She does feel let down by people who could have given her more support. 'But that's life.' Professionally, her reputation has been enhanced.

'I still feel rather frustrated about it all, but at the same time know that this is a better deal for me. . . . I try not to beat myself over the head about the past.'

Claire

OVERVIEW

Claire wanted to stop, to 'get off the roundabout'. She had been very successful, becoming a personnel director in an international organization by her mid-thirties. Her inner confidence had, however, never quite matched other people's high regard for her. She left her post, wanting to nurture other aspects of her life. After nine months of living out her dream she was enticed back into employment, initially as a part-time consultant. Claire's decision to pause in her career was significantly influenced by an earlier choice in which she had become more committed to work. I shall therefore explore this move too in some detail.

EARLY CAREER HISTORY

Claire attended a grammar school, but never flourished academically there. As she prepared to leave at 18 she remembers no helpful career guidance, but was keen to go straight into employment. Her mother was a sound role model for a career woman, having worked all her life in nursing and, later, management. Claire was by then 'a Saturday girl' in a major High Street store. The head of personnel approached her and told her about their management training scheme, which had a non-graduate route. This was the lead Claire needed. She joined the organization and stayed with them for nineteen years, working in personnel and training.

Claire progressed well in the retailing company. It provided a conducive climate, because personnel was seen as central to business and women's talents in this area were appreciated. She was promoted rapidly and regularly, and was often the youngest person to have achieved a given post.

She spoke with special pride about what she had achieved during training, also outlining her beliefs about women and equal opportunities. She, with colleagues, had offered courses and networking activities for women, but had not made women's development a public campaign. She believed they achieved much more by taking direct action but not attracting publicity. She had come to believe, however, that many women look for reasons outside themselves for not achieving, but are secretly frightened to test their own capabilities.

'What I learned was that women aren't always very brave. . . it's easier to say what they can't do or can't have than actually take risks.'

SUCCESS, FRUSTRATION AND STRESS

As she moved from specific functional roles into more general personnel, Claire became less satisfied. In her last post in that company she headed half the personnel function and reported directly to the main board. But she found the company's highly political way of working demotivating. Despite its perceived value, personnel was not as powerful as the commercial functions, and its practitioners had to take a highly persuasive approach. She was disappointed at having to sell her ideas so obliquely, and at how emerging consensus could be destroyed if only a few key managers were unwilling to agree.

'It became very frustrating to have a contribution to make, but to have to go round the houses in order to be able to make it.'

Claire saw politicking as an essential feature of big business, and personnel, a function in which some women do achieve seniority, as often in an ambivalent power position. She doubted whether she would ever have the power she sought to be fully responsible.

'I was never going to be able to be in the ultimate position, where I could actually say "Well it's now down to you" because it's a very highly managed organization.'

She also thought that other people had been better at playing politics than she was. Her management approach was based on natural assertiveness and professional expertise, rather than on engaging in elaborate games of persuasion. Looking back, Claire summarized this career phase as rewarding but demanding.

'There was a lot of success in those years, but there was a lot of stress and self-imposed pain, I think.'

'The words that come to mind are "success" and "status" and meeting all sorts of aspirations and ambitions. What does not come to mind are the words "enjoyment", "fun" or having a good time or feeling the benefits.'

She wondered if this was because of her personality, or was a pattern likely to be shared with other senior women.

'I'd come out at the top of the scale on "Be Perfect", and that is because I think we're [women are] brought up to get it more right than anyone else because we're fighting against the odds and have to be better than anyone else. . . . So I was fairly obsessive about being good at what I did, but not very good at recognizing when I was.'

There was a high 'price to pay' for maintaining the consistent work performance, for 'having to do it all right and not being able to fail'. She saw these as her personal drivers, but also as true of many people, women and men. The personnel role exacerbated them because its influence was so indirect. Part of the price for Claire was the stress she continually felt. She had frequent migraines, engaged in binge eating and was constantly fatigued. She spent most of her spare time sleeping, 'to catch up, and there wasn't much quality of life'. Her self-confidence was also very low. Whilst she could usually perform well, sometimes the easiest things seemed too difficult. She needed constant reassurance about how she looked and how she ran the home. Looking back, Claire could not see how she got into this situation, but once she was there it became a self-reinforcing cycle.

Other people seemed to have much more confidence in Claire's competence than she did.

'I'd achieved all sorts of firsts, which should matter and do matter, and I'm very proud of them, but I couldn't really enjoy them.'

'What it was never possible to explain, almost to anybody, is that no matter how brilliant you're told you are or how brilliant you appear to be by what you've done or what you've achieved, if you don't feel it then actually you don't get the reward.'

Nor could the triumphs compensate for the 'harsher difficulties' of being senior in such a highly political organization.

As she was then working mainly with senior managers, she became more aware that she was a woman in a world still dominated by men. Whilst she did not believe sexism had affected her at all earlier in her career, at this level equality was not guaranteed, especially in day to day interactions:

'There isn't any doubt that you have to manage the relationships with men carefully in order to ensure that they don't feel threatened and feel you're trying to be cleverer than them.'

Thus a double game of subtle influence had to be played: one strand was the difficulty of realizing the potential power of the personnel role; the other was not overstepping acceptable boundaries of gender behaviour. She did, however, largely exempt her own immediate boss from the above description: he was 'one of the most enlightened managers I've ever come across'; he looked at people's abilities, not their gender.

Claire had also to cope with her suspicion that her physical attractiveness was appreciated as much if not more than her competence. This contributed further to her ambivalent self-image, and may well have repercussions as she ages.

'I think, to be perfectly frank, that if anybody had said to any one of the very senior people I worked with "What do you think about Claire?" they would have said things like "She's lovely, gorgeous", and only then "she's also very good at what she does".'

Claire believed her appearance opened doors for her and did her no disservice in an environment where people were very conscious of fashion and looking good. She could have decided not to become part of this aspect of the culture, but thought this would only have drawn a different, less positive, kind of notice. Some 'fitting in' was part of the implicit bargain if she wanted to succeed.

Another discord in Claire's image was her lack of university education. Once she became a senior manager it sometimes affected other people's perceptions of her (especially later when she wanted to move organizations).

> 'My lack of academic achievement has been a big burden for me ... because ... I haven't a degree ... all those things that everyone thinks you ought to have if you're a senior person in business.'

Claire was, then, finding life in senior management stressful for a variety of reasons which were a mixture of organizational, potentially gender-related and personality factors. Her ability to deal with this situation was further complicated by her marriage. For several years before leaving this organization she had been married to a colleague one level ahead of her in the hierarchy. He was her 'biggest supporter', having total faith in her ability and pushing her to be more ambitious. But their combined situation resulted in a high-pressure lifestyle. The organization dominated their working and social lives; there was too little time for them to relax away from very demanding jobs. Recognizing each other's sense of pressure, they tried not to bring problems home, and so communicated less and individually received less help. Claire was often too tired to enjoy weekends, which were further marred by the likelihood of 'getting stress symptoms at 4 p.m. on a Sunday afternoon' as she anticipated the pace and demands of work.

Despite her obvious success and her career being 'good overall', life in the organization was 'getting very sour', and her lifestyle generally was marred by tension and stress.

NEW OPPORTUNITIES

Claire then received her first telephone call from a head-hunter. She engaged in the resulting recruitment process more because she thought it wise as a learning experience than because she felt suitable for the post. The job was as personnel director in the small headquarters team of a division of a large international organization, and was unlike her previous experience in many significant ways. But there were attractions. She would have more potential for direct impact and she would learn about other business functions. The chief executive was impressive and she wanted to work with and learn from him.

'This was a man with as many feminine instincts [meaning intuitive and caring as well as being assertive and so on] as I could have hoped for, highly motivating, very charismatic . . . doing things completely differently from anything I'd experienced . . . and I thought he'd be supportive.'

She also realized that she was unlikely to gain significant promotion in the retailing company. Her husband would probably reach the main board ahead of her, and she was sure they would not accept a couple working together at such a senior level. Further she thought that it might be better for her marriage if they were less intensely involved through work.

'The timing was perfect really, although I think the spirit was willing and the body weak.'

So, with some trepidation at stepping out into the unknown, Claire decided to accept the job. The transition was marked with tension. She felt she was leaving 'home', the safe, known, cosseted environment. Senior managers reacted as if they were the deprived parents; they were disappointed, and implied that she was being disloyal.

MOVING ON

Claire's new job was already changing shape as she entered it. In particular the need for international travel was greater than anticipated. The move was traumatic in some ways, but she felt well supported, especially by the chief executive, and enjoyed learning how to function on the board. The job was full of challenges, and did involve action and implementation in a much more direct style than her previous post.

Her home life was not, however, made easier. They went 'from feast to famine', losing the shared base of industry, company and colleagues which had previously been a mixed blessing, and both travelling extensively, so that it was difficult to find time together.

The discord between other people's perceptions of Claire's competence and her self-image continued. She gave an example. Soon after joining her new company she was offered the main board directorship. She did not accept the job because she doubted her ability to do it. She imagined that many other people would have taken it and worked out the consequences later. She thought her decision was 'fear-driven' and would like the reassurance of knowing that other people have the same 'anxiety about performance' – 'it's a big burden because you're fighting against it constantly'.

Claire had to pay a high price for maintaining the public image of competence and energy which she did not wholly feel internally. In her new job, however, 'it was better because I felt more supported and I was learning new things and growing'. Her previous stress symptoms disappeared initially, as she felt under little pressure to perform. But later they returned, 'self-imposed', because she felt she had not achieved enough. There was no evidence that other people shared this perception.

DECIDING TO LEAVE – 'TO DO NOTHING'

After eighteen months Claire was feeling 'tired, exhausted', and she anticipated major changes in the organization, requiring a restructuring programme of two or three years, which she decided she did not want to see through:

> 'Part of that was a total lack of interest. . . because it didn't seem to me to be what I wanted to do. And part of it was fear that I wouldn't be able to cope with it. Part of it was fatigue and part was just wanting to get off the roundabout. I'd been here, there, and felt I'd done everything. I was supposed to be this high powered career person. . . and I didn't feel like it. There was no fun, I didn't wake up in the morning and look forward to going to work.'

She was very aware of her tiredness, and of all the family and leisure things she was not able to do. She decided to leave. She emphasized that her decision was not dislike of that particular job – 'I couldn't have wished for a better set of circumstances'.

Claire said she took charge of her life, and forced the decision through in the face of everyone's inability to understand. She described it as 'the biggest negotiation' of her life, and said 'the really courageous bit. . . which really shocked people, was that I had to negotiate it from a very emotional base'. No one else wanted her to leave. Her chief executive and colleagues did not doubt her competence. Her mother did not think she would survive long without the challenges of work. This was not a possibility she had discussed in advance with her husband. She needed to 'break the news to him', and he was no better able to understand than other people. He had high regard for her professionally and could not understand why she should throw it all away. Other people assumed that she would do something 'worthwhile' like study, should she really be serious about giving up employment.

'I knew that I didn't want to go and do something else, I just wanted to stop. It's all I knew. I wanted out of the organization, corporate life, power, just to get out. I'd done it for twenty years and it was enough. But I had no clue about doing anything else. I just wanted to do nothing. And that was extremely hard for everyone I talked to to understand.'

She wanted 'to do all those things [she] hadn't done for the past twenty years', such as lunching with friends, going to exhibitions, getting up late, and handing her husband a gin and tonic when he arrived home from work.

'I wanted to switch part of my brain off for a while, so that I could feed another part of it.'

The image of needing different or more nurturing appeared several times in her account. She believed that she was driven by factors in her personality – to regain a sense of self and zest she had lost - and the discomfort she was feeling in 'very demanding senior jobs'.

Looking for an explanation to give others, Claire highlighted another factor in her decision-making. She was unlikely to be able to have a family, given the busy life she was leading, was worried that time was running out as she grew older, and wanted to create space for this to happen. Saying this was 'embellishing a little', but losing control of this option was a significant concern. Ironically this stereotyped women's priority was the reason other people found easiest to believe. That she had had enough of high-pressure employment did not make ready sense to them.

'I did feel some pressure to find a good reason, as opposed to just saying "I want to stop working because I've had enough and want a good rest". I had to find that good reason for everybody, including my husband.'

She found it most difficult to persuade her husband that leaving was wise. He had known and married her as a high-powered, competent, professional woman. This identity, and what she therefore represented, was, she felt, the basis for his respect. He could not understand her apparent change of heart.

'I projected something I decided subsequently I didn't want to be. He wanted me to be that which he married.'

Perhaps he was especially disillusioned because he had played such a strong part in supporting Claire's career success.

Also there were financial implications. Claire contributed 40 per cent of the family income. They might have to make significant changes in their lifestyle.

As they explored these issues further, it seemed as if Claire's husband disliked the notion of dependency. Her apparent strength meant that their relationship could be that of two independent people living a conjoined life. She, instead, saw their marriage as a partnership. Claire felt that her subsequent home-making activities were not appreciated by her partner: he did not see them as contributing to the relationship because they were non-monetary.

After considerable negotiation, Claire's husband conceded. She appreciated that she could not have made her decision had he not finally agreed or been earning a high income. She believed, however, that she would make the same decision in a similar future situation whether or not she has such protection.

As several other research participants have done, Claire tried to take care of company issues at this stage, not wanting to leave the chief executive in the lurch. She stayed on for a few months helping him restructure and recruit for the organization's next phase of development. She was seeing the job through, secure in the knowledge that she had set her limit of involvement.

SO THEN. . .

'So then I had a ball for nine months. It was wonderful, just bliss.'

Claire spent more time with her family; went to exhibitions, the theatre, cinemas; went out to lunch; cooked meals; did the gardening and so on – 'all those things that most women would give anything to stop having to do'. She thoroughly enjoyed herself, did not feel guilty, and regained her sense of vitality. Her husband later said that he had enjoyed her being at home more. The change was less significant financially than anticipated.

But Claire noted that she had become somehow erased as interesting for many people she met socially. She found it difficult to answer the standard 'What do you do?' She said that she was having a sabbatical, taking time out to do 'some wonderful things'. But no one was interested in knowing what these were. Ironically, whilst she was now reading the newspapers for the first time in her life and felt she knew more about the business world, she felt dismissed as uninformed. She found this lack of presentable identity stressful.

BEING ENTICED BACK

Then a request came to help out an old friend by doing some personnel consultancy. Claire accepted, and was soon working part-time, finding it very fulfilling. She felt that her husband and friends could understand her more once she stepped back into employment.

'[My husband] felt I should be doing something because it was a waste. I fought back for a while, but it was a hugely difficult transition for him to make because he hadn't married that person.'

Claire was then invited to join a consultancy with which she had been working. Her role involved career and personal development with senior managers. She enjoyed this and was impressed with the organization's purposes. She looked forward to going to work – one of her main indices of a job's appeal.

I asked her whether her urge to do nothing had been satisfied. She was not sure. She would have been perfectly happy to continue longer, but could not tell how much longer. She was, however, beginning to feel the pricking of her 'working-class conscience', questioning whether it was right and proper for her to be financially dependent, suggesting she should earn a living.

POSSIBLE FUTURES

When we met, Claire was facing some new decision-making. Her marriage had broken down. Her decision to leave work had been a contributory factor but not the main reason. She was experiencing 'a difficult and horrible time'. She had temporarily withdrawn from the consultancy practice because she did not have the energy to do the one-to-one counselling work it involved. She was preoccupied with addressing her own problems.

She wondered whether she needed to become financially independent again. (Her consultancy income would not allow this.) She had been out of mainstream business for nearly three years, and realized that she would have to rebuild her confidence. But she believed she would find the right opportunity, given time. She felt that she had learnt a great deal about herself by taking her step out of employment. In particular she was now fiercely sure that she had to live according to her own dictates, to be suspicious of the many demands and expectations other people try, however subtly, to place on her. In this she was partly repudiating the servicing, caring role of personnel, which encouraged her to look after others and give her own needs low priority.

> 'Having been in a profession where you spend most of your time listening to other people it was very important for me to feed myself and get some nourishment for me.'

As she contemplated possible choices, she described herself as needing courage again to stand out against people's well-meant advice on what she should do. This tension seemed to touch a central conflict in her identity. If she did what people thought she should, she said firmly:

> 'I will only be doing what I've been taught to do all my life, which is doing the right thing. . . . I'm not going to do that because that's what I've got to stop doing, [to stop] trying to please other people at the expense of pleasing myself.'

Her comments are relevant to many traditional women's roles, and present an interesting paradox, that despite reaching senior positions in such functional areas, people risk losing their own voices, whilst outwardly they may seem exceptionally self-seeking in their ambitious career attitudes.

Claire was continuing to spend time on herself, to make sure she learnt what she needed from the process she had set in motion. Her determination to define herself, to do things her way because they felt right, and to escape her self-sacrificing script was strong. It felt, when we met, that she was engaged in a further phase of self-exploration.

One major choice was that between work she enjoyed and gaining a high salary. She would need courage to choose the former, and thought it would be harder to live without money now that she had experienced having it. Whilst she wanted work that made it a joy to get out of bed in the mornings, she believed her well-being was maintained by pastimes such as going to the ballet, opera and theatre. They were part of the 'vitality and enjoyment' in life she had regained: 'There are some things I wouldn't want to give up, they feed my soul.'

Claire was adamant that she would have a different attitude to employment in the future.

'Once I'd stopped working and got rid of all that stress and pressure, I did take a lot of time to think about how I'd do it differently, and if I did how I'd ensure I didn't get myself back into that state.'

She would not be frightened to leave a job again in the future: 'Nothing is for ever any more'.

Claire believed she survived the stress she experienced because when necessary she was willing to 'take control' and address problems head-on. She believed a lot of people are unwilling to do this, and suffer the consequences. She said that leaving her director post was when she took most control in her life. She often talked about courage, particularly the courage women need to act rather than find excuses (such as biased organizational cultures) for their inaction. She saw this too as a requirement for health.

IN REVIEW

After one decision had led Claire towards more career commitment, providing an extreme test of this as a lifestyle, the next took her out of employment. She withdrew because she started to take her own concerns about her lifestyle and her inner sense of self seriously. (Other people did not doubt her competence, but she did.) This story shows how discord between outer and inner self-images can produce a major schism of identity. Perhaps such dynamics are more likely to happen to successful career women of this generation than to many other people. The price of maintaining a competent, consistent professional image is high, when it is driven both by personal injunctions to 'be perfect' and by gender dynamics which encourage women to mask any potential differences from dominant norms. Such acts of impression management favour self-control and rigidity, rather than the flexibility to develop as new challenges emerge. They may therefore impede the learning and reformulations of identity which can accompany career progression.

CLAIRE'S FEEDBACK ON THE DRAFT STORY

Claire went through the draft story thoroughly. We then discussed her reactions by phone and negotiated what changes I would make. She said that she could remember most of our conversation and had no significant problems with the story content – my interpretation was 'mostly right'. She answered my questions and provided extra information on some issues. She wanted to adjust some wording to clarify the sense and occasionally to tone down a comment which now seemed too extreme.

ADDENDUM

Claire has now rebuilt her life and has remarried. She is living in the country and is a housewife and mother. She is delighted with her new situation. She does not plan to go out to work in her child's formative years. When the latter goes to school she will review her life again. She is very glad that she had a career; she has no regrets and does have warm memories. She cannot imagine going back to careerism again. But occasionally she has a 'twinge'. Part of her would like to return to employment because she knows she would do it differently and better. She has reflected on the stress cycles which undermined her, and has planned how to avoid them. She might like a big personnel job, to prove that she can do it.

Jane

OVERVIEW

Jane was in the process of leaving when we met. Then in her early forties, she was taking advantage of her company's voluntary redundancy programme to realize intentions she already had to leave. She had given in her notice, and was to work on for nine months before her final departure.

Jane had not started out with clear career intentions. She had become committed to a professional identity in her later twenties, having settled on personnel as her area, and had then progressed into senior management. One particular job stands out in her story as causing intense depression and stress. At the time she attributed this to various forms of sexual discrimination from her immediate superiors and colleagues, exacerbated by difficulties in her personal life. She later found that a physical illness, candida, may well have contributed to her symptoms.

This experience had made Jane resolve to leave the company at some time. Afterwards she regained her self-confidence and made sure that the organization appreciated her professional competence. She was proud that she had achieved these re-evaluations before she left. Jane was also motivated by her growing sense that she wanted a different lifestyle. With slight trepidation, she was creating space so that what she really wanted could become apparent.

UNCERTAIN CHOICES

Jane's late school, university and early work choices were exploratory, not guided by clear career directions. Often she felt that other people had been unhelpful. Several times she made mistaken choices, by adjusting to limited available options, but felt under pressure to continue with the course or post for a while, until she could achieve a change of direction. Jane attributed this repeated non-assertive pattern to early experiences:

'It was a real lack of self-confidence as a result of my upbringing. . . . Basically I had a very domineering father and any of my opinions were immediately put down, and we all had to do what he said. And I think it's stemmed from that. . . . For a long time I didn't think I had the right to ask for what I wanted. . . . I was quite fearful. . . of other people. . . . It's not a problem now because I think I'm sufficiently assertive.'

She eventually studied psychology and did a variety of jobs, taking on professional caring roles and doing research.

Her options were further affected by marrying during her university course and seeking choices which fitted with her husband's activities. By the time she was 27 Jane had a young daughter and was separated from her husband. She then put herself under pressure to decide what she 'really' wanted to do.

'I thought it was ridiculous and that I should get a proper job, a career. But what on earth was I going to do?'

Through a process of elimination she decided on personnel management. She looked for a suitable graduate trainee scheme, but faced limited opportunities because of her age. Eventually she accepted a job with a large, nationwide, service organization. She was to work at head office in London. This fitted with her personal life, as her boyfriend at the time lived there, but it was not straightforward in career terms. (Jane's daughter disappears from the story at this point as she was mainly raised by her father.)

FURTHER DELAYS

Jane was initially placed in a middle management job in market research because she had relevant experience, although she had applied to join personnel. It was several years before she was allowed to transfer. Looking back, she again felt that she could have been more assertive in pushing for a move, but she was advised that moving too quickly would make a poor impression.

At first Jane was frustrated at the rates of promotion available, even for people like her who entered on a 'fast stream'. The career development system at that time was relatively tradition-bound and rigid. She also felt she was not stretched by the work on offer. As she described these times, Jane sounded rather resentful, as she had about several earlier phases of her work history. She was not in charge of her own situation, and felt that her expressed wishes were not taken into account by those with power. With hindsight, she believed she could have taken more initiative, but at the time she accepted others' advice and the situation she was in.

PERSONNEL: A CLEARER DIRECTION

Jane eventually moved into personnel and soon gained a scholarship to do a one-year diploma in personnel management, which was hard work but enjoyable. At about the same time she passed a promotion board, placing her ready for the first rung of senior management. When she returned from her course, however, there were no positions available, partly because of recent staff cutbacks.

After about nine months of waiting, it became apparent that there would not be a suitable head office job at the appropriate level for the foreseeable future, and that Jane must take another option, moving out into a district to become a local head of personnel. By the time she was eventually offered a specific job she felt she had little choice but to accept. She had been warned against working with the manager who would be her boss because he had 'an awful reputation'. She had been concerned at his argumentative and patronising treatment of her at interview. But the head office person in charge of appointments had issued an ultimatum: 'If you withdraw from this, we'll just take it that you're not interested in being promoted.'

STRESSFUL TIMES

Jane moved to her new position: she was in charge of personnel for the county. She 'enjoyed the actual content of the job very much' – 'under other circumstances it would probably have been my ideal job, at the time'. But she immediately felt under pressure. There were several aspects to this, related to being a woman and coming from head office.

Her manager started harassing Jane sexually. He would, for

example, put his arm round her in front of colleagues and union representatives.

'This guy was just a real bastard. He'd come in and put his arm round me, try to hold my hand. Literally it was like chasing you round the office. . . it was affecting my work and my credibility.'

Telling him to stop had no effect. Jane could not enlist the local welfare manager's help because he was organizationally junior to her. To reach potential informal advisers she had to contact regional head office. She did later make a formal complaint. Her boss was 'spoken to' and stopped harassing her physically.

The move was also a major culture shock.

'But it was so different! First of all they weren't used to people from head office so that was against me from the start, which would have been the same had I been a man. I was relatively young and also I tend to look younger than I actually am so there was this "Look at this young upstart coming down to be head of personnel. Who do they think they are?" And a woman. They'd never had a woman in a senior management job and they just couldn't handle it.'

In previous employment and at head office, apart from one or two minor incidents, she had never felt discriminated against or treated any differently because she was a woman. She had not therefore developed any coping strategies in lower-level, less visible, positions.

Jane's way of working – holding meetings of her team and eliciting ideas from members – was 'totally alien to the office, which ran on macho management'. Most people wanted to be told what to do. The district was suspicious of innovation and resisted change: 'It was really, really difficult.' (A head of finance, recruited a year previously from outside the organization, had faced similar difficulties.)

Jane's efforts to be effective in her job were often ignored, undermined or ridiculed.

'Everything I tried to do was blocked by him [her manager] or by the other managers. They didn't take me seriously. I tried to arrange meetings on things I wanted to do that were directly concerned with their work areas and they wouldn't turn up . . . . It was just dreadful.'

The other senior managers (all men) did nothing to support Jane or to relate to her individually; they took their lead from their joint boss. Her working environment was therefore predominantly hostile. In this she felt particularly unfortunate; most local managers were more positive in their attitudes to women.

Jane gave an example of how the other managers related to her. On her first day back from a holiday, she attended a budgeting meeting. Figures had been produced for her department in her absence, and the head of finance volunteered to explain these if necessary. Instead he remained silent, even when called on by her to speak, leaving her to the wrath and sarcasm of her boss. Jane found such behaviour unsupportive, but typical. Her colleagues would not publicly support agreements they had reached with her privately, leaving her beleaguered and isolated, and undermining her ability in her job.

'In the end I actually started having symptoms of stress. . . . I got very run down and was getting depressed.'

Jane later discovered that she had multiple food allergies and systemic candida which were contributing to the symptoms she was experiencing. She felt depressed and below par. She was still, however, doing her job well.

'The one thing I was clinging to through all this was that no one could say I wasn't doing a good job, because I really felt I was. Even if it wasn't recognized by the people that should have been recognizing it, *I* knew I was doing a good job.'

SUPPORT FROM ELSEWHERE

Jane did have sources of support within the organization nationally and in her social life. She met with the few other women in similar posts occasionally and found this helpful. She met other, male, heads of personnel from neighbouring districts, whom she also found supportive. They knew her manager and said that they would not be able to work with him. But although Jane also met women personnel managers from local companies she did not build close ties with them. There was no one with whom she felt an affinity.

'Just because you're both women it doesn't necessarily mean that you're going to be able to give each other support.'

A further source of support was engaging in psychotherapy, which was highly valuable to her.

> 'Because of my family background and various other things it was something I really needed to get straight. And actually it was really good. It was actually one of the best things I've done in my life.'

Jane was also involved in local activities, which gave her a wide circle of friends.

> 'So I had quite a lot of people I could go and talk to. . . . I did have support outside work and what I would have done if I hadn't I just don't know. It would have been dreadful.'

THE SITUATION ESCALATES

After about two years there was a major reorganization. Six months later Jane's manager left. She hoped that her troubles would be over.

> 'The person who replaced him wasn't at all the same. They were chalk and cheese. But it was like the other side of the male chauvinist, I suppose. Instead of being really aggressive and harassing and "What I say goes". . . it was the patronizing "Look on me as a father figure" sort of thing, which actually was as bad.'

Jane felt belittled by this manager. Polite as he was, he did not accept her as a member of the team.

> 'He'd call a meeting. . . and, I'm sure he wasn't aware of this, but he'd just address himself completely to them and behave as if I wasn't there. He just shut me out.'

Jane and her new manager soon had a significant disagreement about her handling of a disciplinary matter. She had removed a worker from operational duties for inappropriate conduct. Her boss reinstated him, fearing union action. Jane felt totally under-mined by her superior's action.

In the rest of her life Jane was also facing difficulties. Her daughter had health problems, her mother was contacting her by phone and threatening suicide, and an intimate relationship had recently broken down. This combination of work and personal factors and her candida placed Jane under immense pressure, and she was far from well.

'I was feeling really awful. I was irritable, I was losing my temper with people. . . it was. . . becoming harder to hide.'

At this point Jane felt she made a 'very great mistake' in telling her boss that she was involved in therapy. She did so because her regular appointment made her unable to stay late if weekly board meetings overran.

'I think now that was the turning point where he wanted to get rid of me. . . . I realize now I should have kept my mouth shut.'

On the advice of the regional welfare manager, Jane took a week's sick leave. On her return, she was still feeling very depressed, she had to work long hours, and her work situation remained unsupportive. From this point on her position became increasingly stressful and untenable. She consulted the company counsellor and her doctor, but neither was really able to help. Eventually she went back on to sick leave. Her manager was soon pursuing her case aggressively, trying to persuade her to take demotion or medical retirement. Jane felt that she was without allies.

After two or three weeks, a meeting was held to review Jane's situation. She was confronted by the person responsible for senior management appointments in the area. Also present was the company stress counsellor who she thought was invited 'to make sure that [she] didn't have hysterics'. Jane reported that the appointments manager said:

'We're not actually telling you that you can't come back, but if you come back basically we'll make things so hard for you and you'll be put under such a lot of stress that you'd want to leave anyway.'

Negative, but unspecific and therefore unanswerable, comments were made about her past work performance (although she felt secure that annual appraisals had always been satisfactory).

'It was awful and I was very depressed, and the effect of this was to make it ten times worse, because basically what they were saying was, "You haven't got a job here and you're not going to get a job anywhere else".'

This meeting increased Jane's depression and made her feel that she could not return. In the end she was off work for six months.

Jane felt that she was unfairly pressured to make major decisions about her career at a time when she was not well. Initially she felt she needed only a short time off work to recharge her batteries, but she was not allowed this space. Other managers in the district were also on sick leave with stress-related illnesses at the time, but they did not seem to be put under similar pressure.

REGAINING CONFIDENCE AND CREDIBILITY

Help came from head office; as far as Jane was aware she had a good reputation there. When a senior manager offered her a job in his department she felt grateful, but did not think she really should have been. Looking back, she did not feel she could have continued under the circumstances she faced in the district.

Jane returned to London feeling demoralized and wanting to re-establish her self-esteem and credibility. She had to carry her feelings largely alone, and to withstand the aftermath of her experiences. She felt isolated because other people were unwilling to talk about her previous job and difficulties.

'I think what's been the worst thing about it is that nobody since has ever talked to me about it at work.'

She tried to discuss the situation with her new boss, for example, but to no avail. Eventually she gave him a six-page account of the experience from her perspective, concerned at what other views might be on her record. He never mentioned it. This general silence was difficult to live with, making the episode seem unfinished. Rumours also circulated that she had been a failure in the district.

'It was all right in the end because I knew that I could do a good job, but. . . I had more of a hurdle to overcome to show them. . . . In fact it was fine because the job I was put into I enjoyed and I knew I was doing it well and I was getting good reports. . . . I suppose I just started redressing whatever balance I had to redress.'

Jane also watched what happened in her old district with interest. She wanted to check her judgements of the situation and people, and felt these were validated.

PREPARING TO LEAVE

By the time she returned to London, Jane had decided to leave the organization, but only once she had righted other people's, potentially negative, impressions of her.

> 'At the time I moved back I thought "Bugger them. I'm going to work in London just for a couple of years and I'll show what I'm made of and then leave because I'm damned if I'm going to stay with this company."'

Work proved more rewarding and challenging than she expected. In the next few years she developed organizational policies and practices she had previously thought needed improving. She worked on resourcing, promotion, appraisal and equal opportunities.

> 'If I'd left after my job in the district it would have been under this nasty cloud, but now I feel I can leave saying "This is what I've done", and having a reputation for getting things done. . . . I've regained my self-esteem and self-confidence. . . there was a time when I thought "I'm just never going to be able to work again." I just felt so knocked. I thought maybe they were right. I feel fine about leaving now because I feel I'm leaving on a crest.'

She had restored all she lost, and perhaps enhanced her confidence to judge herself. She also had the respect of her new boss. Jane's personal life continued to be very unsettled at times, but she felt secure in her work situation and performance. Her symptoms of candida persisted, but she had no recurrence of the intense depression and stress.

SEEKING A NEW LIFESTYLE

Jane had been tempted out of employment a little earlier than she planned, mainly because the redundancy terms offered were good. Her earlier decision to leave was affirmed by several linked motivations and tentative dreams. She was largely abandoning financial security, but only occasionally felt daunted by this. Once she decided she would leave at some time she started testing out various ideas – including running a garden centre, opening a craft shop, and becoming involved in alternative healing. There are echoes here of her early career, but this time the generation of options was clearly in Jane's own hands. When we met she had no firm idea of what she would do; this sense of open possibilities was part of the appeal of leaving.

There was also the pull of activities for which she had too little time. Her job dominated her week and she was too tired to do other things. She wanted to travel, garden, play the piano, do photography, cook, and make her own clothes again. She accepted that working long hours was 'part of the culture' and what she was being paid to do, but resented employment dominating her life.

'I just don't have the time. I get home late, I'm absolutely knackered. Whatever my good intentions are of doing things they just go out the window when I get in, because I'm tired. Then at weekends I lie in on Saturday because I'm exhausted, and I do things round the house. I sometimes wonder if it's me and whether if I was sufficiently motivated and I really wanted to do these things I would. But I don't think it's the case. I need the space and time to be able to do them.'

Repeatedly there was the strand of wanting space – breathing space, time for other possibilities to emerge.

'I'd like some time just doing nothing at all.'

'What I really want to do is have space and out of that space I trust that something will come that's clear to me I might want to do, and if it doesn't, I won't.'

Jane was also seeking greater congruity between who she is and what she does. Her sense that she was not in harmony had been growing.

'The last few years I've come to realize more and more that the kind of environment I'm working in is just not right for me. It's not nourishing me. I'm not sure if it's just because I'm a woman or because it's me and my particular feelings about it. I just feel really constrained by it, although I have quite a lot of autonomy.'

Jane wondered whether this feeling was because she was a woman working in 'a male world', and what this now common phrase means:

'Maybe it is because I'm a woman. . . . I've been coming to the conclusion that it's all very well saying "It's a man's world" meaning that there are an awful lot of men out there doing it and they're doing it in a man's sort of way. But actually I'm beginning to feel that the whole commercial, business-type world is very much based on a male outlook on life. It's actually a bit ridiculous because of working on equal opportunities, but I'm coming more and more to feel that it's just not right for women to be in that kind of environment at all because it's just not where women are coming from.'

Jane thought that women had been lured away from roles as homemakers and child-rearers because society does not give these equal respect with employment. But she felt that 'something has gone awry somewhere'. Whilst there should not be discriminatory barriers to women working, Jane felt she better understood women who choose not to.

Jane had felt some sense of discord for a long time, despite doing jobs which she thought satisfying and beneficial to other people.

'I've always been aware that there's been some mismatch between me and what I was doing. . . that what I was doing wasn't being true to myself and wasn't right. And really, if I'm honest with myself, that's been the case ever since I've been in this organization.'

She had not acted on these feelings partly because she did not want to lose her income, partly because she had no clear idea what she wanted to do. The redundancy money would give her 'a breathing space', a chance just to wait and see.

Another motivation was Jane's developing interest in spirituality. She felt this sounded 'awfully silly', but it was increasingly important to her. She was following the teachings of a Western spiritual master, not to accept uncritically what he said, but to find what resonated with her and to develop her own understandings. She therefore felt more comfortable, and accepting of potential uncertainty.

'My approach to life has changed over the past year. It's difficult to talk about because it's an inner thing. . . . I take things much more as they come. I worry a lot less. I can see much more that whatever happens is OK, rather than fighting it. . . . I'm not saying that's true all the time. But more so. I no longer feel the need to cling on to the security of my job because it's secure.'

Not knowing what would happen made her anxious occasionally, but was 'really exciting' most of the time.

Jane had mixed views on how seriously to take money in her decision-making. She did not want it to be too significant, and yet admitted that she did 'get a bit panicky about what [she was] going to do when the money runs out.' Her redundancy package would give her a year's salary tax-free. She also had money tied up in a house, and planned to move to reduce the mortgage. She was living with a partner, but he had a 'very intermittent income', and was unable to support both of them at that time. Jane had decided not to worry about financial problems unless they arose, but did find maintaining this attitude difficult at times. But she had survived on little money before, did not feel that more income had made her happier, and did not have expensive tastes.

> 'I'd much rather go back to making my own clothes and cooking from basics . . . and have the time to do that, rather than be driven.'

Jane felt that 'being driven' was something she developed early in life and was only then changing.

> 'I should have said before, that I was really driven on by my father. There were five of us and he pushed us to do well academically. That was everything, to get good marks. So I think I've always carried that with me until recently, that inner drive to do better than everyone else.'

She was not tempted to become a consultant in equal opportunities work, a growing field which she would have been well placed to exploit: 'That's not why I'm leaving and that's not what I want to do.'

There were tensions and contradictions as Jane explained her motivations, especially as she faced the outcome of a major decision which had not yet come to fruition. For all her internal dialogues, she had a very simple way of explaining her move to other people.

> 'I just say I'm going. Basically, I say that a year's tax-free salary is too good an offer to refuse and that I want to do something. . . completely different. . . . Lots of people, particularly at work, can't understand why I'm doing it. The women on the whole understand.'

Jane wondered whether she would have been happier working for a smaller, more informal organization, whether then she would have felt a greater sense of 'fit'. Ironically this was the direction her own organization was taking, just as she had made the decision to leave.

'I feel a bit sad that the way the business is going now I think is great. It's less hierarchical, more towards teamwork and open styles of management, less aggressive macho stuff. It's becoming more of the organization I'd feel comfortable working with. But. . . it's not enough to make me stay. How it would have been if it had been more like that when I first came I don't know.'

MOVING OUT

Jane was excited about leaving employment. Her motivation had crystallized over recent years. In leaving she was hoping to be more 'true' to herself than her career so far had allowed. Her early job choices came from a tense scanning of options and now she was giving herself a breathing space from which new possibilities could emerge. She was holding her own exploratory direction, gently but assertively. I hoped that practical necessities and others' views would not intrude too forcefully, as they had done in the past.

JANE'S FEEDBACK ON THE DRAFT STORY

Jane commented extensively on the story to clarify points and time sequences, and responded to my several questions. She wrote by my last sentence of 'Moving out' – 'They won't – I've changed!!' She said that I had done a 'thorough job' and that she was 'quite happy with [the draft] on the whole'. Some incidents referred to did then seem remote, and she could not remember details fully. She noted several points in the text which seemed especially important.

ADDENDUM

Jane felt well regarded by senior managers as she left. She had decided to become a gardener. She gained appropriate qualifications in gardening and garden design, to foster her own self-confidence and to sell herself to potential clients. So far she has survived well financially. Her redundancy money 'stretched remarkably far', given that it kept her and her partner. They won a car in a competition; its sale funded an extensive trip to Australia, the Far East and India.

She continues to follow the teachings of the Western spiritual master and says this has 'totally changed [her] life – corny but true'.

Jane's candida persists, fluctuating in its effects, but her symptoms are now more manageable because she is aware of their causes. In her recent job she worked under great pressure at times; she did not, however, have any recurrence of depression or stress. Looking back, she says:

'I can see I had to go through all the awful stuff to get to the [positive] point in my life I'm at now.'

Her ideal scenario now would be for her partner to be commercially successful and earn enough to keep them. She has discovered the joys of not working. But she is developing a business plan to launch herself in gardening. She concludes:

'Anyway, whatever happens, I have never for an instant regretted leaving... but I still haven't got time to do all the things I want to. ... I feel much more settled and that I'm making the right choices in my life.'

Is gender at issue?

ENTERTAINING GENDER AS A POSSIBILITY

Whether, to what extent and how gender is at issue in these stories are questions at the heart of this study. You may well already be wondering, and also be wondering what views I hold. Some exploration of these issues is timely.

Gender could be at issue in various ways, ranging from overt to highly implicit processes. For example, gender differences – and associated power differentials – are often created in interaction rather than being fixed attributes of the people involved. Rakow (1986) claims, in relation to communication, that 'gender' is a verb. Many researchers now study how people are involved in 'doing gender' through patterns of relationship (West and Zimmerman, 1991). One implication of this work is that women are active agents in constructing their identities and have some choice about whether they perform or challenge gender-stereotyped behaviours (and what meanings they attribute to their performances). But behaviour is also judged by others, who may reject the individual's intentions or constrain available options.

Gender can also be interpreted as operating more covertly, framing the social world to give primacy to certain values and behaviours – identified as either masculine or feminine – and devalue others, similarly polarized (Marshall, 1994). These 'choices' may seem 'natural' because they have become established in basic cultural assumptions. Feminist and pro-feminist work has done much to deconstruct these value systems as they are mirrored in a wide range of institutional forms such as language (Spender, 1980), assumptions about organizational commitment (Martin, 1990), and career theory (Gallos, 1989; Marshall, 1989).

Gender-related issues can, then, be appreciated as played out in complex interactions of different forms of choice and constraint. Apter and

Garnsey (1994) portray these processes evocatively and provocatively in the approach they call 'social enactment', which 'explores how social actors are both constrained by and can alter social structures' (p. 19).

I believe that gender is often at issue in these stories. Sometimes it is in the background, shaping the context. For example, senior roles in personnel are more accessible to women than are those in most other functional areas. These roles have certain distinctive features which often make power difficult to exercise directly (see Claire, p. 71.) and require the integration of conflicting groups' needs. Women in these roles may also find that they are expected by other people to behave in gender-stereotyped ways. (*Teresa* felt deterred from acknowledging her own stress at work; she was expected to help other people cope: p. 123.) This combination of factors may restrict a person's effectiveness and coping strategies and she may interpret the resulting pressures as an individual matter. The potential patterns and interactions just described are unlikely to be wholly about gender, but it is likely to be one strand in a relevant array of sense-making frames.

In several stories gender dynamics are more obviously in the foreground. *Jane* was sexually harassed by her manager; she believed that having power used against her publicly in this way undermined her credibility with colleagues.

But to claim that gender is always at issue or is the only potential factor is overdetermined. Gender shifts in and out of focus. Often it dissolves into other potential issues, most of which are to do in some way with power. So, for example, some senior men's reactions to women in this study could be interpreted as the dynamics of elite groups managing the insecurity which potential difference represents. They may restrict membership, enforce conformity and marginalize newcomers. These more general processes are equally relevant to the maintenance of race privilege (hooks, 1984). Focusing on gender alone can detract from appreciating the interactions between inequalities.

I believe that gender needs to be entertained as a possible frame of analysis throughout this book. This involves interrogating different levels of possible operation, from overt interactions to the potential gender patterning involved in foundational assumptions of organizational life. The outcome of this interrogation will not usually be clear-cut and will, I hope, produce many puzzles to ponder.

Should Jane have told her manager that she was involved in therapy, for example? In doing so she was contravening a code which makes emotions and potential distress 'dangerous' in the professional-seeming role cultures of organizations. This boundary can be interpreted as potentially gender-related. Emotions are defined out of idealizations of management, but are stereotypically attributed to women; the latter are assigned responsibility for managing their behaviour accordingly. Conforming to this demarcation affirms these several stereotyping processes, with potential stress consequences for women and men (Cooper and Marshall, 1979).

'IT'S NO DIFFERENT FOR MEN. WHAT ARE WOMEN EXPECTING?!'

One resolution of potential gender debates is to see the current organizational world as gender-neutral – 'the way things are and should be' – and to offer women membership on its terms. The data in this book suggests a deeper questioning of the qualities of organizational life. I would like to raise some of the associated issues at this stage, by answering a potential challenge.

One possible reaction to this book – which some people have already offered – is that women have unrealistic expectations, that they want organizations to be friendly, collaborative places, and 'the reality is' that they are hostile and unpleasant for everyone. This argument suggests that women take the coldness of organizational life too seriously, too personally.

As you read these stories you can evaluate whether, in your view, the ways of operating reported are inevitable, effective, appropriate to adapt to or questionable.

I do not believe the rhetoric of organizations as necessarily hostile places (although many I know can be). Not all organizations or departments are like this. Some people, men and women, manage to live by alternative visions of organizing. These possibilities do appear, albeit briefly, in the reported data.

One issue for debate is what kinds of relationships people can expect at work. When is it appropriate to separate professional and personal selves? When is their integration valuable and viable? I believe that ethical concerns are more likely to receive active attention if people bring their whole selves to work, and so I often wonder how this can be achieved. Many of the women in this research favoured more integration. They wanted to be themselves rather than adopt inauthentic public images. They also advocated professionalism and did not like the distorting effects of what they saw as inappropriate emotionality in organizational politics (a delightful irony, given the stereotyping of women as emotional). Perhaps valuable integration depends on what we transport from one environment to another and how well able we are to manage (by which I do not mean repress) it.

A related issue is whether unmoderated competition is a foundational aspect of business life. This is often assumed to be the case in analyses at individual, organizational and national levels. In contrast, various 'new' management models stress partnership, collaboration, empowerment and transformational leadership. The language used seems to herald a revaluing and integration of 'female' values. But this may be co-option, a token effort leaving the dominant base of values largely unreformed. The transformative potential of new approaches is seriously undermined if they are used for instrumental purposes or within frameworks of competitive advantage. Also, taken seriously, the 'new' relational ways of operating advocated are much more demanding of energy, skill and goodwill than most organizations' current practices. I doubt if many people have these competences in suitably robust and complex forms or can trust organizational environments to be safe places to exercise them. I regret that many of these hopeful initiatives may well lead to first-order rather than second-order change.

It seems inappropriate and unhelpful to claim that women's experiences of organizational cultures are wholly different from men's. Men can also be excluded, undermined and bullied. Their socialization as boys may, or may not, make them more familiar than women are with these patterns of behaviour. Sexism can often be interpreted as a subset of bullying. But in this symbolic world of conformity it seems important to acknowledge that women are usually more different from idealized norms than are many of their male colleagues – and are more readily identified as such. People of colour may be seen as more different still.

Life development issues

The four stories introduced so far explicate themes of life development particularly clearly; these themes are also apparent in several other accounts.

CHILDHOOD INFLUENCES

In several women's stories prominent life themes can be traced to childhood influences, but there is much diversity in this material. Several people had parents they considered controlling, although the impact this had on their later attitudes varied. The mothers of two people had died when the research participants were young, affecting their development significantly. A few women believed that needing to be independent or self-sufficient at an early age had given them determination they later found valuable.

It seems that some of the developmental tasks people had acquired in early life had now been completed. This is especially obvious for those who no longer feel driven or have proved their competence to their own satisfaction. Many people now say that they are doing things for themselves.

I did not pursue this form of analysis far. The data was insufficient to support further speculation. I must also admit suspicion about claims that childhood influences are clearly directional in their effects (although I do believe they are powerful) and about assumptions (made in some theories) that parental role models conform to dominant gender stereotypes.

AGE

Some of the women's decision-making reflects life reviews in the late thirties to mid-forties when they were critically appraising their organizational contexts and lifestyles. Some believed their previous development (which they did not regret because it was the path by which they had reached their ability to exercise choice), had led them away from other aspects of their identity or from feelings of basic life vitality. Deciding to move was therefore a bid to reorient their lives and achieve a more dynamic energy base.

I am reminded of an early American study of women managers by Hennig and Jardim (1978). This contrasted the lives of twenty-five women who had reached senior levels with those of twenty-five who had remained in middle management. The women who had been successful had all put their careers on hold temporarily in midlife and attended to aspects of their identities which they had previously neglected. (The authors concluded that these were more 'feminine' or relational aspects.) Doing this integration work seemed a prerequisite for further career progression. Several women in this study had similar experiences (if for different reasons). Their initially disruptive experiences of leaving seemed to provide learning which facilitated later development.

Another review point seems to come at around the age of 50. Some people had wondered whether job opportunities would then become limited, although this does not seem to have happened. Issues of image and personal life expectations may also surface, as they did for *Kim* (see p. 231), who lacked suitable role models for becoming an older woman.

A note about 'male-dominated' organizational cultures

The theme of working in 'male-dominated' organizational cultures, which was a prominent feature of Jane's experience in the district job, appears repeatedly in this book. Statistical studies of women's leaving intentions also affirm the significance of this factor.

I explore what this can mean and how it affected the research participants after the stories (see 'Organizational cultures', p. 300.). This theme impacts most of the other commentary sections in some way. For example, experiences reported in 'Tiredness' (p. 250.) partly result from the self-presentational work women have to do because images of successful management are still strongly shaped by male sex role ideals. The stories of Jane, *Teresa*, *Judith*, *Mercedes*, *Stevie* and *Julia* give extreme examples of 'male-dominated' culture dynamics.

Wanting a more balanced life

The story of: Sarah

Sarah stands alone in some ways in this study. She represents the many women with young children who seek to accommodate both home and work demands. She had recently shown both more career and more family commitment but her career success resulted in her life becoming too unbalanced. So she decided to return to centre and establish a new integration, giving more priority to her family.

In a way, I was pleased that there were not more examples of home–work conflict amongst the sample. This refutes a stereotype and makes it clear that other issues are important to women.

But I could be falling into a trap in this reaction, of devaluing parenting and seeing aspects of the organizational world as more legitimate concerns.

Sarah

OVERVIEW

I met Sarah four months after she had left her job as a manager with a large firm of solicitors. She had decided to do so because her life, and that of her family, had become too unbalanced. She found the price of working in a demanding job in another city, with the attendant travelling, and seeing little of her two young children and husband, too great. She was resting, wanting to return to the centre of her home and achieve a new balance there before taking another step in her own career. She was happy with this situation. It seemed particularly appropriate as she had made four major life changes in the last four years and did not want to hurry into another one. Sarah was weighing different life interests, choosing whether and on what terms to be employed.

EARLY CAREER

Sarah had been to university and then trained as a solicitor. She had moved to follow her husband's very successful medical career, always being employed herself in each location, but with no chance of achieving a partnership position until her husband's career stabilized. She saw the decisions and moves she had made as entirely shaped by being a woman. At times she has resented this fragmentation of her working life, but it has not been a battle: she saw herself as not very career-oriented, or conditioned to be so.

STUDYING FOR AN MBA: SHIFTS IN SELF-CONFIDENCE

Eventually, in the late 1980s, and by then with a young child, Sarah applied to do an MBA degree. This was a significant step, aimed at reorienting her career towards management. The family had settled for at least a while in one town. She applied for courses hesitantly, not at all confident that she would be accepted because of her age – she was then in her mid-thirties– and specialized experience. Gaining a place and finding she did well on the course boosted her self-esteem.

Her next major decision demonstrates an interesting interplay of career and family experiences. Sarah realized that having her first child had shaken her self-confidence. From being a professionally competent woman she had become 'ham-fisted' and isolated.

> 'I felt totally demolished, and I don't think I ever really quite re-established myself.'

Succeeding on the MBA restored Sarah's self-esteem, and she decided to have another child, feeling sure that she could fit everything in and that 'it would all be fine'.

Graduating from the degree, another motivation was also strong: she wanted to prove that it had been worth doing the course, and that having a new baby was not an excuse for doing nothing outside the home.

> 'I was going to justify having had that time to do the MBA, and as I saw it the only way to justify it was by getting a good job.'

A TAILOR-MADE JOB

Sarah found a high-credibility post which might have been designed for her. She was to set up management functions in a department of a large firm of solicitors. She could use her professional understanding and draw on her recent course. The job was a new venture for the firm and innovative in the industry. Sarah spoke with great respect of the organization she joined:

> 'I liked the people I worked for, I had tremendous respect for what they were trying to do. . . . It was a wonderful experience to be in an organization, particularly a legal organization, that was so innovative.'

She described her role as essentially to be 'the interface between the solicitors and the rest of the place', a division marked by them-and-us attitudes. She established formal administrative systems, and initially had to justify her own existence. Administrators were not overly appreciated. She liaised with the functional directors in human resources, finance and business planning.

'I had to be calm and expert on my department for all those purposes.'

'It was a very, very busy job. . . very challenging.'

Sarah had a good working relationship with her immediate senior, who was 'as unsexist as I would expect anyone to be, given his training, the environment and everything else. A very fair person to work for.' He made no concessions to her being female and having a family: 'He just expected the goods to be produced.' Sarah was the most senior woman on the management side of the business. There was a relatively high proportion of female partners (15–20 per cent), which influenced the company culture and meant that women's issues were at least discussed and considered. Some senior people were, however, uncomfortable working with women, and she had to manage herself carefully. She felt she had to modify her behaviour, sometimes she felt silenced, and she did not always achieve the right note.

'Sometimes, just depending on the particular mood I was in, I would feel very bloody-minded about the whole thing, and so it probably wasn't very helpful. On the other hand, there are just so many times when you can take ten steps back before saying anything. And sometimes when you feel strongly enough about something then you say it anyway.'

She also noticed gender at work in relationships between women solicitors and secretaries. The latter generally preferred working for men 'because men are the real bosses. . . they [secretaries] do resent being told what to do by women'. Sarah thought the women solicitors exacerbated this situation by taking secretaries' good work for granted and being less overtly grateful than male colleagues were. Secretaries therefore 'felt underappreciated' by the women. Generally Sarah's own style was to seek consensus. She thought this most likely to achieve cooperation and action, but noted that a man in a parallel role was much more abrasive and seemed effective although he was not liked.

'I think I was managing as a woman will tend to manage. . . by consensus and negotiation. . . . I wasn't confrontational because there wasn't any point.'

Sarah's job was highly demanding of time and energy. Her life was made more pressured because working involved a long commute from her home town, so she often stayed away from home during the week. The family reorganized itself to accommodate these arrangements. They hired a live-in nanny, who proved excellent. Sarah's husband adjusted his schedule to see the children more often, but did not decrease his working hours. He did, however, bond very strongly with the new baby because he spent so much time with it, and was often sole carer.

At first Sarah's job took over her life. Once she had it more under control she felt more discretion about how hard to work. But the long journey, on an unreliable train service, became a significant source of pressure.

> 'I had two half-lives. . . and half and half didn't amount to one at all. It was a grey existence, where one was so tired that you dreaded the weekends because you had to give all your energy to the family, and you didn't have any. And you dreaded the week because you had to give all your energy to the firm. Most of that had been expended by the first train journey.'

DECIDING TO LEAVE

Several factors contributed to Sarah's decision to leave. The 'pivot' was the children. Whilst she was coping, 'it was just coping. I wasn't enjoying anything.' Had she not had children she thought she would have continued for longer. But she became concerned at her own tiredness and lack of energy as a mother, at having little input to her children's lives – some days the children saw neither parent – and at her own limited family life.

> 'Undoubtedly the most important factor for me was that I just wasn't seeing enough of my children and my husband.'

> 'The price was too much. The price is just loss of the rest of yourself, the rest of the things that go to make up a civilized existence. A balance. I just couldn't balance anything.'

She also felt that her overloaded life meant she was not being fair to the job, her colleagues and the firm.

Another aspect of Sarah's decision-making was the nature of the post. Introducing management systems was challenging and full of scope. Running the systems once established would not interest or stretch her. That this was therefore a short-term appointment had been openly acknowledged between her and the firm when she was recruited. She did not see any suitable future opportunities in senior management with the organization, as she would have had to specialize, and greatly preferred a general management role. She would next be looking for a job with more decision-making power.

In some ways, then, Sarah had decided to leave before she started. She had imagined staying two years. In the end she left slightly earlier, because she had completed the initial phase of work, because she could not face another winter of commuting and because she felt her life was so unbalanced. A period of slight physical illness with pneumonia brought a few weeks of enforced rest at home. This reminded her of the sense of space she was missing in her life, and her decision to leave crystallized.

Also relevant were concerns about the nature of her job. She missed the client interaction of being a solicitor, and would like to restore this in the future. Also, she had slight misgivings about the results of her (and other people's) efforts to bring more efficiency to the firm. Significant numbers of support staff were being made redundant, for example.

'I had spent a lot of time and spent a lot of energy making. . . extremely wealthy people extremely wealthier.'

Sarah was not prepared to earn her living long-term doing something she had such reservations about.

In weighing when to leave, Sarah's tiredness was a prime issue. She was also concerned to leave behind a completed first phase of the job, which she did. When she handed over to her successor Sarah was impressed at what she had achieved. She had proved her abilities and made doing the MBA seem worthwhile; she did not have to carry on further.

The decision to leave was solely Sarah's; she prefers not to talk things through with other people. She and her husband did discuss the financial implications, but as she knew 'he was not totally opposed to it', she felt free to decide for herself. She saw herself as privileged to have so much choice. She discussed the timing of leaving with close colleagues at work, but her mind was made up: 'I don't think I'd have listened to anyone who said "Don't give up".'

LEAVING

Sarah explained her decision to the organization in purely professional terms, and felt her reasoning was understood and respected. Running the department once the start-up was over did not require someone with her qualifications; she had given as much as she could. In any case they thought that she should soon be looking for something more challenging. Sarah added that the more limited job satisfaction she was now enjoying did not warrant the family sacrifices she had made. She said that she was looking for a job nearer home, or possibly to do consultancy. She did not want to emphasize the 'personal' factors in her decision, as this might confirm the prejudices of managers who were less accepting of women, and be unfair to future female job candidates.

The office gave her a celebratory send-off, which she found 'very touching', and saw as some indication that she might have made a mark. She was taken to lunch by several of the partners – 'a nice gesture'.

GETTING THE BALANCE RIGHT

Sarah was almost immediately offered a similar job nearer her home. She turned it down: she needed to rest, and having created the space to do so was not going to give it up. She also thought the job offered was potentially more demanding than the one she had left.

At first Sarah felt as if she was on extended holiday: 'immediately afterwards it was wonderful'. She greatly enjoyed being able to work to her own timetable, and not being under pressure to produce things. Jokes about housewives leading lazy lives were now, however, beginning to wear thin. There were times when her life was 'a lot less satisfactory' than it had been when she was working, because of the monotony of domestic chores.

As a family, they were still adjusting to a new lifestyle. Roles had been changed again; the extensive support systems they had previously organized were mostly dismantled, and different ones needed establishing; she and her husband were trying not to step on one another's toes as they renegotiated boundaries. Sarah had taken over most of the domestic work. She thought this 'totally fair' if she was not employed, since her husband works hard at his job. But she did not want his involvement with the children to diminish, otherwise all parties would suffer.

Sarah felt she had learnt a great deal about herself in the time since she applied to do the MBA. She had clear ideas about her immediate life priorities. Whilst she might eventually look for a 'high powered job', this was not an appropriate time. Contributing to her children's development, spending time with her husband and not putting herself under undue stress were more important at the moment.

'It sounds terribly undedicated or whatever, but I keep coming back to getting the balance right. I just felt I'd gone so far one way that I really needed to let the pendulum swing the other way for a while and then find the middle ground.'

REVIEWING OPTIONS

Sarah was trying to decide how much work she wanted to do, of what sort, and how she could make it fit with the rest of her life. She was still enjoying her new situation, and wanted to take advantage of this opportunity to rest. She imagined that at some time she would become keen to work again, but did not want to rush into a job. She had the luxury of time to reflect and choose.

'I'm quite happy to wait. I've always done jobs back to back. . . . I've never had this time before. It's the first time in nineteen years and I'm taking advantage of it, and really am not in a terrible hurry.'

'I am enjoying the time, and there is a great sense at the moment of knowing that I'm not going to have this particular time with my children again. . . so what is the point of just saying "I'm not interested, I must get a job".'

Her daughter seemed happy to have her at home and to be collected from school most days by her mother rather than a nanny. But Sarah said: 'I expect that is more important to me than to her'.

Despite these satisfactions, Sarah did also occasionally think she ought to be looking for a job, but wondered if this was her 'conditioning'. (She was also aware of a prior, conflicting, conditioning that women should look after their children.) She was choosing not to act on this dubious impulse for a while.

One factor which might have prompted Sarah to seek employment sooner rather than later was the pressure she felt because she was not making a financial contribution to the family and had no money of her own.

'It's small things like not being able to buy a Christmas present unless I buy it with [my husband's] salary. I find that very tough.'

Many women she knew had returned to work to regain some financial independence. She was aware, however, that this was her concern, not her husband's. He was more discomforted, she felt, by having a wife who did not work. She noticed that he liked to introduce her to people or talk about her as doing something in career terms. He was not used to her as a housewife; throughout their relationship she had always been something else.

'That is something that I'm just coming to terms with. I seem to be much happier being at home than he seems to be for me to be at home.'

She wondered if these factors would prompt her back into employment for less than wholehearted reasons. She also realized that there were some disadvantages of being based at home, given her background. She did not have an established 'infrastructure' as a housewife, and did not feel good at, or satisfied by, many of the basic tasks involved. Her strong friendships were with people who had followed a similar path to her own – who were 'very much out there doing. . . things' – and she did not want to lose touch with them. She was not finding it easy to develop other ties.

When we met, Sarah did not feel ready to go out and sell herself for a new job. She was not motivated by a burning desire to do anything in particular, and so wanted to wait until something felt right. She imagined various possibilities such as consultancy, teaching, another management job, and working part-time. Part of her problem, she said, was that she was qualified to do all sorts of things. This sounded wonderful, but did not concentrate her mind. She felt (almost) sure that there would be suitable opportunities when she was ready, because people were still contacting her with suggestions of work. But she did wonder if this situation would change; if she delayed too long she might lose her chance to go back into employment.

As she explored different possibilities, Sarah repeatedly returned to her intention to base her lifestyle on her commitment to the family. Achieving the right fit had to start with being an active mother and wife, and having space for herself.

'I am now aware of the price, and I don't think at this point I'm prepared to pay it again. I think there are too many other things in life.'

In deciding what was appropriate, 'flexibility and control are the watchwords'. As long as the job was something she really wanted to do she had no clearer specification. She was slightly concerned, however, at what she called her 'passive attitude', yet felt that it was authentic to her position. She wanted more time, but added:

'I know the truth is that if someone came along tomorrow with THE JOB on the right basis I would say "wonderful, fine". But I just don't feel from my end that I'm motivated enough to go out there and sell myself at the moment.'

Sarah's career had been disjointed. Her husband was dedicated to his work, successful and able to earn far more than her. Her life development had involved accepting the situation, adjusting her employed life to suit. She had been able to create her own space within this family pattern, but this was harder to do once she did not have an identity outside. She was glad not to have been sucked into a pressured, energy-consuming organizational commitment. Her lifestyle offered its own rewards. It was also constraining, and would continue to be demanding as her children grew.

Sarah was cautious about choosing a next step. She had enjoyed the taste of having time to herself again, so part-time work or consultancy seemed appealing possibilities. She felt very confident about shaping her life in the future. The four major changes she had made during the last four years had shown that she was not limited to one lifestyle track: she had proven her ability to change. Sarah balanced the family lifestyle by adjusting herself, and in the process she felt more in touch with her values.

'I wasn't prepared to have a job which would take up my entire existence. Even if I hadn't had children I just couldn't have lived like that.'

SARAH'S FEEDBACK ON THE DRAFT STORY

Sarah described her first reading of the draft story as 'surprisingly emotional'. It took her back to the time reported and reminded her of her tiredness and the decision she had been free to make. Her second reading felt more 'objective'. She suggested a few minor amendments to clarify details.

ADDENDUM

After a year at home, Sarah began working part-time in long-term locum and consultancy posts. Several of her jobs have used knowledge and skills gained during her MBA course. This work fits with her other responsibilities and her motivations: she is making the most of her skills and talents at work and at home. The family have moved house, and Sarah's income is now a necessary contribution to finances, which pleases her. Her situation is not perfect, but is 'as good a balance as [she] will get for the present'. She is doubtful whether she will ever want to devote herself entirely to a career. She has seen the detrimental consequences of doing so affect too many people.

Financial self-reliance

Another stereotype which is quickly challenged by the data (alongside that of women mainly leaving to have babies) is the belief that women have the luxury of choice because someone else will support them financially if they give up employment. For the women in this book this is seldom the case. They took decisions knowing that these could have significant financial consequences.

Table 6 summarizes the women's financial status at the time they left or considered leaving their jobs.

Table 6 Financial status at the time of decision-making

Dual income – household not reliant on their income	Sarah, Claire, *Patricia*, *Stevie*
Dual income – household reliant on their income	*Judith*, *Teresa*, *Dorothy*, *Margaret*
Financially self-reliant – single/divorced	*Julia*, Kathy, Christina
– in relationships	*Mercedes*, Jane
Main/only household income earner	*Pamela*, *Kim*
Not classified	*Ruth*

Even when a woman could expect economic support from a partner this was not necessarily a straightforward matter. *Patricia*, Claire and Sarah were supported by their husbands after leaving. Claire's husband initially resisted her decision because he believed in her career identity. Sarah was pulled back towards employment partly because she felt uncomfortable about not making a financial contribution to the family. Several other research participants placed great emphasis on not wanting to be dependent financially and therefore on earning incomes in their own rights.

Career development themes

The women's stories particularly raise to question the meanings of career. In this section I notice and anticipate some of the career development features they reveal. In 'Decision-making' (p. 291ff.), I look in more detail at their recent career transitions.

INTERNAL AND/OR EXTERNAL GROUNDING

There are many ways of developing a life and career. Elsewhere I have contrasted two broad approaches to planning (Marshall, 1984, 1989) based on women managers' accounts. 'Agentic' planning is forward looking, goal-directed, clear, pursuing external ideals, often against expected timescales. 'Communion-based' planning is more present-focused. It involves being open to opportunities, listening to the next inner need without concern about longer-term consequences and generating change if a given situation becomes unsatisfactory.

Much career planning literature favours agentic planning, especially for women who cannot rely on other people to develop their careers for them and may meet obstacles. Women are therefore advised to set clear, ambitious goals and plan steps for achieving them. (They have often been criticized for concentrating on their jobs rather than on career building.) Pursued uncritically this advice has its individual and organizational dangers. Engagement, effectiveness and satisfaction in a particular job are devalued. Also, people may become attached to career aspirations they cannot realize because organizational opportunities change, creating frustration and disillusion.

I am not advocating either extreme of career planning. They each have their different strengths, and can best be used in combination. I am not comparing these women's development to one ideal, and certainly not suggesting that people should plan their careers early and pursue them with determination. The stories show a mixture of approaches, with many decisions incorporating strong communion-based elements. The five accounts presented so far are especially strong in taking the inner grounding for life decision-making seriously. Perhaps people whose careers are shaped by wholly agentic or externally based factors are unlikely to initiate discontinuous changes of the sort described here in case they are difficult to describe credibly to future employers.

UNCLEAR STARTS

It is interesting how many of the women in this research (at least eight) had unclear starts to their employed careers. (Two others trained in nursing, but only later became consciously career-oriented.) A few married and had children, later (re)entering employment. Several talked about lack of advice, direction, aspiration or support for them from home and from educational sources. Their diffuse images of what their lives might become echo other research findings, and seem more typical of women than men. (More recent generations may have different experiences.)

In a world of portfolio careers (Handy, 1989), and three careers in a lifetime (Still, 1993), perhaps openness is helpful. But without a more developed awareness of choice, openness has a sting in the tail. It did not foster self-images of competence and potential for most of the women in this study. Nor did it encourage committed experimentation. Self-confidence came later for some of them, as did finding jobs which would allow them to demonstrate their full capabilities. Several people became deliberately career-minded in their late twenties or early thirties. But outward success could be achieved without the person feeling a full sense of internal commitment. Christina, *Julia* and *Pamela*, for example, expressed some distance in their senses of career.

ORGANIZATIONAL MOBILITY

Women managers now seem more likely to move between companies than they were ten years ago (Still, 1993). This suggests both more openness from organizations in recruitment and less concern about the security of known territory on women's part. Only three women (Jane, *Judith* and *Margaret*) in this study had not made a change of organization after they became committed to their careers. The data therefore supports this suggested trend. But it also seems that moves may have unanticipated long-term consequences. Three women (*Patricia*, *Teresa* and *Ruth*) had been successful in previous, highly similar, jobs and so were unprepared, surprised and disappointed when they experienced difficulties in their posts. Five women had departed from their usual pattern of career movement in taking the jobs they subsequently left, some showing greater career commitment, others entering unknown organizations as managers for the first time. Perhaps the radical nature of these previous moves helped to set the scene for leaving.

Job moves at the levels research participants had reached seem more dependent on fitting with cultural patterns and less about professional competence than are those earlier in a career. Perhaps they are therefore more risky for women because their acceptability is still often in doubt. Senior managers are also particularly vulnerable to changes in company fortunes. Two women had lost their power-bases because their organizations had been taken over. (This had happened to Christina earlier in her career.) Another was forced to leave by an incoming chief executive who wanted to create his own team.

How to judge environments and what risks to take are issues for women moving company. Some research participants found new organizations more hostile to women or to their specific functional roles, and some found them less hostile than their previous employers. In the workshops I held people discussed these issues and concluded that it is difficult to make safe choices. Some moved to apparently more favourable environments only to find that circumstances very similar to those they had escaped were now affecting them again.

Leaving change roles which became untenable

The stories of: Teresa, Judith, Patricia and Dorothy

All the research participants' roles involved change in some form (see 'Change agent roles', p. 188). In four cases, however, change initiatives eventually became difficult, despite early successes. The resulting pressures on them were central in prompting the women to leave; one (Patricia) was forced to resign. These stories overlap and contrast with each other in various ways. Patricia and Dorothy were the two nursing managers in the study. (Both were working in non-UK settings at the time.) Teresa and Judith often appeared in more general analyses alongside each other, for example they had very similar strategies for coping with pressure. The stories together show a range of potential change strategies.

Teresa

OVERVIEW

Teresa volunteered to participate in the research, having read about it in a journal. She thought her industry – construction – was a comparatively harsh environment for women and would provide a valuable reference point.

She had been with her organization for four years in training, organizational development and personnel roles. The culture was highly male-dominated and not sympathetic to human resources initiatives. Senior managers were confrontational and abusive amongst themselves, and adopted the same style towards Teresa. They often seemed to be testing her out. She was either feared, ignored or patronized. She developed various strategies for coping in this hostile environment, becoming more tough and aggressive herself. Despite resistance, she did introduce some key human resources practices, but her working life was a continual fight. Teresa was feeling stressed and depressed and wanted to leave. Eventually a relatively minor incident crystallized her decision. She then found a way to engineer her own redundancy.

We met in Teresa's last week at work. She found our conversation cathartic, an opportunity to tell her story fully. She wanted to spend the next month resting and then decide what to do. She had received a limited pay-off from the organization, and so thought she needed to find work again within three months.

BACKGROUND

Teresa married, had children when she was young, and went to university when she was in her mid-twenties. This was 'the most wonderful thing' she ever did. Until then she had been 'aimless'. Studying psychology opened her eyes to a world of possible learning.

After graduating Teresa taught for a while on part-time contracts. Later she joined a community team working with drug misusers and then went into full-time research. This last move was disappointing; she and the engineers with whom she collaborated spoke different languages.

Teresa was relieved to be offered another job, as training manager in a large manufacturing unit. She learnt rapidly, reorganized the function, had great fun and experienced no problems with initially being the only woman manager on a site of a thousand people. But she became bored and wanted a challenge. Looking round, she found two possible positions. One seemed well structured, too orderly. The other, with the construction company, was a 'blank page'. She chose the latter.

UNCERTAINTY AND LONELINESS

Teresa's first months in her new organization were confusing and shocking. She found the company very old-fashioned, formal and hierarchical. There were no other women managers. There was no formalized personnel function. There was no induction, even informally. She could not understand how she fitted in.

She had been recruited by the group personnel director to work in training, but with no specified responsibilities. She asked for direction and was told to do what she thought fit. She set herself projects such as conducting an attitude survey on recently recruited graduates. The reports she wrote were ignored. After three months Teresa told the person who had appointed her that she was dissatisfied. He suggested she work with him on organizational development initiatives.

INITIAL EXPERIENCES IN A MALE-DOMINATED CULTURE

By this time Teresa had assessed the company culture. Characteristics of building site life seemed to have been converted into styles of organizing. Managers dealt with each other and other staff aggressively, using blunt, confronting language. People were told what to do and expected to obey. Sometimes when she went to speak to managers she was told to 'get out' and sworn at. Asserting power in this way is apparently part of building site life. Success and respect come from being tough with workers, architects and clients.

'I've never experienced such open hostility and aggression. . . . People [said]. . . . that was how it was on sites.'

'Just have a shrieking stand-up row and it's OK. You can be really abusive and it's OK.'

Working on sites, there is 'powerful bonding' in the all-male work teams. Women are either peripheral or idealized figures – 'Women are for looking at and ogling. They like girlie, female types.' The culture was:

'totally male-dominated. Women had their place and were maltreated. . . . It wasn't unusual to walk along a corridor and hear someone being bawled out.'

Teresa would often find secretaries crying in the toilets because of their treatment. She was totally unused to aggression and had no strategies for coping with someone being openly hostile to her. She was initially quite frightened, but hid her feelings, not wanting people to see that they had upset her. She reacted either by turning away or laughing because she 'didn't believe it to be real'.

UNINTENTIONALLY THREATENING BEHAVIOUR

Teresa soon learnt that her professional expertise was not welcomed in the organization: 'there was quite a lot of hostility to the function, regardless of me'. People saw attention to human resources as unnecessary and costly, something they had succeeded without. The culture favoured short-term problem-solving. Whilst they were 'technically very clever people', senior managers were not very confident in management skills such as planning and commercial decision-making. Teresa's activities exposed their areas of potential weakness, and generated hostility.

'I. . . realized how incredibly insecure and vulnerable they were as managers. . . . If you start. . . to talk about things which are unacceptable, you instantly hit defence mechanisms.'

During this phase Teresa conducted several attitude surveys
and company audits (in divisions) which revealed concern about
issues such as poor communication and changes in the company
culture. Although the results often seemed 'quite bland' to her,
managers would either react violently to her attempts to report
them or totally ignore her. Teresa persisted in trying to speak 'the
truth' despite this resistance. She felt in conflict with the atmosphere of secrecy and control, both personally – she prefers
openness – and professionally – she felt the resulting culture was
'unhealthy'.

BEING PLACED AS A WOMAN

Teresa was also out of place as a woman in the culture. She was
surprised to be called a 'dolly bird' and 'Sindy in the Dream
Factory', since she is relatively formal, but believes that because
she was blonde she was not taken seriously. Around her, personalized sexual joking was commonplace. She gave the example
of one very senior manager who said to one of her staff:

'Have you had a chest transplant then? You're looking loads
bigger now than you used to.'

When challenged by Teresa later, the manager said that he was
only joking, that the woman involved knew what life was like on
site. Women were apparently meant to accept such behaviour
without comment.

'There was a lot of [sexual] innuendo and you have to be careful
how you handle that'.

She felt she could not openly reject comments because 'they
would perpetuate something that they knew annoyed you'. Signs
of potential sensitivity offered opportunities to bully. Instead,
Teresa ignored sexual innuendo or talked over it – 'I'm quite a
strong personality and I do take control quite a lot'. She was
surprised at other women who did seem to enjoy flirting with
managers, unaware that the latter would laugh about them behind
their backs and not take them seriously.

Male colleagues did not have appropriate images to fit Teresa:

'I. . . was the one they couldn't recognize. I was neither the flirty
tart type, which they can relate to, the old spinster who was

bitter and twisted, and who they were frightened of. . . . They didn't understand professional women or know what I was.'

When she first arrived, she also 'hit amazing hostility' from women in the organization. They were jealous, because she had a company car, and suspicious of her. They would not let her sit with them at lunchtimes: 'They would look the other way, not acknowledge me.' Later she learnt that some people believed she must have been sleeping with senior managers to be appointed.

WORKING RELATIONSHIPS

Teresa found it difficult to develop alliances with men.

'I was either feared, ignored or patronized. . . by everyone apart from the group personnel director.'

Senior staff were not used to having women as peers, and saw her role as 'totally unnecessary' and threatening. One told her: 'You frighten us because you know the answers to things that we don't, and we don't like that.' They would dismiss her function and her, partly citing her lack of building site experience and therefore her lack of appreciation of 'real life'.

Teresa was also feared because her psychology background might mean she 'could read their innermost souls'. People often told her their personal problems. She gave a typical example of feeling patronized: 'If you could do anything there was real surprise.' Presenting proposals to a senior manager she was asked, 'Did you do this?. . . Well aren't you clever?' She was furious afterwards, but her male colleague thought her a bit sensitive.

During one initiative, jointly running development assessment workshops with colleagues, Teresa established more satisfactory relationships. She was consulted, her expertise recognized; she felt accepted and a lot happier. But these improvements did not transfer; outside this context she was ignored again.

She also encountered institutional practices which had so far excluded women. One day she attended a seminar; lunch was to be in the senior staff dining room. 'There was horror as lunch approached because I couldn't go.' Eventually a senior director gave permission for Teresa to enter this male preserve. She was later asked if she wanted to join the dining room. Although she qualified in status terms, membership was by invitation only.

She declined – 'I said I wouldn't on principle attend this boys' club.' Teresa sometimes spoke to people outside her organization about examples of its sexism, to check her impression that these were unusual – 'they'd be quite stunned'. She did this to maintain some sense of perspective.

The role she most often adopted, or was invited into, was that of counsellor. Senior men would tell her how hard their lives in the organization were, how difficult the bullying was, and she would counsel them. This frequently happened after she had initiated discussions to address a particular organizational development issue. Typically, the original discussion was deflected. Instead Teresa would find herself helping apparently powerful individuals feel more comfortable with the situation as it was. Whilst she built relationships with senior people in this way, she also saw their vulnerability and so became a potential threat. Some subsequently treated her less aggressively, but warily. In such 'role reversal' relationships she felt used rather than accepted for her potential contribution.

A NEW ROLE

When Teresa had been in the company about two years her role changed. A more formal personnel and training function was to be established to act as a consultancy and devolve good practice throughout the company. Prevailing practice of 'everyone doing their own thing' was to be countered. She was to head the new department. She resisted this, anticipating significant difficulties with the strategy, seeing this as demotion because the role was largely operational and potentially less influential, and wanting to persist with the company-wide development she thought was much needed. She was not, however, given a choice. She acquiesced reluctantly.

This move placed Teresa in a more alienated organizational position. Her new reporting relationship severed her ties with the group personnel director, her only supporter. She was assigned a large staff, some of whom other people had not wanted. She soon had to make two redundant to keep her activities within budget. One of her 'subordinates' was an older man who had previously run personnel-related administrative areas. Because of his long service and previous importance as an engineer it was never made clear that he should report to Teresa. In fact no standard memo appointing her in post was issued, to avoid 'humiliating' him. She challenged this, but was told that 'he didn't deserve that' and that she was 'big enough to take it'. She had considerable difficulties 'managing' this man, who undermined apparently agreed tasks and her position with other staff. Her boss would not let her discipline him. She was told: 'Don't do it. Leave it. He's been a good bloke.' She was relieved when she was later able to have him transferred elsewhere.

BEING TESTED OUT

There was considerable resistance to the devolution of personnel practices Teresa was charged with implementing. Senior managers were aggressive and blunt at the meetings she called, some of which 'ended up as huge punch-ups'. One very powerful, charismatic manager adopted an extremely oppositional stance, directed at Teresa.

'He was one of the biggest underminers of the philosophy and the way I operated. We used to have the most horrendous rows. He would come and have stand-up arguments with me, and because I wouldn't do what he wanted he couldn't relate to me. . . .'

He would sometimes try to make her feel stupid, shouting at her in public if she did not immediately know the answers to his questions or would not agree that he was right.

A focus of tension in Teresa's life was strategy meetings for the directors, which she chaired. She saw these as her 'biggest mistake', because she acquired multiple bosses, each trying to tell *her* what to do. Her purpose for the meetings was to encourage *them* to think through how they were going to implement human resources in their divisions. The directors preferred to discuss clear operational details, and resisted her agendas. Teresa thought they were too involved in political battles amongst themselves to address wider issues. The meetings often seemed like multi-directional arguments in which people were 'virtually screaming and shouting and swearing in the board room. . . . There weren't debates, there was Teresa baiting.'

When she tried to confront these dynamics, the meetings would sometimes turn into group counselling sessions, with the directors 'moaning' about things they found difficult and using her 'to get things off their chests'.

As these meetings were so unproductive, Teresa tried repeatedly either to reposition or cancel them. Her boss ignored or resisted her suggestions. Later, he stopped the meetings himself to avoid asking one member, who had effectively been demoted, to withdraw and thus hurting his feelings. She saw this as an example (of which there were others) of subtle protectiveness between men, which was not accorded to her.

TOUGHENING UP

By this stage Teresa had developed her working strategies. She still favoured a counselling approach rather than open confrontation, but she also became much tougher, partly so that she was not exploited as a woman:

'I realized two years ago I was on my own, without support, and I had to fight like mad to survive. I acquired a lot more stand-up aggression.'

'I would behave much more aggressively deliberately to fight like with like. There were certain female traits that they knew and they tried to exploit, and I had to hold out against. For example, to try to get you to cry. They wanted that desperately. A lot of the bullying came in there.'

She also learnt to make points indirectly, through analogy, to avoid personalizing and provoking retaliation. But people's comments to her were often direct, personal and seeking to provoke.

Teresa used her more confrontational style to canvass directors one by one and establish agreement on forthcoming human resources issues. But this private support usually evaporated in public meetings, when they would change their minds. After one strategy meeting she formed the image of the directors as 13-year-old boys and herself as 'Mummy', trying to discipline and cajole them:

'I suddenly realized they were very childish and the stupidity of their behaviour became more overt. And in every meeting I went to. . . I sat there and listened to the nonsense that was talked and the nasty way people were slapped down if they dared to oppose the views of senior players.'

She knew this image seemed patronizing, but 'every day was a fight' – and her resulting action strategies often worked. This approach became counterproductive if she challenged them for changing their minds and letting her down. They then resisted her canvassing, and she had to find other ways to work. She found this manoeuvring 'exceptionally tiring'. Teresa's own department now worked well and she enjoyed the sense of team. Her secretary was also a support and an ally. Teresa had become very friendly with some women subordinates and associates. They would lunch together and have tea in her office. The men, however, made fun of this, calling them 'the knitting club'.

SPEARHEADING CHANGE

In many instances Teresa was her managing director's agent for change, but he seemed unable to help her with the several levels of resistance she was encountering. He gave her some public support, but Teresa believed that this was insufficient. When she told him of her difficulties often 'he just said "tough"', and described his own problems. He would not help her by confronting the powerful opponent.

But Teresa did not always ask the managing director for help. As he was disliked by some of the board, she calculated that his support would bring overt acquiescence but covert resistance, so she chose the alternative strategy of trying to 'win hearts and minds' by her own efforts. This sometimes worked. But she was also a pawn in the tensions amongst the directors. The managing director sometimes used her to test out strategies. If they proved unpopular or problematic, he would withdraw and side with the other directors, leaving her to take the consequences and handle the resulting loss of credibility. Other directors sometimes attacked Teresa as a way of challenging the managing director. The group personnel director, with whom Teresa had a good relationship, would not intervene either. She offered various possible reasons for this, from insufficient organizational status to his perception that Teresa was tough enough to handle the situation. But she still felt abandoned – 'I resented that intensely because he was protecting himself.'

Teresa described her role as going into battle. She used phrases such as 'front line', 'being handed the bullets', knowing that she would 'get shot' and 'coming back bleeding'. But when, despite this, she had achieved their agreed strategies, her immediate bosses would minimize the difficulties, making her feel betrayed.

Teresa looked back with regret at the ineffectiveness of the working norms among these senior managers. Sometimes the people could be bright and witty, good company. But more often they played political games.

'If we'd stopped playing silly games and taken it on a professional level we would have achieved a lot more a lot earlier. The women in the organization actually get on with the job and men don't. They want to play political intrigues and muck about and build their empires. The fact that I didn't floored them.'

Internal rivalries were perhaps accentuated because recession had hit the business: energies became focused inwards, political infighting was rife. Teresa said: 'I just happened to be one of the more baitable people because it was a nonsense function and I was female.'

She described how she preferred to behave at work. She liked to be informal, using humour, imagery and analogy. But when she did, her remarks 'fell like lead balloons'. She liked 'the naturalness of being ordinary', but her colleagues were unresponsive or seemed confused – 'because it wasn't the game. I didn't know the boys' game. . . . I was just being me, until I had to acquire roles and they were OK, but they took their toll.' Teresa's intellectual appreciation of her area of work may also have set her apart from colleagues.

Despite the challenging environment, Teresa continued to speak her mind openly, sometimes criticising proposed human resources initiatives which would be inappropriate in this culture. She even tried to introduce some equal opportunities policies, but was unsuccessful.

'It was like a red flag to a bull. I couldn't even get it on the table. If I mentioned it, I'd get "Oh, here's the feminist again. Look, love. . . ."'

Teresa's relationships with male senior managers were predominantly characterized by conflict. She was thus both mirroring their behaviour and standing for her own beliefs, which became strengthened in the process. Her change agenda and theories shaped her stance.

'I believed my role was one of organizational catalyst – that to change the prevailing culture I had to tackle it on all fronts. I *did* let them win unimportant battles, but would never give in on what I believed was core. They soon realized that. Also they *hated* it when I shrugged my shoulders and said "OK you do it if you want to." I was often canvassed later to know why I didn't stick to my guns. It created a sense of insecurity that I might just be right and they would find themselves in trouble.'

NOT LIKING HERSELF

Helpful as her toughness was, Teresa did not like what she was becoming.

'I didn't like myself very much. I actually acquired more what I see as masculine traits in order to cope. And these were the more hostile and aggressive ones, where I had to make myself more unreasonable to gain a particular foothold on occasions. That's what I found most stressful.'

She later noticed, for example, how she had treated her father's death. She had stepped in to take control and manage things, expressing little emotional reaction. The shielding she was doing at work was becoming generalized.

She did receive some support from friends she had made at university – 'kindred spirits'. Some were in similar roles to her, but not facing similar pressures. But Teresa seldom told them her problems fully, thinking she might be seen as exaggerating or unable to cope in industry. She would, however, gladly counsel them – 'it's a role I tend to constantly take'.

Her husband ran the house, relieving her of such demands. But he was not interested in her work or sympathetic about its pressures. Her children were then in their late teens and needed support themselves. She took home her accumulated stress and tiredness (determined not to let them show at work), and did not find support.

'When I got home I just wanted nothingness. . . . I was utterly jaded. . . and at weekends I wanted to do nothing or things I wanted to do, which isn't terribly sharing when you have a family.'

She now thinks this behaviour was selfish and wrong, but at the time was too 'totally exhausted' to act differently. She was suffering her own stress warning symptoms of diarrhoea and loss of sense of humour. Long working hours, a feature of the culture, were also taxing.

She took up conversational French and wine appreciation to provide some counterbalance in her life.

'I felt I was becoming boring and far too serious and narrow, and I didn't like that. I felt all my creativity was being used negatively.'

She could see that she was achieving some organizational changes, but 'the personal cost was too great'.

'It did cost too much, and I don't think that for my mental well-being it was good. I was getting very, very stressed and more agitated.'

Her defence mechanism of seeing the managers as children, and therefore not frightening, alleviated the situation. But some of her coping strategies may have helped cut Teresa off from potential support. Both at work and at home she maintained control, not revealing how stressed she was. She was much more likely to help others – particularly through her counselling – than to receive help herself. At work no support seems to have been available. Levels of stress were high. People upbraided Teresa if she showed any vulnerability or uncertainty because she was meant to be helping them cope. Also she feared that she would be bullied more if she showed any weakness. These were further incentives to maintain her tough façade. She described herself as a strong personality, but perhaps her strength encouraged her to persist too long in this unhealthy environment.

DECIDING TO LEAVE

Teresa had wanted to leave for at least a year, but had not given herself permission to do so. This was partly because she had internalized company values which would interpret this as 'giving in', and partly because she felt responsible for her staff, who depended on her for protection.

Eventually a minor incident revealed how stressed she was. For some time major arguments with her chief opponent had been sapping her energy. Her boss phoned her about a budget detail

and asked her now to pass all claims to him for authorization
because finances were tight. Losing her signing rights was 'total
trivia', but Teresa was taken aback at her reaction.

'When I put the phone down I could feel my throat constricting,
and I really didn't believe it. . . . I got in the car and just burst
into tears, and I'd never in four years done that. It seemed too
petty and over-sensitive, but I couldn't see the point any more.
If it was getting to that level of frustration I wasn't going to make
it any better. I hadn't wanted it for a year, but that was the final
straw.'

She made her decision to go: her situation was 'no longer
tenable'.

Still not wanting 'to just walk away from things', Teresa took
care of the organization before leaving. A reorganization was
planned. She formulated three alternatives for repositioning
training and personnel functions. The one she favoured, and
which made most organizational sense, did not include a position
for her: she thus made herself redundant. She presented her ideas
to the managing director. What she intended gradually dawned
on him.

'I said it was a logical situation because we had people needing
to consolidate the good practice that I'd set up.'

(Other personnel-related staff were available to support this.)

'So I then asked what they'd need me for. And he said: "Of
course it's logical, but I don't often get women being logical." I
said I thought that was disgusting and he boyishly laughed.'

Teresa told the managing director that she had had the most
unhappy eighteen months of her life, and he seemed genuinely
saddened; he said he loved his work.

THE PROCESS OF LEAVING

The official announcement that Teresa was leaving departed from
traditional – blandly factual – form by saying at some length that
she had made a considerable contribution to the company. She
interpreted this as acknowledgement from senior managers that
her job was unreasonably difficult, that she had gained some
grudging respect for meeting their challenges and achieving

some change, and a sign that they felt some guilt about how they had treated her.

She believed that she had some impact, although an outsider might not appreciate how radical change had been, because elsewhere what she facilitated 'would be par for the course'. She had also made the organization question things and prompted more openness. Despite her struggles, she appreciated having learnt a lot more about herself, particularly that she is 'a lot more resilient' than she thought and that she can hold her own in an extremely aggressive environment.

Some people were sorry that she was leaving, and she received some unexpected letters of appreciation. She was sad to leave her department, her secretary, someone she had helped develop, and a manager for whom she had sympathy; but that was all.

Teresa visited each director and explained that she was unhappy as a result of their behaviour. Some expressed regret. One thought she 'would have had more staying power'. She thinks this is demanding too much. Her chief opponent explained that he had used his aggressive style to try to build a relationship with her.

> 'He said "I was only trying to get you to respond to me in the right way. I wanted to make you angry and aggressive."'

Teresa replied that by becoming aggressive she would have lost. She also resented his intention to separate her from her boss's influence – 'he still didn't realize I had a mind of my own'.

She regretted that she and the directors had not been able to work together to put the organization in good form to emerge from the recession. She saw this as a major missed opportunity.

When we met, Teresa was in her last week with the company. She was seldom in, but no one seemed to care; it was all 'slightly embarrassing'. All she knew for certain was that she did not want to repeat the last four years, and that she wanted to rest for a month, to do nothing.

She next wanted a job that was personally worthwhile, and offered a more creative environment. She had applied for one post, which looked promising. She liked organizational development, but was not eager to become an external consultant because she believed that most apparent change disappears once the consultant leaves. She may have had little choice about employment, as she thought she needed to start earning an income again in three months. But she did not want to do something just for the sake of it, especially as she might replicate her previous situation. Some time in the future she would like to write and/or set up her own business.

Teresa's personal life was also in transition. Her children were leaving home, and she expected that her relationship with her husband would change.

TERESA'S FEEDBACK ON THE DRAFT STORY

Teresa suggested a few changes to the draft for clarification, and supplied more explanatory detail to enhance points I had queried. She said: 'I found it clear, concise and a good representation of my experience.... I enjoyed listening to my story from another perspective.'

ADDENDUM

Teresa had a month off work and rested. She then took a job in local government as head of personnel and training. She had 'extreme reservations' about the post, but felt she needed to resume earning. The move was not successful. She was the council's first female chief officer, and people were wary of her. Her role was highly constrained by the organization's culture and procedures, and by her boss's domineering behaviour. Her previous coping strategies were inappropriate.

'After three months it was institutionally accepted that I had no status.'

She had still been tired when she entered the job. Within three months she was depressed, sleeping badly and experiencing other stress symptoms. Her unhappiness was greater because she felt she had brought the situation upon herself. She wondered whether the problem was her inability to fit in. At last she concluded that it would not be valuable to fit into what was 'a very unhealthy, unproductive environment', in which she had clear evidence of discrimination against her. She stayed for more than a year; she believes she did 'a very good job' within the organization's somewhat limited requirements. When she left, she was exhausted and depressed, and her self-esteem was 'at rock bottom'.

Since then Teresa has done some extended consultancy for an

international organization. As soon as she began this she 'had bags of energy and looked fine', despite extensive travelling. She is financially solvent for the moment, but she is unclear how to move forward. She feels emotionally drained and intellectually stagnant. She is giving herself more thinking time following this move, but is worried that it has not yet resulted in positive action. She has started writing as a hobby, which she finds satisfying.

In the meantime she is contemplating her style. A male psychologist, a colleague on a project, recently suggested that she intimidates men, and that because she is intellectually able they find her pushy. He suggested she make more effort to be 'softer, feminine and cuddly'. She thinks he interpreted what she feels is professional demeanour as coldness, and that she was being warned for failing to behave in supportive, female-stereotyped, ways. Teresa appreciates that this is only one person's opinion, but it does echo previous feedback she has received. She wonders if other men share this reaction.

Judith

OVERVIEW

Judith was a senior manager in local government. As the only woman at her level, she had to establish her credibility and status in the face of people's devaluing expectations. Her role as county officer for community development involved bringing about equality-related change internally and externally, working in an inherently conflicted boundary position. The organization was resistant to these agendas, despite espoused support. Judith became a figurehead for threatening disruption. Her relationship with a male superior became strained. In this situation, she found it difficult to maintain a coherent sense of self. She was, none-theless, partly successful. She developed her department into a strong team. Her work had impacts. Her own coping strategies strengthened. But she was bombarded by needs and challenges from many directions. Eventually she left because the stress involved became too unhealthy for her.

Judith's account shows the learning she did, in what was her first major management role. It also incorporates a retrospective self-critique. While in post, she had held a feminist, political view of gender and power in organizations. She later believed that she had played some part in creating situations she found stressful, and had underestimated the importance of psychodynamic factors in change situations. She felt she had, at times, been naive, too aggressive, insufficiently strategic. This analysis was based on the more complex, multi-stranded, perspective she had developed.

Judith told her story with energy, speaking her critiques and values clearly. I felt I learnt something of her style, and of the challenge or inspiration she might be for people.

FROM OUTSIDER TO INSIDER

Judith's working-class background has significantly shaped her life. At university it meant a lack of self-confidence. In later experiences she was better able to affirm her own values. She had often chosen to live with, rather than resolve, feelings of marginality.

Judith went into teaching and loved it. After several years she left to have children. As they grew, she did various voluntary activities. Particularly significant was her involvement in political campaigning against local authority spending cuts in the late 1970s, and the experience this gave her of public speaking.

She moved progressively into part-time and full-time community work, funded by local government. In these jobs she felt at one with herself, authentic to her values.

'I felt I had a political mission that was very grounded in practical action.'

Working for the local authority, with whom she had sometimes been in conflict, created some tensions, but these remained in the background because Judith was very autonomous in her work role and there was little management involvement. Her next move took her into the heart of these contradictions.

After several years, Judith applied for the post of county officer for community development. She did so 'in a spirit of complete cheek', as a marker to show she thought herself competent. At interview she felt she had little to lose. She was very clear about her ideas for the post; these included introducing management processes, equal opportunities practices and staff development.

'It felt like an open book. Nobody had done proper management, it seemed to me.'

Judith was offered the job. She felt she had the director's backing and had been recruited for what she could do. Community development involved bringing about change towards greater equality, internally and through relationships with outside groups. The area was so undeveloped that her job description had twenty-eight points to it, all key areas of work which needed taking in hand. She was to manage thirteen full-time staff, introduce new posts and manage external relationships with community groups. She was the only woman on the senior management team; the other eight members were white men.

STARTING FROM SCRATCH

Judith received no induction into the organization or her role, and so taught herself. She discussed with administrative staff how to set up appropriate basic systems, for example. As she found the advice she needed she began to make good lateral relationships; networking was a key feature of her style. Her department had previously been relatively isolated and received little manage-ment attention.

> 'I had what I would now call "hungry babies" of staff, clamour-ing for love, attention, support – and also, in some cases, saying, "Who the hell do you think you are? You're one of us, and how are you going to be as a manager?"'

Whilst people did like and trust her, there was also some ambivalence about her appointment. Initially she felt supported by the people to whom she reported. Amongst the senior manage-ment team there were other partial allies, but also 'lots of people tried to trip [her] up'.

IN-TRAY EXERCISES

Judith's in-tray symbolized how she initially felt about her job. How she coped with it shows her determination and attitude of learning. When she arrived she had been shown to her desk and her in-tray, which was piled about a foot high. As she knew little about the organization's bureaucratic systems for processing paper many items seemed challenging at first. That many looked to her like human situations needing careful attention added to her uncertainty.

> 'So at those early stages I used to take the in-tray home with me every night and weep over it. Do it all, but weeping splashes of tears on the papers. Thinking, "How am I going to deal with this enormous workload?" And of course the phone was ringing all the time and all the stuff was piling in.'

A colleague in a parallel position appeared unable to cope, and had a desk piled high with paper. Judith was determined this should not happen to her. She was scared of being seen not to be able to manage, and scared of drowning in a pile which grew every day. By the end of a year she could deal with her in-tray by

9.30 a.m. She achieved this partly by learning how to look after herself and how to set clear boundaries and priorities. These were core issues she worked on continuously throughout her three years in the job.

BEING SEEN THROUGH GENDERED FRAMEWORKS

Her success in dealing with her paperwork did not bring Judith recognition. She felt that, throughout her time in the organization, she was seen from within what she called 'gendered frameworks'. This phrase shows her readiness to analyse her situation in feminist terms. By it she meant that gender stereotypes prevailed as ways of judging women. For example, they were not expected to be as competent as men, and what they did achieve had to be explained away as not that difficult (since they were able to do it).

'So there was no getting it right, and, as the only senior woman, everything I did was under a spotlight.'

She felt that women as a group were being judged by what she did and whether she could prove herself.

With everyone she met, and continually, Judith felt she had to establish who she was as a manager and what were appropriate forms for the relationship. The stereotypes of women on which people drew did not attribute to her the competence, power and diversity she was seeking in her role.

'I felt I was defining myself as a manager every minute of every day, wherever I went. And that was so wearing. It was exhausting.'

In this ambiguous context, small signals were unclear in meaning, many potentially carrying gendered associations. Typical, often repeated, examples, happened when she went to make formal presentations, such as funding requests, to committee, the policy-making forum in which elected members and employed officers of the organization met. A man might well ask whether she had his name for the minutes, assuming she was the secretary. Alternatively, while they greeted each other by name, shook hands and exchanged pleasantries, other attendees would greet Judith by catching her eye and winking:

'I was winked at by men at every level in the organization from caretakers to the chief executive. You would walk into a meeting and sit down and a man would look across the room at you and wink. And I never knew quite what they meant by it. That was the jokey end of the babble of sexualized noise that was around all the time.'

Judith emphasized that this behaviour was 'not a big deal' on the spectrum of possible offences, and that it was meant to be friendly. It was, however, one of an array of thoughtless ways that people positioned her as a woman rather than as a senior manager. As she made her presentation – wanting to do a good job, perhaps feeling slightly nervous – she had to create an image of credibility which counteracted habitual assumptions about women's status. Judith felt she was constantly being positioned by other people's expectations, and that her intentions were often 'mis'-interpreted, translated through unsympathetic frames of reference. She continually felt tested and challenged. Creating a viable identity was demanding and tiring.

'I guess, in the end, that was the fundamental thing which made me leave, because over a period of time it was just too difficult to hold together a coherent sense of self within all those competing expectations.'

In this context, many aspects of Judith's role were ambiguous, conflicting, simultaneously affirming and confronting. Her many achievements were closely intertwined with difficult features she had to work to contain.

Building her department was one example. She was pleased with the appointments she made and the gender balance she achieved. She supported individuals and provided rigorous supervision. In time, and in the face of initial resistance, she helped the team work collectively as a learning group, introducing training to encourage this. She received a lot of support from them. This placed her in an ambivalent position. She had to manage and discipline staff, while also needing their backing. They were very demanding: as they received support, they came to want more. Sometimes Judith had to hold them at arm's length to protect her own boundaries; she would then be accused of withholding help. Their relationship had a potentially more destructive side.

Judith handled these dilemmas, as she did others, by being clear about boundaries and very explicit in her communications. To reduce the confusion of people living with conflicting covert expectations, partly gender-related, she overtly addressed the issues involved. This 'meta-communication' sought to redefine frameworks of sense-making, and attribute her own meanings to her behaviour. These meanings might not, however, be understood or accepted by others.

ACHIEVING COMMUNITY WORK

Similar dynamics and dilemmas arose in other aspects of her role. Judith did a lot of 'very conscious' equal opportunities work internally, building alliances with training officers and groups of women staff. She came to represent equality issues, potential change and – for some people – threat; resistance became directed at her.

External, Judith's role involved facilitating open access, empowering community groups, and offering support to those such as women's and black groups previously marginalized from funding. She introduced practices to achieve these goals; she received positive feedback on the difference she made. But the pressures of acting for others – a mandate she took very seriously – were considerable.

Judith was sometimes criticized as heavily from outside the organization as she was from inside, particularly by women's groups. (Her ambivalent position – as a professional, high-earning woman – was also contentious.)

'They were right to be impatient with what was happening, but I needed their support more than their criticism. And that was the criticism that wounded and undermined me, I think. I could cope much better with the criticism from inside, which is what I expected.'

The community development role was inherently contradictory and problematic. In this boundary position, Judith described herself as both 'in and out of the organization'. She was a member, but also opposed to fundamental aspects of its working, such as senior managers' decision-making power. She sympathized with external groups, whose voices she had to represent, but was also aware of organizational issues which necessarily slowed the pace of change. She felt a sense of mission about trying to reconcile these tensions.

Judith deliberately maintained her sense of being marginal. This fitted her personal and political values. It also placed her under enormous strain, meant that she became a focusing point for latent conflicts in the organization as a whole, and provided constant challenges to her sense of self. She wanted to stand for others' interests, and promote fundamental change towards equality. But she also took on a burden of guilt about how well she was doing this.

On reflection, Judith felt that she could have handled these issues better. She criticized some of the approaches she took, but believed that she had probably done what she could at that time, in that organization.

FIGHTING MEN

As she tried to maintain faith with her internal and external allies, Judith very soon 'got into a position of fight with men'. She was raising agendas which others wanted to ignore; she was therefore 'getting up people's noses'. The issues became associated with her, as a person and as a woman. Judith now thinks this position of fight was not strategically effective, but was inescapable for her at the time as the only senior woman in the department. Often she was too open and direct, too impatient. Sometimes she would confront people about their sexism, and they would become defensive. Her senior colleagues were more politically astute than her and resisted well, sometimes covertly undermining initiatives they had publicly agreed to support. She felt wounded by this behaviour towards her.

She described her way of understanding the world then as mainly political, seeing conflicts of interest between different social groups. She thought white men were particularly able to maintain their power and privilege in local government, against the interests of women and black people. In retrospect she added a more psychological analysis to complement and refine this view. She believed that attacking people's values is likely to evoke threat and retaliation; and that recognizing only group interests and public power can create battle-lines which have to be defended.

With hindsight, she was particularly critical of the stance she took towards one chief officer. Her sense of fight became targeted at him. She stereotyped him as epitomizing all she despised in the organization: its political expediency, conservatism, lack of aware-ness about race and gender, lip-service to change and failure to be more humane. She realized later that he had adopted a common strategy of attacking when under threat. His subsequent use of authority power antagonized her, as did his covert sexual innuendo, and she would 'spit back'. A battle developed between them. But Judith was not on equal terms. She was very scared of meeting with the officer on her own. She felt that he could manipulate her, make her feel small, encourage her into revealing more than she intended, and force her to take a collusive, traditionally female, role, by which she felt compromised. She later saw these fears as partly an inevitable consequence of a battle which she had helped to create but could not possibly win. Although at the time, as she said in a self-mocking tone:

'I was the honourable victim claiming the high moral ground, and he was obviously the immediate representative of what was known to be a horrendously patriarchal and racist organ-ization.'

In a critical incident Judith tried to resist the manager's author-itarian approach to a particular issue. She used memos to express her views, to avoid being undermined by meeting with him. But the manager demanded she retract, and she was forced to do so. He was furious at being challenged; he said that she had betrayed his trust, that their relationship was fundamentally and irrevocably damaged. This incident significantly strengthened Judith's developing decision to leave.

'At the time he was the baddy, and he was the reason I left, almost. That relationship was the final straw. It was no longer possible for me to do my job.'

She later felt she had been naive or unwise to clash openly with someone in a superior position, someone moreover who was not afraid to exercise his power.

SUPPORT, LEARNING, STRESS

Judith's role was extensive and demanding, especially given the work she had to do to maintain and develop her own sense of identity and power. She found women's management training

courses she attended particularly helpful. She exchanged experiences with people in similar positions.

'It was really good. . . to have reinforced that things I was feeling
were my individual fault on my bad days, were in actual fact
the nature of management and women's experience as well, and
were things that needed structural changes.'

Other participants encouraged Judith not to try to achieve too
much, especially as she was acting largely alone at her level. She
remembers two striking role models. One was a black woman who
was very clear about what she could and could not offer. She
would, for example, attend meetings only for the limited time she
had promised.

'She suggested that there was all the work in the world to do on
race and gender, it had been there for 2,000 years or more. And
the small amount I could pick up would be useful, but there was
no need to pick up two armfuls when one was all I could carry.'

In stark contrast was the woman who never ate lunch because
she was too tense to digest her food. She was what Judith did not
want to become, a 'wounded woman' or overworked martyr.

These encounters gave Judith permission to start managing her
work even more effectively. She already advised her staff to leave
at 6 p.m., not take work home, relax, exercise, and be clear about
priorities. She started living up to these injunctions more herself,
and was explicit about doing so. This worked well. But rumours
circulated that she was 'working to rule'. Her explanations were
interpreted in relation to people's habitual value frameworks,
limiting her power to name her own experience.

Outside work Judith received a lot of support from her family.
Her teenage children were a worry and pressure at times, especially as her job took so much of her time:

'But also they just changed the colour of the world every now
and then and made everything completely different.'

She needed a lot of help from her partner: 'I didn't take my in-
tray home any more, but I took home my emotionally battered
self'. She felt she had placed a 'ridiculous burden' on him; he had
nonetheless been actively supportive. Much of her time, even her
weekend country walks, was taken up by her expressing her pain
about work and putting herself back together to be able to face it

again. She was frustrated by this use of energy, but became dependent on it to survive.

She used other strategies to help her cope with the pressure and look after herself physically and emotionally. She had super-vision, attended a gym, went to a health farm, had homoeopathy and instigated a departmental women's support group. But she experienced many symptoms of stress. She was never without a stiff neck and headache, and had difficulty sleeping. She felt tense during the week; she cried and recovered at the weekend.

'I did my job in the week and had my feelings on Saturday morning. Sunday was a better day.'

Judith saw her weight as an indicator of how she felt:

'I always think of myself by nature as a kind of tall, skinny woman and. . . I became a very solid, statuesque tall woman, because I had put on two to three stone in weight. It was as if physically I had to build a barrier between myself and other people.'

She knew she needed to look after herself, but there were limits to her self-awareness. She did not fully acknowledge how close she felt to falling apart.

An additional strain was noticing the effects of the self-protective strategies she was adopting at work. She coped partly by recognizing that people were creating and responding to gendered images of her, and by holding her own sense of self separate. She increasingly felt armoured, watchful and manip-ulative. She liked her development of political skill, but not the tough, hard, brittle, outer shell which was beginning to form. Judith was under too much pressure to have space to reconcile these competing images and find more flexible responses.

She was unable to express her vulnerability, uncertainty and emotions at work, partly because she had to be strong for others, but also to protect herself. Necessary and inevitable as this guarded coping strategy was, it ironically mirrored the culture's defendedness.

Despite the challenges, she said she was seen as a good manager, able to deal with difficult issues, someone from whom to learn. She was invited to take on the role of informal 'trainer' on equal opportunities in many situations, and would then encounter people's resistance to change. This too she found draining.

Looking back, Judith believed that had she stayed longer in the organization she would have burnt out.

DECIDING TO LEAVE

Judith realized that she wanted to leave after about eighteen months, influenced by the crisis in her relationship with the senior manager. She then had difficulty justifying this wish to herself. She had a sense of responsibility to others, particularly to women's and black groups. She was often 'operating on guilt towards other people'. She felt she had to stay to protect their interests, and was reinforced in this view by feedback and by her own successes.

She would also, however, often be 'screaming inside', feeling she could not take it any longer. She talked often with trusted key people outside the organization about whether to leave, trying to come to terms with her desire to do so. Later, plans for a reorganization threatened the existence of her area of work and further eroded her motivation. But it took another critical incident to clarify her intentions.

Part of Judith already 'just wanted to walk out'. One day she did so – literally. She heard, from one of her best allies, a black officer, about a negative response to work they had both been promoting. She found this 'completely outrageous', and burst into tears.

> 'I thought, "This is the first time I've ever burst into tears at work", and somehow that undermined me terribly. . . . You don't cry at work was my notion (and certainly the organization's) then. That's changed. . . . But basically I was saying to myself "Shit. This is what they've done to me. They've reduced me to this."'

Judith had crossed an important boundary. By crying she contravened her implicit agenda of proving women strong and competent. She immediately packed her bag and left; it was 4 p.m. This too confronted her: she had not stayed to try to solve the problem. Shocked at her own behaviour, but taking it as a clear statement, she made her decision.

> '"I am now in a state of leaving," I thought, whatever that meant.'

She no longer needed to justify leaving; instead she talked through the implications for family finances and how she could make it happen. Despite her resolve, she was not willing to compromise. She wanted an appropriate job at a suitable salary, and was not prepared to take 'just any job' in order to escape. Part of this motivation came from her sense of personal worth, part from her strong feeling of being responsible financially for herself and her children, which she has been since the end of her first marriage.

As fears that she could be ruining her career and doubts about whether she was 'finished' or 'done for' rumbled in the background, Judith applied for other jobs. Eventually she was offered a part-time lectureship in professional training. She was jubilant. She wanted the space of working fewer hours to think through what had happened to her and to look after herself more. She also wanted to explore possibilities of becoming a freelance trainer or writer, or doing therapy training. By then she had concluded that individuals and groups also need to work on their personal issues to achieve organizational change, that revolution and therapy are necessary companions. This conclusion also applied to herself.

> 'Subconsciously I think I knew that I really needed to find out what was happening inside as well, and take some care of that, which is what I did.'

In the two months before she left Judith set about creating the 'proper ending' she thought she deserved after all her struggles. She deliberately planned her goodbyes. She wrote appreciative letters to people who had supported her. She invited her immediate staff to lunch at her house and talked candidly about how she valued them, her experiences of the organization, and how it felt to leave. She found their responses to her very affirming. Together they planned how the department would operate once she left, while reorganization was awaited.

She planned a party for all the women she had worked with outside the organization but unfortunately she was ill and unable to attend this herself; she thinks it was too much to cope with. The participants showered her with messages of acknowledgement. There was a formal party for her, at which she gave an 'outrageous speech'. She felt glad to be going and lighter. She was able to refer to problematic issues in the department with humour, and was able to carry people with her.

Throughout, she spoke honestly about her experiences and views of people, hoping others would reciprocate. She thus took away validations as well as her memories of the pain. Although some people's feedback will have been guarded, she was satisfied with the impression she felt she left behind.

> 'I think people are left there with "Well she was good, wasn't she?" And people can say "We had some fights" and leave it at that. . . . Undoubtedly there are people who said that I couldn't stand the heat and had to get out, but the people who mattered are left with the same view I have, I think.'

Looking back at what her previous organization had become she was impressed. There was a 'more mixed management team of black and white, male and female'.

ON REFLECTION

Since leaving, Judith had reviewed her experience in various ways, exploring what she personally brought to the situation, and developing more complex ways of understanding organizations and change.

> 'So I walked out of that place and felt that I'd finished with it. I've discovered since that I haven't. I've worked on a lot of the things that I was playing out there in a therapeutic way, and come to understand them more. I think I've also become more tolerant and strategic in the way I work. I'm not such a politically correct radical as I was at the time. I still feel that I've got radical politics, but I've more strategy, experience and humanity and more realism about how to implement them, and more patience.'

From this learning, her view of the senior manager she confronted had changed. She could see more of the wisdom in his approach. Had circumstances been different, had the senior team been more mixed, had she been 'a little bit more grown-up inside', she thought they might have made a good team.

In telling her story, Judith was surprised and delighted at the 'warmth' she felt towards the experience. The learning she had done, most of which was 'in agony', felt really solid.

'I can look back and see that some of the pain and the wounds
of that time have healed.'

She had become more empowered, more centred personally.
She felt better able to act in situations shaped by people's gendered
expectations and yet able to define herself.

This is a tale of personal and professional learning, illuminating
some of the potential dynamics when a woman change agent
works on equality issues in a challenging role and resistant
environment. Judith thought she would act very differently in the
future. I am impressed by her insights, and simultaneously wary.
There is a danger that focusing on Judith as an individual obscures
an interactive appreciation of the woman manager in context. By
developing greater abilities to handle such situations, she and other
women could be creating new superwomen images, and absolving
other people of responsibility for becoming more aware and
helping cultures change.

JUDITH'S FEEDBACK ON THE DRAFT STORY

Judith said the draft was very recognizable. Her first reading was
unsettling, it made the woman described seem so vulnerable. She
felt a sense of shock at re-entering the situation. Later she enjoyed
reading the story, and reported that the process – like the initial
interview – had been 'stimulating, moving, provoking a lot of
thought'. She again critiqued some of her previous approaches,
believing such behaviour likely to lead to trouble, and felt that she
had been driving herself too hard.

In one way she was surprised. The draft struck her as a personal
story, whilst she had thought of the experience as political, typical
of what was (and is often still) happening to women. (She also
identified the 'very vulnerable experience' being described as 'the
truth'.) I took this comment very seriously. The storytelling form
could encourage individualized explanations of the experiences
recounted. It is important to bear in mind simultaneously wider
social and political issues. These are evoked more fully in other
sections of the book. (See 'Assigning responsibility', p. 159.) In
revising the text I sought to make political themes in the story
clearer.

Judith suggested some corrections to the draft. Most were
clarifications; two emphasized the inherent challenges of the
community development role.

ADDENDUM

Judith's part-time post became full-time within a year. She later moved to another university post, which she enjoys. In current lecturing and consulting she draws significantly on her experiences of senior management and on the enhanced theories of action and change she has developed, then and since. She says she now knows more about her limits and boundaries, feels more powerful, and is more strategic and able to build alliances.

Inclusion, influence and marginality

It seems, from these stories and other available evidence, that women are not widely accepted as legitimate in the senior management environments they have now entered.

Various theories suggest that there are stages in group formation, at each of which certain key issues need resolving sufficiently if progress is to be made (Srivastva *et al.*, 1977). Inclusion issues are seen as paramount at early stages, as individuals try to find viable places in the group. Once these are sufficiently resolved, group members move, in sequence, to concerns about control (achieving personally acceptable levels of power and influence) and affection (achieving appropriate levels of intimacy).

From research reports, much of women managers' behaviour could be interpreted as having the subtext of gaining or not prejudicing their membership, legitimacy and credibility (Marshall, 1993c). Group theory would suggest that people need to establish a *satisfactory* level of inclusion as a necessary precondition to exercising influence and power. Are women often perched on this divide? If they look to men to legitimize them, can they only expect this to happen if they conform to male images of management? Does being rebuffed in attempts at influence throw women back to doubting their inclusion?

Judith's story shows a manager living knowingly with marginality. This was not a comfortable position for her to maintain. But for many women being marginal (perhaps proudly and playfully) offers another option which may feel more authentic than disguising feelings of difference.

Can appreciating one's marginality and difference, and maintaining an alternative view, paradoxically be a form of self-attributed inclusion? (*Dorothy* adopted a similar approach, but found it lonely and conflicted: p. 176.) Can organizations cope with people choosing to do this? Does diversity management allow this much potential discomfort?

Feeling undermined

A recurring theme in the data was 'feeling undermined' by features of organizational structure or aspects of particular relationships. Teresa's story gives several examples. By this phrase research participants meant that their organizational position had been made unclear, their status or power had been placed in doubt or their ability to act effectively had been compromised. It is interesting to speculate on whether these dynamics are currently more likely to happen to women than to men.

Claiming to be undermined is a contentious interpretation to make. People can be accused of paranoia, of taking trivial issues too seriously, of creating the situations in which they then feel trapped. Some of these dynamics may happen sometimes. Particular patterns of interaction can also arise because they are readily available in the organizational culture or society generally. For example, until recently men have tended to be in more senior and women in more junior organizational positions. Expectations of status and interaction are therefore generated which shape many situations, but are often not open to conscious awareness. In any given instance acting contrary to habitual patterns of expectations can prove inconsequential, can provide an alternative which is readily accepted, or can so disrupt other people's views of 'normality' that they feel threatened and retaliate. Women managers often describe themselves as 'walking a tightrope', meaning that they frequently negotiate these possibilities, aware that the penalties of making a mistake could be significant.

Several women felt that organizational structures had been created which masked or detracted from their status. For example, Teresa and *Julia* were assigned as subordinates people who had previously performed their functions in the organization. The new reporting relationships were never made clear, creating tensions and obstructing the women's work performance. Several other people had dealt with confusions of organizational status, role or reporting relationships which had complicated already difficult jobs. The women were left to cope with the resulting disruptions. In some cases it seemed that the pride or previous power of men was being protected at the women's expense.

In other cases the undermining came through patterns of relationship. Jane felt her competence and status were compromised when she was sexually harassed in public by her boss. Judith felt undermined by the lack of images for women managers in her organization, which meant she had to create her rights to status in each new encounter. Some women felt their credibility was detrimentally affected by superiors who ignored or patronized them. Other organizational members were likely to take these behaviours as examples, discounting the woman's formal position and avoiding her.

People also felt undermined when they were criticized by people on whose behalf they were acting. This was particularly wounding, and contributed to feelings of isolation. It implied that no one understood what the research participants were trying to achieve.

Gender stereotypes can also affect cultural rules. Women may engage in behaviour that seems culturally acceptable, but discover it is not acceptable *from women*. Judith provides a possible example. Having previously avoided confrontation, she decided to stand up to her boss on a particular issue, in a style she saw other (male) people adopt. Her approach was rebuffed. She was told she had overstepped an unspoken boundary and caused irreparable damage to their relationship. Her 'mistake' may have several elements. Her behaviour unsettled the gender balance of the relationship. Her challenge was also hierarchic: she may have been considered insufficiently deferential. *Stevie's* case has similarities (see p. 211). She was assertive towards the manager who challenged her to join the sauna. She was satisfied that she had stood her ground, but her willingness to engage in overt combat also made her a threat. The field of possible power moves can, then, subtly marginalize and undermine women, whichever 'rules' they seek to play by.

This material suggests that women's inclusion in organizational power systems is still often in doubt. Attributed status lags behind formal role status (see 'Inclusion', p. 154). Further support for this possibility is men's reluctance to treat women seriously as political allies (see 'Organizational cultures', p. 300). Ambiguities about women's status can, however, sometimes be used to advantage. Christina capitalized on being an unknown element in the early phases of her change work.

This section shows how important relationships with more senior people are. Their signalling about acceptance can confirm or undermine women's inclusion status in current organizational cultures.

Finding ways to judge themselves

Repeated themes in the stories were whether and how people were able to judge their competence and performance. This often proved contentious because either they received little feedback from other organizational members or messages to them seemed hostile or devaluing.

Several people talked about the importance of professional standards and knowing that they were performing well against these even if their work was not appreciated by others. In this way they were also able to judge how much they had achieved in their companies by the time they left. Others looked outside for reference points to help them assess what they faced within. For example people confirmed Teresa's impression that hers was a very sexist organization, and Jane's that her boss was difficult.

Lack of trusted information could be highly detrimental and become self-reinforcing. Whilst *Margaret* (p. 241) was unable to obtain evaluations she could believe she doubted her own competence. By keeping her doubts to herself she reduced opportunities for receiving contradictory, positive, feedback. Only later, when she discovered that male colleagues also felt stressed, was she able to improve her self-evaluations. In contrast, *Dorothy* (p. 176) deliberately set up situations to receive feedback so that she would not 'live in a fog'.

Several people looked back at their organizations once they had left to assess how much the problems they had experienced could be attributed to them or to the situation. Several felt validated to find that their successors or previous colleagues also faced difficulties or that people who had betrayed them had not flourished.

This material suggests that people were often judging situations from more than one frame of reference, deliberately using several perspectives to assess themselves because readily available frames and norms felt inappropriate or devaluing. This approach seems helpful when working in cultures whose values are potentially inhospitable. But talking multiple languages in this way involves complex processes and gives no 'right' answers. Several women's self-images were affected by this sense of contradictory views (see 'Incongruity', p. 224). For example, *Stevie* was affirmed at work for being tough, but did not like herself for this. Judith was aware of being seen through gendered stereotypes. She did not share these, but knew they affected other people's responses to her. Similarly, Teresa was digesting feedback that what she saw as a professional style was experienced by some people as 'cold' and intimidating. These women faced choices about how to balance different frames of judgement and particularly whether or not to seek acceptance within dominant cultural norms.

Appreciating multiple perspectives can provide insights and power. It can also be tiring, adding another source of pressure as people seek to create identities which are organizationally viable and sufficiently authentic personally. But *public* identity creation is not wholly under the individual's influence. Several stories show how people tried to exercise control over impressions they projected. They were largely successful in being accepted. But they also at times restricted the selves they could be.

A linked theme was how much people personalized their experiences as failure. Judith, Patricia and *Julia*, for example, did take their situations personally at the time, believing that animosity was directed at them specifically. Only later did *Julia* realize that all of the old regime of management were targeted. In retrospect Judith believed she had contributed to the situation of fight in which she became entrapped. In contrast Dorothy and *Pamela* did not attribute their situations to themselves, but to irreconcilable organizational forces and a specific power clash respectively. *Pamela* felt secure that she could not be criticized when she was invited to resign, and this did not happen. Jane and *Margaret* were shocked, in contrast, that previous positive appraisals were cast into doubt retrospectively when senior people wanted to undermine them.

At one of the workshops I held people discussed how to leave others with a suitably positive impression of their behaviour. They felt both that they could contribute to achieving this by taking appropriate and overtly legitimized steps in decision-making *and* that this is an impossible wish. Other people would judge them in relation to their own frameworks; their motives could be reinterpreted in retrospect. This is one of the penalties of being senior and taking initiatives.

Making sense, assigning responsibility, having choice

As I have worked with this research these change agent accounts have seemed particularly contentious. I have imagined that readers will want to identify 'mistakes' the women made to explain away their experiences. I want to pause here and reflect on processes of sense-making which affect all of the stories. I want to question whether individualizing responsibility is appropriate or helpful.

The issue of whether the managers helped to create situations they then found difficult lurks in the background of this research. Some people with whom I have discussed the project have wanted to assign responsibility or blame, come to clear conclusions, or take sides. I anticipate that some readers will seek to do so. I hope it will be difficult to summarize this data simply. I urge you not to. Usually the interaction of person and context is complex, shifting and dynamic.

Research participants could not tell their stories without attributing responsibility in some way or openly reflecting on this issue. In this they varied greatly, as the stories show. Some questioned themselves searchingly. Some noted and disliked what they interpreted as tones of paranoia or self-pity. Many used me as a sounding board, wanting to be understood, assured that other people have similar experiences, but not fooled or patronized. Some judged themselves harshly. Many reviewed their explanations as the experience receded, some assigning themselves less influence, some more, in the process.

Actively considering different explanations for their experiences was often associated with taking charge of their situations and being able to move on (see 'Judging', p. 157). Overall, people took on more responsibility than they attributed to others. Even when situations or relationships seemed difficult, the women managed their own reactions and repeatedly sought new strategies for being effective and surviving.

The processes of making sense amidst an array of plausible interpretations have been a continuing preoccupation, delight and concern for me throughout the research. As I wrote each story, for example, I was aware that I could 'choose' story lines with different tones. I could, for example, select innocent victim, political *ingénue*, righteous rejector of ineffectual organizational norms or unaware provocateur. I have sought to write an account which honours the story I was told (checking this with the person concerned), which incorporates my own reactions, and which poses questions about choices of interpretation rather than resolving them. (But what I have just written is an espoused story line in itself, of course, one with authenticity – which may involve naming contradictions – as its theme.) (See 'Inquiring in practice', p. 23ff.)

And yet I do favour certain 'readings' of the material. I would dissemble to claim otherwise. I do believe that the women in this research experienced their organizations and roles as difficult and stressful at times, and that their experiences are worthy of consideration and respect. I believe that these situations were framed by structural and political factors which in turn take their shape within broader social contexts. This backcloth of organizational life is influential and often unawarely incorporates gender inequalities. These circumstances make available certain patterns of possibility – such as typical interactions or potential career expectations – which can be readily invoked and repeated. This broader, social and political, level of appreciation needs to be held in mind alongside any individualized sense-making.

The story form on which this book is based may lead readers to look for individual-based explanations. Gender issues are so often personalized and assigned to women that I am very suspicious of using such sense-making alone. The repetition of certain circumstances in a story, for example, may suggest that this reveals someone's personal pattern, that they attract these kinds of experiences. This is unlikely to be wholly untrue; people can be triggers for particular kinds of interaction. They are often, however, triggers because of their social rather than personal characteristics. The attribution of total personal responsibility seems inappropriate in the cases reported here. The experiences could as readily be seen as available patterns of possibility, in these worlds, at these levels – the current frontiers of women's entry into management – which are being played out in some individuals' lives. My many further meetings with women who have left organizational roles or would like to do so give weight to this possibility.

Of interest in the stories is what the women do with their confronting circumstances. Many use them as development opportunities. But perhaps they have less choice than this phrase implies; if they are to survive they must learn from them. Their experiences were digested, come to terms with, reviewed as a base for learning and for moving on. Thus making sense is also making choices, an active process through which people create meanings to live by.

Patricia

OVERVIEW

I met Patricia at a conference. I had just presented a paper on women managers and organizational cultures, depicting women as often under pressure to adapt to established norms and values. Patricia said that she had had such experiences. A year and a half previously she had been forced out of her job as vice-president of patient services in a large North American hospital. She had been leading a major organizational change initiative, against which there had eventually been retaliation. Her chief executive officer (CEO) had planned changes with her privately, but not supported her in public. She had become the scapegoat when change was resisted. Her story echoed those of other women I had spoken to and I therefore asked to interview her formally.

Patricia is one of the two non-UK participants (both nurses) in the study, and one of the few who had been asked to leave. Her account offers insights into the potentially complex power dynamics involved in organizational culture change which has significant gender associations.

Patricia wanted her story to be told, but did not feel able to do this herself. She knew of several women in similar positions, mostly nurses, who had also been forced out of top management jobs. She was surprised at how much emotion was still stirred by recounting her experiences: she thought she had come to terms with them. The interview proved a further step in doing so.

EARLY CAREER MOVES

Patricia was in her early fifties when we met. She had started her career as a nurse. She took a short break when her children were young, and organized some later job moves to accommodate family responsibilities. She spent some time in nursing education, especially enjoying developing new courses. She also did further training, including taking a Master's degree course in organizational change. Only when her children were older did she move into senior management.

By the early 1980s, Patricia was working as a nurse practitioner in a 150-bed paediatric hospital, reporting to the vice-president of nursing. She had moved geographically to follow her husband's career. When her boss was fired, the CEO asked Patricia to take over the role. This was initially seen as a temporary appointment, but she stayed in it for four years. Patricia initiated a major reorganization of nursing, which she and others judged highly successful. She described this organization as 'very open to change'. She admired the CEO and felt they were 'on the same wavelength'.

'I didn't see myself as working in a male-contexted environment. It was a very open environment, there was a lot of opportunity.'

Nursing was restructured to become more autonomous and have more power in decision-making. Patricia described this change work as related to issues of gender and relative power.

'I was looking for the inclusion of nurses in the decision-making processes, the inclusion of women. . . . The doctors were almost all men. The nurses were the guts of the organization. They were there 24 hours a day, but had little power. . . . So nursing became more valued in the organization: nurses became more able to select patients, to be in control of decisions about patient care.'

At that time Patricia's children were in their early teens. She thought that having a family had been a healthful rather than stressful influence.

'Getting home to the family was a relief, a necessary change of pace, a balance in my life.'

Patricia was then invited, by its CEO, to join a newly opened hospital, 'to try to utilize some of these new theories and ways of interacting in this environment'. She accepted. This time her husband moved to follow her.

AN INVITATION TO INITIATE CHANGE

A year after the hospital opened Patricia became the first full-time vice-president of nursing. She stayed with the organization for six and a half years.

For the first few years Patricia's change of work was very successful. Initially she had to bring together 'three very disparate groups of nurses' to form a new nursing structure. A strong, cohesive management group developed in nursing, with 'a lot of openness to change'. Nurses became more involved in decision-making. Concepts of primary nursing were also introduced, meaning that one nurse would work with one patient and their family, getting to know them and contributing to decision-making about them.

Then some of the changes began to impact doctors, administrators and other parts of the organization. People began to ask if nursing was acquiring too much power, whether they were 'moving ahead' of the rest of the organization too quickly, and who was in control.

From this point on Patricia had to live with three major forces, which together eventually eroded her ability to influence change and her position in the organization. Firstly, powerful organizational players, especially the doctors, felt threatened by the changes she was initiating and reacted against them. Secondly, the CEO's behaviour was ambivalent and contradictory. He advocated and planned change with her in private, but would not affirm it in public, leaving her isolated and facing opposition alone. Thirdly, as the resulting power processes worked themselves through, some nurses withdrew support from Patricia and the directions of change. These issues interweave in the account that follows.

CHANGE AND RESISTANCE

One effect of the changes in nursing was an improvement in patient care which other members of the organization, including doctors, recognized. The CEO wanted such changes spread throughout the organization, to improve quality and devolve decision-making. He saw Patricia as a prime champion of change and in a reorganization redesignated her vice-president of patient services: 'My mandate then was to help clean up the act of a number of other departments as well as nursing.'

This move happened about three years into Patricia's time with the hospital. She was by then known, and respected in some quarters. But she thought the CEO did not realize that she was also perceived as a potential threat by managers whose areas were slow to change. Following the reorganization people were suspicious of her and saw her as power-hungry. Yet Patricia felt that she was clearly mandated by the CEO to progress significant change.

'I took over other areas and began to build them into participative, self-directed units. They were happy about this. But again, that became more threatening to the people who were not in those parts of the organization. So the change was very lopsided. Because although we were all mandated to. . . [change] our areas, the only place that was really changing in the organization was the part under my direction.'

As this became more apparent, the people who did not like change began to fight it strongly, and to direct their challenges and anger at Patricia personally. The conflict was partly about professional standing, but may also have had gender associations. As a nurse she was organizationally out of place, upsetting established patterns of culture and power. Patricia recalled the tone of comments: 'nurses are getting too strong, too powerful, who is this nurse, is she running this hospital?'

During this time, Patricia worked closely with some directors of services on specific initiatives. These people became allies. But even when changes had been widely agreed within an area, Patricia felt she was singled out for comment and resistance. For example, it was decided to remove incongruities about nurses' pay scales and reporting relationships in a particular care area.

'Then the director of [that area] came under fire. But I came under fire because I was promoting that new change. . . . So it didn't matter that it was a combined team of nursing who were really committed to the objective. It was me personally.'

PERSISTENCE AND ISOLATION

In retrospect Patricia saw this as a critical time. The battle-lines became hardened, her position and behaviour became more visible, more tested out, and she became more isolated.

'If I'd been smart, at that point I would probably have got out.'

She would thus have been a woman who left of her own accord, having decided that the situation was weighted against her. But this option did not appeal: 'I really had a vision that things could and would change.' Her conviction rested firmly on believing that she had the CEO's backing and encouragement.

'And through all this I was very supported by the CEO. When I would go back to him and say "In this meeting, when some of these things were questioned you didn't really come out and support this, is this indeed what you still want to happen?" he would absolutely assure me that "yes, it must go on, it cannot be stopped, they will come round to our way of thinking, but we must proceed ahead". And so there was a lot of encouragement to continue with this change process.'

It seems that change was not being carefully managed organization-wide, that the positioning of powerful interest groups and the dynamics of resistance were not being addressed.

Patricia repeatedly challenged the CEO about his failure to support the changes and her in public. She was given renewed reassurances of his faith in both. But the lavish resources of organizational status, money and decision-making power she had were never overtly underwritten with the CEO's public approval.

'So in the back room I was very supported. . . but when it came to the open forum with the other administrators I always felt that I was being hung out to dry a little bit.'

The CEO adopted a similar style with other senior managers. Patricia was not the only one for whom it created problems. But it does seem that Patricia relied heavily on this somewhat dubious relationship for both support and power. Explaining this, she said that she knew the changes could work, but that they would be hard to achieve on her own. She wanted her new CEO to be like her previous boss, and hoped that he might change. But this did not happen. Also she had limited access to other senior power networks. Her allies were mainly in nursing or at lower organizational levels. She felt barred from developing alliances with her male peers.

Patricia believed that she was perceived *as a woman* who had become too powerful, and so transgressed deep-rooted organizational and social expectations. She thought that resistance to her would have been less had she been a man. She was different in too many ways to her peers – as a nurse and woman and an advocate of changes which emphasized empowerment and de-centralization – for relationships to be developed to ease the tensions involved. Patricia did not feel accepted by her male peers. She quoted the words of Rosemary Brown (1989), a black politician, to express her sense of exclusion from possible com-radeship, and work-effectiveness:

Throughout my time in office I was able to observe the ease with which the men twisted each other's arms, to see that even when they opposed each other's views there was an underlying respect, a feeling of family between them. My approach, on the other hand, even to those members I considered friends, was met with wariness.

(Brown, 1989: 229)

Patricia thought that women are therefore more likely to work through influence than by directly exercising power, and that they do not 'really have a chance to play the power game', because fundamentally different terms underlie their membership of senior management.

An anomaly of organizational power also seriously affected Patricia's situation. The decision-making structure retained the individual power of doctors, who were becoming her main opponents. They reported directly to the CEO, and on the management group, the hospital's main decision-making forum, were *represented* by a medical director, so named to show that this was not someone medical staff reported to. (Other functions were headed by vice-presidents.)

Patricia was, then, relatively isolated politically in the manage-ment group. She was not the only woman, but did not identify with the other two female members. She saw them as 'very passive, very non-aggressive, not decision-makers at all. . . very, very controlled, directed people'. Having women colleagues who adapted to prevailing norms put Patricia under additional pressure. Her initiative-taking and straightforwardness made her the more visible violator of female stereotypes.

When we met, Patricia wondered why she had not trusted her own gut reaction more, which was telling her: 'slow down, there's something wrong here'. She became caught between this message and the others telling her she was supported and should proceed. She thinks that women are more likely than men to find themselves trapped in this way, that when they have goals they tend to believe that they will achieve them.

'So, with any encouragement at all, we will go forward and continue to pursue those goals. I think men are more political than women. We look at what the value is, and I think men look at whether this is going to fly. They're maybe not so committed. So I think sometimes women tend to push more than men in some situations. And I really wanted to believe the CEO.'

Patricia was too committed to the potential changes to heed her own concerns. But she did not want to be 'smart' enough not to try for what is sometimes unattainable. She had to be committed to her job and, as an organizational leader, to have thoughts on how the organization could be different, to make her working life worthwhile.

Patricia thought she probably knew two years before she left that the CEO's failure to support her publicly was dangerous. But she carried on trying to work through other sources of power and influence. Her focus was on the changes, not on her own security.

'I wanted to believe in what was happening. It wasn't that important to me to keep my job *per se*, but we were building something, it was important for both patient care and the profession of nursing. . . .'

She also felt she could not have left the organization at that time because nursing as a function was under stress and lacked support from other directions.

Her actions continued to be challenged publicly, and the CEO continued to 'fudge'. But despite her difficult situation, Patricia deliberately 'did not want to resort to playing politics'; she wanted to 'play it straight'. She did not, for example, describe initiatives to build bridges to doctors or their concerns. She wanted the value of organizational improvements to be persuasive in themselves. Her strategies were to increase openness and decentralization, and empower staff by changing structures and processes and encouraging team participation. These proved successful in changing the organizational culture in nursing and other areas under her direction. Her leadership also encouraged nurses' professional development.

On the wider organizational stage, she had much less power. Here, the CEO was leaving Patricia to be the public face of change initiatives. But, by not speaking clearly as their advocate, he left the arena open for other power-holders to challenge.

Doctors' concerns about nurses' power increased.

'The doctors. . . saw nursing changing. . . saw it coming out from under their control. They wanted to be able to make decisions about what nurses were going to do, and nurses were saying "No, that's a nursing responsibility to do that." And they didn't like the fact the nurses were then not responding to them, but were listening more to their professional intuition. Through this time the nurses were beginning to get very self-directed, very interested in their jobs.'

As the pressure increased, and it became more obvious that there had to be support or the whole change programme would be undermined, the CEO continued to play an ambivalent role.

THE SITUATION CAME TO A HEAD

The doctors' resistance to increased nurse power eventually found an issue to focus it. Bed space was under pressure and at times they were unable to admit patients.

'And they needed someone to blame. They certainly couldn't blame the CEO because they felt that he was their spokesperson, and there was a very close affinity between them. And they saw me as the second in line, also as the person who was promoting a lot of changes they weren't sure they liked.'

Although Patricia was not directly responsible for admissions, nursing generally and she specifically were becoming identified as troublesome.

'It was easy to say "It's all her fault", and that blaming context was quite strong.'

At this point, too, Patricia felt betrayed by some of her previous allies within nursing. This she found especially painful. Some people exercised their new-found power to improve their own career chances. They no longer supported the direction of change if it threatened their individual prospects. Nurses began to 'hedge their bets', and be more supportive of doctors.

Patricia felt particularly regretful about the behaviour of one senior nurse manager, someone whose development she had aided, who did this. Patricia believed her dissent was significant in eroding the potential for change, and therefore 'very destructive'. (Noting that this person had not been successful in the organization subsequently, Patricia thought this was because her integrity had been compromised by her behaviour.) When people lower down the organization saw divisions within nursing administration they became cautious. If they were not supported from above they could not be advocates of change.

Patricia believed the nurses began to understand how much power they had to destabilize the organization, and that this created uncertainty for them. They recognized the signs of backlash, and expected little support from the CEO should things become difficult. Once Patricia, their strong champion, became vulnerable, they doubted their own power. In this combative situation, rather than speak up for quality care and more participative organization, 'the nurses came out from underneath'.

The potential for change had somehow receded, and people sensed this. As they wavered, concerned about personal ambitions and self-protection, the push for new ways of working was further compromised. Neither she nor her allies could maintain the vision, and the power-base crumbled.

Finally, the doctors forced an organizational confrontation about bed utilization and patient admissions. There were nurse and bed shortages in neighbouring hospitals. In other organizations senior nursing people were also targeted, blamed and forced to leave. Patricia said 'this had happened in five other hospitals before I went'. When these administrators left, the most senior nursing post was often demoted organizationally.

The doctors asked to meet the CEO without Patricia present. He agreed, despite Patricia's protests that patient care was central to her organizational responsibilities and that she had the relevant data on staffing levels. At the meeting, the CEO apparently did nothing to support Patricia. She became the scapegoat, as other parties would not take responsibility.

The doctors showed that they could exercise power to 'turn the whole organization round', despite the widespread lip-service being paid to organizational change goals. The nurses could not withstand these developments.

'The women [in nursing], rather than continuing to be powerful and stand up for what they believed, began to just drift away.'

During the next month, Patricia became increasingly marginalized, relating mainly to the CEO she still wanted to believe.

LAST DAYS IN THE ORGANIZATION

Patricia met with the CEO several times to discuss the directions of change and his trust in her. Again he assured her that she was doing the right thing, that he trusted her decision-making. She wanted to test his views because she needed to take certain actions before going on vacation. By this stage she was very tired, needing a break. She wondered later whether her tiredness had contributed to the situation's deterioration, whether she had been insufficiently watchful.

Patricia felt that there was a lot of unrest and concern within the organization and suggested that she and the CEO tour round, showing cohesiveness, making the CEO visible. She used such tactics to facilitate the CEO's effectiveness, also aligning with him symbolically and personally. Even at this stage he had her loyalty and support. During this tour they discussed future change possibilities.

The next morning, Patricia visited the CEO to tie up loose ends and was told that her services were no longer needed. She was offered the choice of resigning or being fired. Her suggestion that they both think matters through and discuss them in the afternoon was initially accepted. (She already had ideas on appropriate financial terms for leaving, as she thought any senior executive should.) But this pause was pre-empted by the CEO's sense of hurry to have her go; within the hour he had informed her secretary that she was leaving and demanded her keys. Patricia did receive 'a very nice settlement', but thinks that the CEO was on such poor ground in dismissing her that this was made partly to deter her from legal action.

When Patricia left, some people in the organization were 'devastated', greatly disappointed at the hospital's return to its earlier self, dominated by doctors and with a weak CEO. These included the directors of services who had become allies and nurses who had moved to the hospital because of its organizational developments. Many of the latter subsequently left.

Individually these people did not have the power to sustain the new culture.

STRESS AND EXHAUSTION

Looking back, Patricia was struck by how much stress she had experienced in this job. She contrasted this with earlier, potentially highly demanding, phases in her career. While in this vice-president role she was over-committed to work. Her home life was not the source of 'interesting diversion and revitalization' it had been before. The role seemed to overtake her. Also she was continually being given extra duties – 'the expectations grew and grew'. Having compared notes with other nursing administrators, she felt that overloading is particularly common in this function, that other people hold unrealistic expectations of (senior) nurses.

By the end of her time in the organization, Patricia was exhausted, 'glad to get out of it'. She felt betrayed and upset by the hostility displayed towards her. She was also very angry. She had not been able to adapt and forget her visions and hopes for change. As she became aware of her trapped situation, her sense of frustration had mounted.

'I saw my commitment becoming more one of anger. I've been given this task to do, I've done it and what am I getting out of it?'

In the end Patricia was powerless. Her success in her previous organization was a reminder of her competence, but made her situation even more difficult to accept.

REGRETS

Whilst she later believed that the CEO had lied repeatedly and she was taken in by it, Patricia did not see this as the 'real essence' of her disappointment with her experience. She was more upset by the parts played by other women – the nurses who withdrew their energy – and by the supremacy of the doctors' power.

'I think my disappointment was in the support from women, and amongst women. And also the fact that the male dominant, doctor group could have a really double standard. They could have so much power to have their way, even though it meant returning from good patient care, nurses' satisfaction with their jobs and so on. Which were perceived by many people as going backwards after I left.'

She believed that the nurses had the power to maintain the new ways of working if they had stayed together, but that they did not recognize this. She felt they were too strongly influenced by the original culture and their previous, subordinate, position. The political power of a core group was able to overturn an emerging alternative reality. In the testing of organizational power which occurred, women's roles were therefore demoted.

The changes Patricia offered the organization, which were perceived as so threatening, seem highly symbolic in gender terms. They challenged the power of a dominant group of men, the doctors, and had the potential to empower a previously subordinate group of women, the nurses. Perhaps some of the force of the situation derived from this confrontation.

Women's reactions to each other contributed to the complexities. Patricia believed that women are uneasy and ambivalent about women with power.

'So often. . . we want nursing leaders to be powerful, but many times once nurses become powerful in their own ranks they are unsupported by their own peers or their own colleagues. It's almost as if we can't stand success and we don't want a hierarchy.'

As women with power discomfort both men and women, they are challenged from all sides.

AFTER LEAVING

Patricia took six months to look after herself and recuperate from her experience. She had to cope with the emotional consequences, and her sense of exhaustion. She then decided she needed 'some time back at the bedside', and took a short-term contract with a local hospital as a clinical nurse specialist. She found this direct work with patients and families very rewarding. After a period of travel, and almost two years after leaving, she registered on a postgraduate research programme to do a PhD. Her studies are funded by the hospital. She sees this as guilt money from the CEO.

IN REFLECTION

In telling her story, Patricia highlighted her CEO's lack of public support, the doctors' power and nurses' lack of faith in potential change, and subsequent withdrawal, to explain her eventual marginalization. A further significant theme is what power and change strategies she was able to use. She relied heavily on legitimate and expert power. These seemed insufficiently robust to deal with the complex situation she faced. Patricia was unwilling to use political strategies. She also believed she was constrained in developing power through alliances in this environment, because as a nurse and woman she was never fully accepted as a peer by male colleagues, despite her senior rank.

PATRICIA'S FEEDBACK ON THE DRAFT STORY

I met Patricia on a trip to London to talk through my first draft of her story. She said I had done an 'excellent job' of capturing the essence of her experience, and confirmed my interpretations of her actions, for example about not wanting to engage in politics. She said she could be more critical of the experience as she felt much less emotionally involved than when we had first met. We agreed some minor amendments to clarify the sense. I later radically reorganized the story to avoid repetition and shorten it. I submitted this draft to Patricia. She was entirely happy with it.

ADDENDUM

Patricia was encouraged to apply for a CEO post with a major charity. She was offered the job and accepted, taking leave of absence from her PhD programme. (She had received other job offers; her experiences in the hospital, and the manner in which she left, did not seem to have damaged her career prospects.) The charity's board had recently reviewed its role, and promised to concentrate on policy development, leaving her to manage. She immediately set about making changes, moving the organization from a hierarchy to a flatter, team-oriented structure. She benefited from being able to recruit new personnel, including senior people. She delighted in her new role; she liked being in charge, dependent on her own abilities not on someone else. She felt appreciated by her staff for combining strong people and task management skills. The changes began to take effect.

Patricia left this organization after two years, because the board started to interfere in management again, in ways which she could not condone ethically. She believes she re-encountered the difficulties of working in a male-dominated culture, but at a more senior level. The board was 'content having senior women work themselves to death, but didn't want women making decisions or showing initiative'.

This time, leaving was much easier. She had learnt from her previous experience, and was able to protect herself and her energies. Her stress was minimal and her self-confidence remained intact.

She has now moved into consultancy, concentrating on organizational development in health care and not-for-profit institutions. She likes being able to choose who to work with; she is confident in her abilities. Patricia feels she has developed remarkably in the last few years: this is partly new growth, gained through maturity and facing adversity.

'Some of it is returning to some traits that I had lost, that were overcome by corporate oppressiveness.'

Her PhD is still on hold, but this is not a problem. She is very satisfied: 'I truly feel in control of my life and my future.' She is wary of rejoining corporate life, and concludes:

'My final analysis is that corporate/male-dominated business is unhealthy for caring women.'

Dorothy

OVERVIEW

Dorothy had been a senior nursing manager in New Zealand. She had left this job, and the country, several years before we met. Her role had involved acting as a change agent on several fundamental issues simultaneously. She and a small team of allies had facilitated significant developments, particularly supporting Maori people to develop culturally appropriate mental health services. But the resulting organizational tensions became difficult to contain. Dorothy's base of allies weakened. She decided that she could not, and should not, hold the change process together. She left to preserve her sanity, and to allow other solutions space to emerge. Moving to the UK suited her husband's career as well as her need for a complete break. She imagined finding relatively undemanding work. She was then just 50 and not feeling significantly career-minded.

This story is as much about Dorothy's understandings of how organizations work and her associated strategies for facilitating change as it is about her decision to leave.

WORKING CONTEXT

Dorothy is English by birth. Her career has been in nursing and nurse education. By the mid-1980s she was the regional director of nursing in a large psychiatric service in New Zealand. Her role was primarily that of a change agent and had various interrelated components which placed her at the centre of organizational tensions.

Firstly, Dorothy was developing the nursing function by explicit work on its philosophy and mission. This involved helping nurses look at their roles and boundaries, and how they worked with other professional groups. Secondly, she was generating initiatives to transform the region's mental health provision, strongly favouring a move to more community-based services. Thirdly, she had accepted the Maori people's challenge to help them develop culturally appropriate mental health facilities. Whilst in practice the three components were simultaneous and interwoven, in this story the third is highlighted, because it proved so challenging to the organization.

Dorothy was liaising with the Maori community to identify and meet their health care needs. Doing so involved appreciating fundamental racial inequalities. Maori people have been suppressed for about a hundred years, stifling their cultural development. Gender was also a significant issue. Men are currently more dominant in this culture than women, partly reinforced by the male domination of Western systems with which they have contact. Maori women therefore face a fundamental conflict between supporting the men in their communities in negotiations with white groups, and wanting more social power themselves. Into this work Dorothy took a strong concern for the rights of indigenous peoples, and a willingness to listen to their voices. She addressed women's health needs, and so was also very aware of the gender tensions.

Dorothy's style involved building alliances widely and pursuing change where it seemed possible and on different fronts simultaneously.

CHANGE APPROACHES

During her years as a manager, Dorothy had developed understandings about how organizations work, how change happens and what roles are available for her to play in different kinds of contexts. She saw two broad, complementary, paths to change.

Her favoured approach can be called 'systemic'. It requires seeing any situation as a complex system of interacting forces, lived out by people with different needs, some of which are unconscious. The system achieves a certain stability and force of habit even if those involved are dissatisfied with it. It may have the potential to act differently, but it will typically need to overcome major resistances before doing so. A change agent can encourage parts of the system to innovate, but initially has to work *with* rather than *against* established patterns. So actions may be introduced as 'probes' to see how the organization reacts and whether it is appropriate to move in that direction, or whether an alternative arises. This approach is sensing, not pushing issues publicly if the time does not seem right. Whether change will emerge and what form it will take is difficult to predict. Intervention hopes to create an open and flexible culture. The facilitator must be willing to handle new issues as they arise in the process.

Dorothy believes her preferred style is more likely to be adopted by women than men because it involves empathizing with others as a way of understanding, and seeks action which respects diverse views.

An alternative change strategy is that of introducing different ways of behaving in a top-down, command way. Interventions claim to know what is best for the organization and introduce processes for achieving this – such as new reporting relationships – and rewards for adapting to new norms. These approaches have their value and can be successful. They can, for example, introduce initiatives such as equality programmes which the organization would not easily imagine from its current way of operating. They can, however, be ineffective if new patterns of behaviour never become enacted aspects of the dominant culture, but are only accorded lip-service.

BUILDING ALLIANCES

In her work Dorothy combined the two approaches to change, but also faced many dilemmas about what she could achieve from her social position as a pakeha (white) woman, and how she could help people work with the threatening material about race and gender which change initiatives were raising.

One of her main strategies was to build alliances with people in different social groups. It was important that some of these were white men in positions of organizational power. She had to work with the dominant system, even if she wanted to change it. She described her recent work in these terms.

'I believe that we, as women [nurses], can't change the world by just changing the women's world. We can only change the world by finding alliances with men in their world, and getting them to change their world. We can't do it for them, but we can do it with them, and we can support them. . . . It's hard to explain to a lot of women because they think it's a cop-out.'

She did not feel that this was compromising, as she was building relationships with people with similar values rather than being manipulative. She was careful in selecting allies.

'What I try to do. . . is choose men that underneath have a sensitivity to those issues that are troublesome, that often cause conflict, that involve a lot of soul searching. Often they're the least obvious men. You have to delve.'

Dorothy thought some women try to undermine men to compensate for their own (women's) perceived lack of power. But she saw this as unproductive and tried to ensure that her actions did not have such effects. Also, she was very aware of the potential gap in power between doctors and nurses and felt that she needed to bridge this for any change work to be successful. Dorothy, then, typically worked with and through others. She initiated the change processes referred to here jointly with a small group of like-minded colleagues, which included a senior male doctor, a long-standing ally who was appreciative of women's issues.

She saw herself as able to create visions of the future by incorporating different parties' views, but did not want to be the sole person pushing these through. This offended her belief that for change to happen it must become part of the system, advocated by different actors. She was therefore reluctant to assert her voice independently. Sometimes she would not be given public credit for her work, but she felt that achieving change was more important than personal glory.

'So long as it happens, and so long as someone addresses it, you don't have to be at the front all the time.'

Also, taking the lead often meant visibility and stress she would rather not cope with.

Dorothy and her allies worked to influence the organizational climate, each encouraging key people in their areas to take Maori concerns more seriously. A major next step – which took much careful negotiation in various directions – was creating a post of Maori co-ordinator to represent the communities' views. Making this a paid position ratified by institutional systems was a formal acknowledgement of Maori rights.

As discussion of Maori issues strengthened, the Maori people offered to provide institutional racism programmes for all staff, beginning with those in senior positions. Dorothy helped to introduce these.

> 'I needed to facilitate it, leave it to those who had experience to do it, and to the people who participated to make their own sense of it. If the time was right then energy would flow towards supporting Maori activity within the institution and tolerance of difference in decision-making practices.'

Some people felt threatened and withdrew their staff from the programmes, but a large proportion of staff attended. Their greater understanding opened more flexible ways of working, including a willingness to co-operate with Maori healers. Within a year a Maori community and out-patients centre had been established, providing support for families of patients, and opportunities for tribal healers to work with people admitted for treatment. Dorothy said that there was a 'manageable tension' in these arrangements.

> 'My role in it was to try and understand the various points of view and respond positively to requests, concerns and conflicts.'

These various developments had been challenging, but containable. There were signs of 'the beginnings of a real partnership' between the staff and Maori people. The organization 'arrived at a temporary sense of stability'.

DEVELOPING TENSIONS

But, Dorothy commented, often in change work you reach a plateau and are able to breathe for a while, and then the tensions build again.

In the background, since before her appointment, had been concerns about the hospital's medium secure unit. This was used to house prisoners who could not cope with prison life. It had a relatively high proportion of Maori admissions. Many people suspected that Maori men were often put into the unit as a means of social control, when they were neither dangerous nor violent but had other mental health care needs. Over the years there had been several inquiries into potential malpractice and accidental deaths. The most recent death had caused a great furore because it involved a Maori youth whose case seemed to have been mishandled in several ways. Conflicts and anxieties were building around what to do with the unit.

The hospital board eventually decided to close it. This precipitated a strike by staff on other wards who refused to take the unit's patients into their areas. These developments placed a major strain on Dorothy. Her response was to manage the consequences. She acted in a way which she knew would create conflict *and* opportunity, hoping to prompt the organization to engage with the challenges to its value system the Maori people posed. Whilst other people may have viewed what she did as a 'finite solution', she intended it as a next move in what could become a process of dilemma resolution.

She opened one of the hospital's new in-patients units to the Maoris, to be dedicated to their health. Many Maoris were not professionally trained, but took on the role of caring for their people. Dorothy and other committed staff stayed day and night for a while, to stabilize the situation and support the Maoris in developing a suitable infrastructure. It was particularly helpful that one of Dorothy's male allies was able to work with the Maori men, thus facilitating co-operation between them and the women.

But Dorothy began to realize that her systemic approach to change had limitations in this situation. Her attempts to empower the Maori community were only partially accepted by the dominant system.

'When you have a culture which is oppressed... the normal growth is to destroy that population. . . . So you need to force people to look at it in a different way.'

Developments were confronting people with their own beliefs and values, which was painful for all parties. Dorothy, as the change agent, had to stay open in order to understand the processes which were being lived out and respond appropriately to them. She felt under stress and at risk.

ORGANIZATIONAL CONFRONTATIONS

Dorothy became caught in the middle of conflict. Working with a combination of intellect, intuition and empathy was a major source of her skill and power as a change facilitator. But it also rendered her vulnerable when people become threatened and attacking. She tried to honour the diversity of voices, even when she did not agree with individual viewpoints. She wanted to preserve the complexity of the situation, and help people face its inherent dilemmas, rather than resolve it in any group's favour. But this strategy brought her into conflict with most groups involved, because they wanted her to take their side and felt betrayed when she did not.

White people at the hospital confronted her for supporting the Maoris. Nursing staff accused her of betraying them because she was not supporting their strike action or views. They complained that she was giving the Maoris preferential treatment. Maori women wanted her to help them establish their own health services. Her regional director wanted her to manage a proposed reorganization. She continually felt 'caught in the middle'.

'So one of the reasons I couldn't stay was because I'd got myself torn. I couldn't not support the Maori people. I also couldn't not support nursing, because I am a nurse and that's my particular concern. I couldn't not be a woman. And also, because I do understand a lot of the male world, I couldn't not support some of the men and what they were trying to do. I got absolutely torn between so many worlds that I felt I had to move for my own sake and others'. They had to find a new way of doing things.'

It was significant that by this time Dorothy had lost her strong male ally. The hospital board had encouraged him to retire, partly because his support for community involvement was seen by other senior doctors as reducing their power. The changes were beginning to have impacts and be felt as disruptive. His replacement was close to retirement and said that he did not want to be troubled by radical groups of women and Maoris. Dorothy had no other male allies in sufficiently senior positions.

'In every situation where I've managed to make headway and do something different there's been a [senior] man who has been able to see it my way.'

The person who by then most nearly filled the position of senior advocate was actually 'a powerful woman who acted like a man'. But Dorothy believed that this was detrimental, that women are not given the liberty of challenging norms in male-dominated cultures.

APPRECIATING MULTIPLE VOICES

Dorothy's alliance with the Maori community was also creating conflicts she could not contain. Her approach was to empathize, seeking to appreciate their voices, rather than impose her own cultural values. It was therefore difficult to maintain a sense of who she was. She became attuned to their conflicts between women and men, but did not want to take sides, further fragmenting her. She struggled to live with the complex interplay of agendas, but found this intellectually and emotionally difficult.

'When do you actually say "But this is me. I am who I am"? And when do you say "I'm trying not to be who I am so I can understand who you are"? It's terribly difficult. I just used to get massive headaches.'

One critical incident illustrates Dorothy's tensions. A major meeting about Maori health had been organized, involving health department representatives. The Maori men wanted to present a united front to the government, but the women did not feel their health concerns were being represented and did not agree with aligning behind the men. As Dorothy sat in the meeting she felt the conflict rather than identifying with any side. As a Maori orator praised the government, the women jangled their bracelets, signalling their irritation.

'You sit there knowing that something is going to happen any moment. And it started to get into conflict. I was at the point where I could just not take on any more of these double messages. I just blocked. And when I blocked I actually started seeing things, I saw images coming out of the panels that were carved in the meeting house. . . . I felt terribly, terribly sad.'

Her Maori friends made sense of the images Dorothy reported. For them it showed her deep empathy with their culture. But Dorothy decided she could not contain the contradictions for which she was acting as a collector.

'At that point I said to myself, I couldn't be involved because I wasn't in control of what was going on. I was in a different state. And if I did stay in control I was just torn.'

LIMITS TO CHANGE

From a systemic perspective it is as important to recognize when to yield or desist as it is to pursue change when appropriate.

Dorothy's multi-faceted strategy had facilitated some significant changes. But she eventually became caught in the dynamics of difference and resistance which erupted rather than being able to act as mediator and integrator, as she had in other settings.

Finally Dorothy decided that the chances for further change were limited. She then had choices to make. New possibilities can become co-opted, incorporated into the established culture but diluted in the process. This time she did not want to let this happen. Holding out against this and finding ways to support allies whose courage might begin to fade was 'very exhausting'. She had to decide how to protect the changes already happening, and herself. She was worried that if she forced issues too prominently the system would retreat and lose previous gains.

'If you go backwards and lose credibility, unless you hold on tenaciously, what gets left gets pulled into the existing order, and you haven't got the difference any more.'

But Dorothy could not hang on and stay central in the change: 'It would have destroyed me.' Neither did she think she was the right person to do it. She could not act authentically for too long on the Maoris' behalf: this would usurp their agenda, undermine their power and be patronising. The organizational system, with its different voices, had to 'decide' what was possible at that time.

'If I left and it failed, then maybe it needed to and something new could come out of it. If it stayed together they [the Maoris] could lead it in the direction they wanted.'

It is interesting and significant that it is the attempted change which might have failed, not Dorothy personally. Her ideas on how organizations work did not leave her feeling individually responsible for a situation she could not eventually transform.

Dorothy engaged in a scrutinizing assessment of her purposes and what was possible.

'I have to say "What's my bottom line? What can I and can't I do? Where do I stand on this? What am I compromising? Who am I hurting?" And I have to take the consequences of that. And that's often to be misunderstood, to be accused of things you've never intended and to let go of things you highly valued.'

She was largely without allies, there was 'nobody to hold hands with you because they didn't see it that way'. And she was continually under attack. She decided that she could no longer hold together the change process and be true to herself.

'Leaving was first of all about keeping my sanity. I just couldn't take the strain of holding it together.'

DECIDING TO LEAVE

Dorothy decided to leave because her role was impossible at that time and she needed to regain a sense of her own boundaries.

'I got caught in so many ways and it was just too much. I just wanted to be myself'.

'I've learnt. . . that to be yourself and to be a woman is quite lonely.'

She decided that she must not only leave that job, but also New Zealand: 'I had to get out. I couldn't stay.' Once she announced her intentions, she was approached to take on several other, equally demanding, jobs. She declined, thinking that if she stayed in the country, because it is relatively small and she was widely known, people would expect her to perform in a similar way. In order to regain her sense of self she had to change her context.

Dorothy gave four months' notice, but stayed for nine months to help the Maori unit become sufficiently established.

'Professionally I could not have left at that point. And my relationship with the Maori people was such that a sense of shared responsibility and spirituality bound us.'

She engaged in a thorough leaving process. She feels that people can only leave behind situations which they have paid attention to closing appropriately. She wrote reports on everything she had done. She said goodbyes publicly, affirming different people and different places, tailoring her parting to the different social groups. She was concerned about what would happen to her own immediate team of senior nurses. She wrote a poem – about the wind – which she cut into pieces to make a puzzle, then gave each person a piece, inviting them to meet once she had gone and complete the puzzle. She thus hoped to encourage them to unite and act together.

(After Dorothy left, the Maori people were officially ordered out of the unit by the hospital board. But the issue of what should happen to them was avoided. Years later they were still in place and running their own service.)

STARTING AFRESH

Dorothy and her husband decided to move to England. This satisfied several motives. She was now 50 and was content to find a low-key job while supporting her husband in expanding his career and her son in finishing his education. Her attitude then was: 'I really don't need to have any more career. I've had enough of it. I just need a job I feel happy about.' She also wanted to return to her country of birth.

'I wanted to be part of the indigenous population, and just wanted to have the right to put my needs first'.

She was offered several jobs on arrival in the UK and chose one in nursing education because it would give her a break and allow more energy for other life activities. After two years she was offered a more challenging post, inviting her back into the role of change agent. She accepted, partly because her husband and son were by then well settled. Her job again became her first interest in life. She was working with, and developing, her understanding of change. She had registered for postgraduate research, partly to help her do this more systematically. She had built strong relationships with powerful figures in her organization. She was beginning to see an opening of attitudes, and felt that she could play a prominent role in contributing to change, working along-side other people.

DOROTHY'S FEEDBACK ON THE DRAFT STORY

Dorothy said that she was comfortable with the draft, that it fitted with her own understanding. She provided some clarifying explanations about the Maori issues. She also responded to my request for illustrations of changes that had been achieved.

ADDENDUM

Dorothy is now a director of nursing and associated functions in a National Health Service Mental Health Trust. She is fully engaged in and enjoying this demanding role, building alliances for change as she has in the past. She is also watchful about assessing whether she should sometime move on, if the job becomes strategically 'undoable' or too constraining. Dorothy believes that her work for her research degree has increased her insight into the change situation described here, allowing her to tell a richer story and to do herself more justice than she might have done in the past.

Change agent roles

The prominence of organizational change themes in the stories as a collection was initially a surprise to me. In this section I shall first review participants' involvement in change. I shall then concentrate on the four situations featured above, in which change initiatives became especially difficult, and explore the factors that characterize them.

CHANGE ROLES

Dorothy and Patricia, as nursing directors, introduced changes with organization-wide repercussions. Kathy and Christina were personnel directors: the former had been central in creating the culture and practices of her company as it grew, the latter introduced successive phases of change into an established organization. *Pamela* took on organizational units of various sizes and reorganized them. Teresa, Judith, Julia, Jane and Sarah introduced functions into organizations which had previously paid limited attention to these areas, with potentially widespread impacts (especially in the cases of Teresa and Judith). Claire, *Stevie* and *Mercedes* were innovators within their functional areas, but did not dwell on these aspects of their work. *Margaret* implemented changes as her company responded to difficult economic conditions. *Kim* was the champion for particular activities in her organization. (*Ruth's* work is not specified here – see p. 257.)

Whether there was a readiness for change, where the research participants were placed in relation to power and the congruity of their styles and visions with the organizational contexts seem important influencing factors in this data. Some women encountered relatively favourable conditions; others found ways to manage and contain potential challenges. *Pamela* and Kathy were centrally placed organizationally, architects of initiatives. Both received positive feedback through company successes. *Pamela* particularly liked company turnarounds and succeeding in difficult economic times. Christina developed and sustained her own power-base through networking. Each phase of her change work was challenging in different ways, but ultimately successful. Sarah was appointed to create management systems in a relatively willing organization. She had to proceed with care, but achieved this in a relatively short timescale. *Julia* and Jane introduced selective change in their established areas of expertise. *Julia's*'s skills were not rebuffed, although she personally was. *Mercedes* and Claire had devised relatively non-confrontational change strategies, the former having some legitimation through equal opportunities responsibilities.

These people had mostly been successful in their change intentions. They did not discuss the processes of change in detail, as these had not been central in their leaving decisions.

FOCUSING ON FOUR DIFFICULT CASES

In the remainder of this section I shall concentrate on change roles which eventually proved difficult and were a major contributing factor to the stress of the four women concerned – Patricia, Dorothy, Judith and Teresa – and their leaving. I explore the factors that distinguish these stories or seem common amongst them.

Lack of organizational support

In three cases senior people seemed ambivalent about change, and this affected the women's positions. (This was partly true for Dorothy later in the change process.) Patricia and Teresa spearheaded change which was contentious and contested, and received limited support from their chief executives and colleagues. Similarly, Judith became a figurehead for equal opportunities issues, officially mandated by her role. As organization-wide endeavours these change initiatives seemed somewhat weak, placing the women in compromised and vulnerable power positions. Teresa and Patricia were, for example, supported in private, but not in public, despite their requests for more backing.

The failure of those with symbolic power to back change wholeheartedly undermines initiatives. (It is common in equal-opportunities-related work: Hammond, 1992.) This projects the organization's ambivalence publicly. Resulting tensions can become focused on the change agent and may be personalized (especially if they are symbolically appropriate – see p. 19). Teresa's and Patricia's chief executives appeared to be using ambiguity about the women's organizational status and power to probe the viability of change. When situations proved difficult they withdrew support. Subsequent rebuffs may undermine women's organizational inclusion and power – in their own or other people's eyes.

Commitment

You may wonder whether the managers were wise to accept the change roles. Patricia was clear about her motivations. She had a vision and enthusiasm and believed it was possible to introduce different ways of working. Pursuing these brought her into conflict with the established culture. Creating change requires a certain grandiosity, an unwillingness to believe that obstacles have power. It is difficult to know when moderating one's vision is unacceptable compromise. There are similar themes in the other stories: action is driven by values, commitment and loyalty. In these cases, culture transforming change seemed possible. Patricia and Teresa initially felt optimistic, partly because they had been successful in similar roles previously. The women concerned were so committed that they went ahead of the organization's energies and ways of operating. They wanted to believe the change intent mandated in their roles or espoused by senior people, some of which appears to have been lip-service. They varied in how much they assessed or heeded other sources of organizational support or resistance. Their high levels of attachment made them potentially more effective, but also potentially more vulnerable and less likely to allow themselves to stop.

These four (and other research participants such as *Kathy* and *Mercedes*) believed that other people would not pursue change as they were doing, that their vision or value system was distinctive and potentially indispensable. This deterred them from contemplating leaving.

Becoming over-extended

These four research participants seemed to become over-extended as they tried to seed and nourish new visions of organizational possibility. The changes involved organization-wide interventions, which they managed largely alone. Dorothy had deliberately worked to create allies, believing that change needs advocates within established power systems. Her situation became difficult to manage once her fellow initiator left. Dorothy and Judith were particularly open and accessible to people, especially those marginalized by organizational power structures. Despite these extensive network systems (this description does not apply to Teresa), increasing isolation was another theme in all four stories. Patricia's allies withdrew as powerful people's resistance to change seemed to be having effects. Judith felt particularly wounded by criticism from the disadvantaged groups on whose behalf she had been operating. Her demanding situation was exacerbated because she had little time, space or support (except in her marriage) to reconcile the pressures she was under. All four became partly inured to certain forms of challenge and resistance. Whether they could have done more to build alliances is difficult to tell. Patricia and Teresa certainly felt that such relationships were largely closed to them (see 'Organizational cultures', p.104)

In these conflicted and demanding situations, it became difficult to know what messages to heed. Patricia ignored her own doubts. Judith received positive feedback which encouraged her to continue. Dorothy was pulled in different directions by the groups involved. None of the four gave their own safety high priority. Each was willing, to some extent, to set unsettling processes in motion and live with the consequences. All also actively developed their change and coping strategies. Judith became astute at boundary management; Teresa learnt how to retaliate in kind when faced with aggressive behaviour.

Being disruptive

Change of the sort these women were pursuing is bound to be disruptive. It challenges fundamental aspects of organizations' cultures. If it begins to have effects the culture will be disturbed, prompting optimism for some, fear of change and resistance from others. Established patterns of power will be threatened, realignments may occur. These change agents were trying to achieve second-order cultural change. But most were operating from somewhat marginalized positions themselves, despite their apparent seniority. From her extensive experience, Dorothy believes that women are not allowed power to challenge the culture, unless – as in her case – senior people fail to recognize the likely effects of proposals. Given these situations, the failure of key symbolic managers to signal their support for change had profound effects.

It seemed as if the four managers came to symbolize the changes they were advocating. Perhaps this identification was more powerful because they were women rather than having majority group characteristics. Their change initiatives were gender or minority interest related in a broad sense, for example empowering previously subordinate groups such as nurses or developing more participative ways of working. They were therefore representing repressed or shadow issues in the culture. All four seemed to have become focusing points for latent conflicts, and to have evoked resistance which became directed at them personally.

Raising questions

The power and care dynamics of change initiatives which are on behalf of marginalized groups or suppressed issues are inherently problematic. These cases raise many dilemmas. For example: how much collaboration can change initiators expect from other women or disadvantaged groups with less organizational power than themselves? Should or can the manager defend their supporters? Does the change initiator need other people's consent or permission to make them vulnerable? How much support from each other can women expect if they are differently placed in organizational hierarchies and life situations? Can these issues be negotiated explicitly? How can the change agent know whether the disturbance they are helping to create is appropriate, in the service of future transformation, or beyond their and the organization's abilities to contain?

These change roles are, then, precarious to undertake. Much energy is required to maintain personal and organizational viability. Being a destabilizing force tends to be uncomfortable and lonely. Having someone willing to take this stance could be beneficial, prompting necessary organizational experimentation (Torbert, 1991). But the conditions in these four cases proved unfavourable. Dorothy, Teresa and Judith eventually decided to desist. They were achieving some change, but the personal costs were too high. The tide of possible change had turned against Patricia: she was dismissed.

Relating to other women

It was striking how little data relatively there was about research participants' relationships with other women. This was mainly because there had been so few around at their organizational levels. Some people wished that more female role models had been available.

Male-dominated cultures provided the backcloth against which most women related, and this made certain kinds of interaction more likely. In such environments women may be covertly or explicitly discouraged from meeting, identifying themselves as women or aligning with each other, lest they appear to threaten cultural stability. Women find their own individual ways of coping with cultural pressures and creating acceptable identities. For example, some stress their professional roles, some become 'one of the boys', some emphasize caring and some use their sexuality overtly. Their resulting styles may set them apart from women who have made different choices. Several research participants commented that – contrary to popular belief – other women were not necessarily instant allies or people with whom they had an affinity. Some had felt uncomfortable and undermined by being in the same team as women who were 'over-adaptive' or used a sexualized self-presentation. Two believed that they might initially have been wary about having other women at their level.

Some research participants' relationships with other women had at times been strained. Hostility and ambivalence about women with power was occasionally reported from female employees lower down the organization, against which the managers had learnt to defend themselves. Sometimes it seemed that other women had judged them against prevailing cultural norms and found them confusing. For example, few women applied to be Teresa's secretary when the post was advertised internally because there was more *perceived* status in working for men on more junior organizational grades. Several research participants had felt wounded and betrayed because women they saw as allies had withdrawn support when difficulties arose.

Some people did have very supportive relationships with other women, mostly outside their organizations. This base of friends was a highly significant reference group for discussing career aspirations and work challenges.

Some people later worked in companies which had several women at senior levels and felt this was associated with generally more open cultures. As the research drew to a close I was being told both about the delights of having strong female colleagues and about the tensions that could arise if distrust and rivalry developed in these relationships.

Isolation

As their relationships with both men and women were limited, many research participants seemed to be operating in evacuated relational spaces. This made them feel isolated, and increased their sense of pressure. It reduced their feedback and other information. Acting effectively, and judging their own performance, became more difficult.

This theme can be interpreted as women placing importance on relationships at work. They certainly do to some extent, but not mainly to make them friendly and supportive. Their attention is more often directed towards making potentially difficult relationships work and towards safeguarding their power and effectiveness.

The stories do not suggest that the women's sense of isolation is greater because their expectations of relationships are idealized. Their potential relationships were blocked in too many ways to make this a viable interpretation (see 'Organizational cultures', p.104). At the same time male colleagues seemed to have their own forms of comradeship (although some men would protest that these are superficial, antagonistic and so on).

Some people's sense of isolation was exacerbated because their high commitment to work and their tiredness meant they had too little time or energy to use or enjoy sources of support that were available in their lives from friends and family.

It does also seem that feelings of isolation and alienation are currently affecting many managers, despite increasing organizational rhetoric about participation, teamwork and partnership. This could be a sign of changing times, influenced, for example, by a continuing emphasis on individualism which strengthened during the 1980s, and the interpersonal competition fostered in organizations which are 'downsizing' and 'de-layering'. Lee (1994), for example, graphically portrays the 'isolation inherent in the role of the manager as change agent' (p. 123) felt by eighty training course participants she consulted, and links this to current changes in formulations of management and organizations. It could well be argued that the climate is colder for everyone.

At the workshops research participants discussed how they run their lives knowing that isolation is a probability. For example, they reported networking a lot and making sure they included in their schedules some meetings or seminars which would interest or support them; as one put it, 'times when I am not on show and can explore freely'.

Blocked promotion prospects

The stories of: Mercedes and Stevie

These two stories come from very different employment sectors, but both contain the theme of blocked career prospects in male-dominated organizational cultures. These are classic tales in their way, with which many women would identify. Their experiences presented Stevie and Mercedes with major challenges about what styles to adopt. Stevie decided to leave her organization as a result. Mercedes was determinedly staying in hers, but hoped soon to find a senior appointment elsewhere.

Mercedes

OVERVIEW

Mercedes was a deputy director in local government. When we met she had just decided to stay in employment for the time being, and pursue her ambition to become a director. Her hopes of being promoted within her authority had recently been thwarted. The disappointment of this rejection was compounded by having to adjust to working with her new director, whose values and style seemed significantly at odds with hers. Mercedes was reflectively accommodating to this situation, reviewing her aspirations, work competences and needs.

In the past Mercedes had left jobs in similar circumstances. For the time being three factors were encouraging her to stay: her sense of interest and achievement in the work she was doing, her determination to be promoted sooner or later, and her satisfaction with her salary. She was applying for a director post in another authority and wondered how to present herself, what chances she stood of a fair assessment and how stressful the job might prove.

BACKGROUND

On leaving school Mercedes studied art. Her main motivation at this time, which had been formulated with determination at 16, was to leave home to escape the controlling influence of her mother. By her early twenties she had settled in London. She did a series of jobs, strongly influenced by her socialist values, and was sometimes unemployed. The most settled post she had was with an estate agent. Here she was aware for the first time of being affected by gender inequalities: whilst the female staff were bright and highly competent, it was the male employee who was starred for promotion to partner.

In her early thirties Mercedes decided to look for work that would be more intellectually challenging. She moved into local government to train in a professional field, mainly because friends she knew there were earning 'very good salaries'. She wanted more financial security, having just taken on her first mortgage. She set herself the goal of becoming a director by the time she was 40.

After four years in her first authority, Mercedes applied for promotion. Three posts were available; all of them went to men. Mercedes was rated fourth and led to believe that she would be awarded the next vacancy. But the next post was advertised internally in case more people wanted to apply. Mercedes was not interviewed again, and a male colleague was successful. It was a very male-dominated organization and seemed unlikely to change. Mercedes realized that 'there was no future there' and decided to leave.

> 'As soon as I didn't get that internal promotion I vowed to leave, because that's really been my pattern. If I didn't get what I wanted I left.'

Mercedes moved authority three times over the next eight years, to gain career progression when it seemed blocked in her previous organization. In her second authority she was promoted internally twice, but was unsuccessful in applying for an assistant director post. She vowed to move on when the director 'brought in an incompetent, for whom I had no respect whatsoever and he was useless at his job'.

In her third authority, her job suddenly went from being enjoyable to 'undoable', again because someone Mercedes judged incapable was appointed as her manager. He created unnecessary paperwork over minor details, causing overload and resentment. She decided to leave whatever the consequences because of the stress she was experiencing. Her partner volunteered to support her financially to make this possible. Only later did Mercedes discover that she was not physically well at this time (she subsequently needed a hysterectomy). She had became excessively tired and was unable to keep pace with the culture of late night meetings and drinking. She had not minded this working pattern at the time, but described it, when we met, as 'not a woman's

culture, in a sense'. As other participants in the research have
done, she initially interpreted physical illness as work-related
stress, for which she took on responsibility. The decision to
leave, whatever the consequences, was the resulting coping
strategy.

Mercedes had slowed down her own career development twice.
On one occasion there had been a tragic death in her department,
so she stayed to provide stability at a time when she would
otherwise have been looking for a move. Once, she was advised
to apply for a significant promotion, but declined because her
mother had recently died and she did not think that she could
handle the job. She saw this as 'a typical way a woman behaves'.

> 'Women wait until they can do the job and then they apply,
> whereas blokes apply all the time, whether they can or can't do
> the job, have a good interview and they get the job. And women
> prop them up.'

ASSESSING HER CHANCES

As she told her story, Mercedes judged the authorities she applied
to and the appointment processes she faced by several key criteria.
She was interested in whether the organization was male dominated or had shown some willingness to promote women. She also
assessed how tough the working situation would be from the
political composition of the council and the nature of the local
community's needs. She judged the appointment panels by their
proportion of women members (identifying some women as
biased against other women), commitment to equal opportunities
principles and their possible propensity to recruit people who
fitted traditional (white, male) stereotypes of management. She
also rigorously assessed her skills and credentials against those of
other candidates. Sometimes she was competing with people who
already held the rank applied for in another authority; this made
the competition stiffer.

I was impressed with the information to which Mercedes had
access, based on her own extensive experience and her many
contacts. I also noted how essential it seemed for her to do these
calculations, because of the highly political nature (in power,
influence and gender, rather than party, terms) of the organizations she worked in.

Sometimes she judged that she had had 'a fair chance', and was satisfied with this. In other cases she was disappointed and angered by the selection made, especially when a white man whose skills she could not respect was appointed. She thinks that appointments are often in the image of the recruiters – 'people. . . they feel comfortable with, can have a drink with' – and so an established elite is maintained. In one case especially she could show how good practice had been neglected to achieve this, with detrimental long-term consequences. Recently, the dynamics of recruitment had become even more confused. Many men in local government now knew the politically correct language of equal opportunities, but most used it, Mercedes believed, without awareness or commitment.

Mercedes described her jobs and promotion attempts – successful and failed – in detail, often with intense feeling. She carried an accumulated sense of frustration that promotion practices favour white men over women and black people. This general social injustice has affected her personally. Several times, jobs she was enjoying had become extremely stressful from a combination of changed work demands and having to find ways to work with, but not overtly challenge, a new male boss she thought incompetent.

Mercedes therefore presented starkly conflicting images. She seemed highly competent and confident, and could point to an extensive record of achievement and positive feedback from others. And yet she had often experienced significantly stressful situations and had to develop new coping strategies. Much of the stress had come from or been accentuated by being a woman in a male-dominated world. This had been 'immense strife on the whole. I've been challenged all along the line by groups. . . or individual male staff.' She thought she partly attracted reaction as a strong and visible woman: 'If you're weak, I suppose other things happen.' From subordinates, at least, the sense of challenge had decreased with increasing seniority and credibility in the organization. In the post she was holding when we met, Mercedes felt free to be herself, not emphasizing her status as a boss, because that was secure.

Despite her forthright comments about male-dominated cultures, Mercedes would not identify herself as feminist, although she *is* publicly committed to empowering women.

'I've never said I am a feminist or identified with it particularly. I think it's too confrontational. Sometimes you have to have confrontation to win a debate, but that particular one puts 48 per cent of the population's hackles up, and I think there are other ways of winning.'

Mercedes favoured strategies which might lead to attitude change, preferring to pick her moments for speaking on gender-related issues.

BLOCKED PROMOTION PROSPECTS – AGAIN

Mercedes was recommended to me as a candidate for the research because she had again been considering leaving and was feeling highly cynical about employment. Although she had accrued considerable credibility and goodwill in her authority, her promotion prospects were blocked again. By the time we met she had moved through her initial anger at this situation and was attempting to stay in employment and, for the moment, in her current post. But she described it as a very stressful time, preceded by nine stressful months. We discussed her mix of motivations as she reacted to this situation, her strategies for coping and her prospects. Her reflections provide valuable insights into the dynamics of staying despite adverse conditions, and reveal the frustrations of one woman whose prospects seem restricted more by prevailing organizational norms than by her own potential.

Mercedes had joined her authority as an assistant director in the mid-1980s. It was a well starred move: she respected the director and he supported her appointment; she felt that the appointment panel was well-balanced and fair; she was keen to help bring in equal opportunities, to which the organization was newly committed; and she judged herself the best candidate. Her enthusiasm was marred, however, when she discovered only one month later that she needed a hysterectomy, news she described as 'life shattering' and 'devastating'. But her new boss was highly supportive, the time she needed off work was not resented, and she returned 'a new woman'.

For the next four years, Mercedes (who was soon promoted to deputy director), thoroughly enjoyed her work. Her director left much of the running of the department to her. She learnt a lot, took pride in her developing competence, and was able to effect changes in the culture. One result of her activities was the significant numbers of women and black people in senior posts, and their participation in training. She had encouraged more open access, and good candidates had been forthcoming.

'I think there has to be that openness and commitment, and the word has to be out that if you apply for jobs in certain boroughs you stand an even chance.'

Mercedes was also proud of the confidence that customers had in her. She cared about their interests and felt that this was understood and her work therefore respected.

But a year before we met, Mercedes' life had been subjected to major change. Her director, whose interest in his post had significantly waned, had been forced to leave. Mercedes had been carrying the department, but had not let this be known, partly motivated by loyalty to someone who had given her opportunities and with whom she still worked well, and partly by the growth further responsibility offered. But her director's departure was a stressful experience for her. She was asked to be acting director until the post could be filled. Realizing that people would see her as strongly identified with the outgoing incumbent, Mercedes says: 'I kind of knew all along I wasn't going to get the job.'

But she could not refuse to act up for the intervening eight months: it was one of her formal responsibilities to do so, she wanted to continue the learning she had been doing, and she had agendas for change in the department – 'I wanted to continue at that level for as long as possible'. The experience was highly stressful, particularly once interviews had been conducted and she knew that she had not been appointed. Also she did not judge the selection fair. A powerful panel member favoured another candidate, and Mercedes had been forthright in challenging another member with sexism only months before. She thought that only one person 'would take an even view'.

Mercedes was furious when the director designate started coming into the department, weeks before his official starting date, talking to senior staff. She felt he was undermining her. She persuaded the chief executive to warn him against such behaviour, but staff began to align either with the new director or with her.

Mercedes tried to secure a secondment to avoid working with her new boss, but was unsuccessful. She found his first weeks in post very difficult – 'I had to drag myself in'. Initially he made few demands on her, but he consulted with her staff, making her feel bypassed, and excluded her from important meetings with clients.

ACCOMMODATING AND REAPPRAISING

In the two months between the new director's formal arrival and my meeting with her, Mercedes had taken various steps to consolidate her position and learn to live with the new circumstances. She saw her manager's behaviour towards her as partly unskilled – she judged him poor at communicating – and had therefore made statements about what she expected from him, to which he had responded similarly. He seemed open to working as a team with her. He had involved her in a departmental reorganization, taken her advice and given her the biggest job in the structure. At the same time, there was a sense of continuing friction, with the director at times trying to 'rubbish' her achievements and 'trying to prove his superiority'. Her relationship with her new boss was a preoccupation during our conversation, an issue to which Mercedes often returned.

Mercedes was assessing whether she could stay in this situation. She had applied for a director post in another authority, but saw it as 'one of the most stressful jobs going', because of the particular (party) political context. She thought the appointment process would be 'as even as anything could be really', although doubting the openness of some of the panel members. She had used her networks to make herself known and meet some potentially influential people.

However her relationship with the new director developed, she was ambivalent about staying in this post. She was not fully stretched by it.

'At this moment I feel I have a job I can do standing on my head, being paid a very fat salary for it.'

She would, however, be taking on new responsibilities for customer services through the restructuring. These gave her the opportunity to implement changes she had previously nurtured. She had already enjoyed exercising dormant skills in dealing with different staff groups. These changes gave her work new dimensions and interest.

Another factor which was making Mercedes stay was the attachment she had developed to having a high salary. Her income had increased significantly over the last year, due to changes in contracting arrangements, and she had 'started to live up to it'. This made her feel uneasy because she espouses socialist principles, and because she does not like to think that she can be bought. On the other hand, she was enjoying her designer clothes, sports car and home comforts. She felt she had worked for them and so deserved to maintain them.

Mercedes also wondered whether the changes she had encouraged the organization to make towards more diversity of senior staff were about to be reversed. Restructuring, to cut costs, would result in fewer management jobs but at more senior levels. She thought that revised jobs previously filled by women would go to men. This seemed more likely to happen if she left, partly because the new director seemed more comfortable working with men than with women and would be able to exert more influence: 'He's feet on the table, swearing, bad language, all that. It's much more comfortable for him to have men around.' Mercedes saw similar changes happening in many local authorities, with the result that some women had disappeared from senior positions.

So Mercedes was faced with various dilemmas, with many factors beyond her control. Her views had significantly developed since our initial telephone conversation. She was involved in a major process of review.

'It's good that you saw me now rather than any earlier. I would have been fairly incoherent and angry.'

There was still, however, a sense of pent-up frustration she needed to discharge and explore through talking. Part of her appraisal was to accept rather than inflate the tensions in her position. She said of the director: 'He has mended his ways a bit.' She was warmed by the confidence shown in her by customers. She believed that most staff and politicians knew where she was coming from and respected her. From these various directions she had received overt affirmations of support recently.

But she believed her situation was unstable. This was accentuated by differences in values between herself and her director. He was excited by finance and money, and less motivated by customer satisfaction, clients' needs and equal opportunities, all of which are vitally important to her. She imagined that these differences would be played out in the department and could cause her problems.

'I tell you where things can start to go wrong. Where I won't
bite my tongue.'

One difficult instance had already arisen. Mercedes had found
herself challenging a committee chair in public as she spoke
against one of her director's proposals, about which she had not
had prior warning. She had been in danger of making a significant
enemy.

Mercedes could not hold on to her initial anger at her new boss's
appointment: 'There's no point. . . it's soul destroying'. She was
seeking to live up to her pattern of leaving if she is dissatisfied.

'There are two things you can do if you're going to whinge. One,
you can come to terms with what you're whingeing about and
make the best of it and keep quiet. Or you can leave. And I go
by the latter code really.'

EXPLORING POSSIBLE OPTIONS

But this time Mercedes was not taking exit as her immediate
strategy, partly inhibited by the limited number of senior jobs
available. She did, however, vow to leave somehow if her situation
became totally unbearable. One possibility was to retire at 50.

A major reason why Mercedes was not inflaming her potential
dissatisfactions was the pressure it would put on her home
relationship. Her partner had supported her well during the time
that she was acting director. But Mercedes did not think it
reasonable to continue taking her stress home, particularly as her
partner was facing her own work and life pressures.

Mercedes was assessing just how ambitious she was, how much
stress she was willing to tolerate to gain promotion and what her
prospects were. She was beginning to feel that she had age as well
as being a woman against her. Directors in her area are often
appointed aged 35 to 40; she was then in her late forties.

Mercedes debated her chances of being selected for the director's post she had applied for. She had dilemmas about how to
present herself to best effect. She was not sure that she came across
well at interview. Some feedback had suggested that male panel
members were ambivalent about her.

'The men say "We think she might tick us off", but that's their
vision of how an older woman is. Or they say. . . . "She'd be a

good number two. She looks as though she might need support." That's to do with my being smallish, I suppose.'

Trying to judge herself, Mercedes reflected on her style, its
strengths and conflicts. In the past she had been relatively willing
to adapt to male values and the resulting assertive culture. Now,
and encouraged by her current partner, she avoided this way of
fitting in. She thought she handled organizational politics well, by
using her interpersonal skills, having wide-ranging information
networks and not becoming aligned with any of the politicians'
camps. She described ways many men operate which do not feel
authentic for her, but which she might need to explore:

> 'I don't believe in banging tables and shouting and telling
> people to do things, but that is a mode of operating that men
> have. . . . I think they play games, but I wonder if they need
> to. . . . But one thing I've noticed of late is that they never stop
> talking. . . . So that seems to be a new style, which I wondered
> if I should adopt. I don't usually say a lot.'

Rather than position herself against others' norms, Mercedes
wants to assert her individual identity. She does this partly
through dress, now wearing bright colours and designer clothes.
(But what to wear for interview – particularly how sober or
flamboyant to be – was still a matter for consideration.) As she
weighed different options she was torn. She wondered whether
to 'play the game', to moderate herself, for this next interview. But
she really wants to be wanted for who she is. She would prefer
this recognition of her to include acceptance of her sexuality. She
was not open about this, although some people in the organization
might know that she is a lesbian. Not being able to be open added
further pressures to her life.

> 'I hate it. . . . At the moment it feels like a threat. It's something
> where I could be exposed.'

A recent episode had made her more aware of this possibility.
It also meant that she had, in some ways, to betray her partner for
her own self-protection. She felt compromised by this.

OTHER WOMEN

Mercedes referred often to a network of women who share
information and are a source of support and comparison for her –

'If you haven't got a good women's network it's absolutely hopeless.' They are mostly as ambitious as she is, and advise and counsel each other about achieving senior appointments. They are also understanding listeners when someone wants to discuss the pressures these roles often place on women, or wants to debate why they take them on. There was a sense of friendly rivalry here and sometimes slight jealousy at seeing someone else succeed while her own prospects were blocked.

In the past, there have sometimes been several senior women of sufficiently similar mind within Mercedes' organization to lunch with and exchange views. This heyday had passed for a while, and she was feeling more isolated. (She was also noticing that individual men who had previously been supportive of women were less so, now that the gender balance had changed: 'there are more men on the team now, and less women to call them to task'.) But Mercedes does not feel that people are truly friends unless they know that she is a lesbian, and she is uncertain about making this widely known. Outside the organization she is more open about her identity.

DETERMINATION

Mercedes was righting herself after an unsettling time. She wanted to pursue her ambitions. She considered other possibilities, but did not talk them through with any energy. She wanted to go out as a director. She was wondering whether to compromise in order to achieve this move, or whether she could be accepted as she is. Ideally, she wanted recruiters to come to her; she wanted to be invited, as men are. Three statements seemed to summarize her position:

'There are other things in life, but I am very involved with my job.'

'I'm still an optimist.'

'I feel it must be my turn soon.'

MERCEDES' FEEDBACK ON THE DRAFT STORY

Mercedes made several minor amendments to the draft story, to clarify details and change a few colloquial phrases in quotations.

Reading the story prompted a self-review, partly because she had recently been criticized at work for lack of consultation. She wrote: 'It was a shock to read how accurately you had interpreted me.' Because of this combination of feedback, she was reflecting on her 'driving ambitions', the speed with which she was trying to introduce change, and 'how to become a more relaxed person'.

ADDENDUM

Mercedes applied for two further jobs in other organizations and was eventually successful in being appointed a director. She *was* encouraged to apply (as she had hoped). The new organization's culture was very different from her previous authority, so the move has been a challenge. Directors are allowed a great deal of discretion, giving her plenty of scope. Her new management team, in which there are other women, are open to change and supportive. She is exploring how to build sound working relationships with her colleagues, and how to be effective organizationally. She is really enjoying herself.

Stevie

OVERVIEW

Stevie was in her mid-thirties when we met, one of the youngest people I interviewed. She had worked in the chemical industry and was very much a pioneer for women in her company. She had been successful up to a point, adopting the strategy she called being a 'female man'. But her career prospects had become limited, and she had become disillusioned with her competitive lifestyle and its effects on her. Her growing sense of alienation had crystallized suddenly in her decision to leave.

Stevie had travelled for a year, regaining her sense of self. When we met she was setting up a business with a partner: both were keen to prove that they could succeed and not be constrained by dominant, hierarchic organizational systems and their ways of operating.

BACKGROUND AND EARLY CAREER

Stevie's family were working class, and she was the first member to go to university. She studied sciences and her first job was as a graduate trainee in a technology-based organization. This company gave Stevie plenty of scientific interest and challenge. She had various jobs, and within a few years had been appointed a section head within the development laboratories. It was 'a wonderful position at quite an early age', and involved supervisory responsibilities. Stevie attributed her success in this company to working hard, being keen and being a good communicator (not always characteristic of scientists).

But after a few years two factors prompted her to move. Stevie believed she could not progress much further as a scientist without gaining a PhD, and she was dealing with new products and developing a taste for marketing. Her boyfriend had moved to London. She had initially decided not to join him because she had recently been promoted and was 'career-minded', but two years later she needed to move on and found a job with an international chemical company in the south-east. They married soon afterwards.

Stevie remained with the chemical company for nine demanding years. Development was a little slow initially, but she enjoyed the excitement of joining a big company, seeing the range of activities involved. She was given responsibility, was able to make things happen, and soon achieved senior management exposure. She said, 'I was running on adrenalin half the time'.

CAREER EROSION

It took a little while for Stevie to gain a job in sales, the area she had identified as her interest. She was one of the first women to do so and had few female role models in Europe or the United States. She believed that being a pioneer had its costs, and that women now may have a somewhat easier time. Whilst there was little overt discrimination, she came to believe that covert processes were operating.

'For a long time I was of the opinion that... if you were good you'd make it. I hung on to this for about five years until the overwhelming evidence was that it's not enough to be good or better. There's accumulated stuff that's unconscious discrimination.'

Stevie described the 'general erosion' which she later realized had been happening. She was not progressing as quickly as she thought she should, or as quickly as men recruited at the same time as her. She had to push hard for promotions. Whilst she then described the excitements and satisfactions of each role, she also thought that reaching them was overdue; she was not particularly stretched.

Stevie enjoyed her first sales job. It came with the trappings of 'a nice company car and rushing around', and she was negotiating large agreements quarterly with significant UK customers. But after two years when she looked for her next move, none had been planned or was forthcoming. She went outside to secure an alternative offer and force the issue. This time she was successful, but she could not use this strategy again.

A later post was as a new business development manager. Stevie enjoyed the creativity in this role, its European connections and the sense of team. But in other ways it was disappointing.

'My attitude at the time was "Big Deal! It should have happened years ago." I was going into jobs I should have had a couple of years previously because of the erosion effect, and I wasn't being challenged by it either. It was a piece of cake.'

Also, around her, she could see the company cutting back, losing jobs, and so reducing her opportunities. By then Stevie had consciously decided to become a 'female man', which she saw other senior women in technical areas doing – 'They were rough and tough and "I'm as good as you mate"'. She knew the political games to play.

'I knew how to piss in the corners. . . . I hate this jargon, but it's endemic. It's a good phrase because it's about territoriality and that's what working with men is about in big organizations. "This is my patch. This is mine." And people establish boundaries all the time. You constantly piss in the corners to make it clear what is your patch and what isn't, and if you're aggressive and challenging then you challenge other people and piss in their corners sometimes.'

Another factor, which Stevie believed contributed to her sense of erosion and applies much more to women than to men, was having to prove herself anew in each job.

'When you get into a job you have to prove yourself all over again. . . and the fact that you're a woman means that they're looking at you a lot more carefully. When you're continually doing this your reputation doesn't carry with you through the steps.'

Stevie believed she could not have taken her suspicions of disadvantage too seriously while still in the organization.

'It's very risky. . . . If you're going to be successful you have to have a perception or view that is safe, and being overtly feminist is very risky in a big organization. You're attacking everything that men stand for. . . . I was approaching 30 before I thought it wasn't really fair, that they were issues about women.'

Instead, she was self-reliant, believing that her abilities were all that mattered.

MAKING A POWERFUL ENEMY

While in new business development Stevie crossed a senior manager in ways which both reflected and reinforced her marginality as a woman. In 'one of the many reorganizations' her group was amalgamated with another. It was unclear whether she or a team member from a different group should be assigned overall responsibility for the new unit. The indecision dragged on, involving more top people than necessary, but not being resolved. Stevie believed that a particular senior manager did not approve of asking her (male) peer – who was older and slightly more senior in management grades – to report to her (although such arrangements were common organizational practice). The two of them therefore came to their own amicable agreement to work together.

Eventually Stevie's colleague received a memo asking for annual appraisals to be done and for him to do Stevie's appraisal, effectively establishing his managerial superiority. He showed Stevie the message, expressing his discomfort. Stevie was angered, not so much by the decision, but by the process through which it had been reached. She sent a reply stating her views very baldly, knowing that she was breaking cultural rules.

'That's the first time I've ever done anything like that. I thought about it really carefully and thought it was a really dangerous thing to do, but I did it.'

The senior manager who had finally made the decision came to see her the following week.

'He admitted that it had been a difficult decision but basically said "Like it or lump it" and I said I'd lump it.'

They discussed Stevie's frustrations about her career progression, but the manager was unsympathetic. He suggested she look elsewhere, and she said she would.

'So there was a clear understanding that I wasn't just going to fit in and be nice and say "yes, sir". And that really was a turning point in some ways.'

Unfortunately for Stevie this incident happened just before a major round of future management 'potential' ratings in the company's formal system. She believed it was ultimately her manager's negative opinions which reduced her designated rating from 'high potential/executive positions' to one of reaching only senior management.

> 'I was a HiPo (High Potential) and then fell off the HiPo track, mainly because I crossed one particularly dominant and aggressive manager. I did the unspeakable, I challenged a senior manager.'

By this stage too, she believed that her track record in the company could not outweigh the dominant cultural image of success.

> 'People have an image of what a successful [company] manager is, how they behave, how they look and are, how they communicate and manage. And that is a [company] clone. Typically it's a man who has a wife who doesn't work, so he's geographically flexible, he probably has kids, if he hasn't he is a good sportsman and has a wonderful social life. He's one of the boys, he doesn't do anything excessively, he doesn't challenge or make waves. Pretty smart. A good guy. So when women come along they don't fit into any of those things.'

Perceived geographic mobility is especially important.

RESPONDING TO CHALLENGE

Stevie also encountered more overt discrimination at this time. One of the regular international sales meetings was held in Scandinavia. The senior manager who she had crossed announced that they would all have a team sauna together. At a large drinks reception he asked her publicly: 'You are coming, aren't you?' She took this as a challenge, 'an out and out gauntlet'. There were two other women at the meeting, but they were not in her team and therefore not 'invited' to attend. One tried to help Stevie by offering to talk things through with her, but the latter declined – 'I wanted to get on on my own'.

Stevie was not going to let the senior manager win. She said she did not feel concerned about taking off her clothes because of all the sports she has done, but did think it was an 'awkward' situation. The French men at the meeting stayed away because they did not approve of the position she had been forced into. The Italian men arrived with their swimming trunks on, but were teased about this and took them off. With some nervousness Stevie went to the sauna. A colleague her age helped by welcoming her and talking through the initially difficult moments.

> '[The senior manager] arrived last and said "So you made it then." So I said "Yes. You'd better come and sit next to me. Nobody else will." And it was fine and everyone relaxed and it was quite jolly.... The most embarrassing thing was getting dressed again. It was like reaffirming that you didn't have any clothes on. .... I felt I'd won that battle all round because he'd put weight on and the other guys ribbed him about his beer belly. But it was in the background as another challenge and I faced him on that.'

The other women were appalled that she had gone.

At a later sales meeting people were planning to go skiing. Stevie asked the senior manager whether he had topless skiing planned for her this time. 'He just shrivelled and said. . . . "That was a really stupid thing to do. I shouldn't have done that." ' Stevie believed that she had become too dangerous, she could threaten the manager with his treatment of her – 'So I won, but I lost.'

DECIDING TO LEAVE

Stevie's final decision to leave had several professional and personal strands. She was feeling a sense of 'mounting frustration with being good and in many cases better consistently, working hard and being seen by subordinates and many people in the organization as a good egg, and yet not having that expressed in terms of career progression'. She knew, for example, that fast-track employees needed at least one international posting to consolidate their careers. She had been considered twice for such postings, but they had not happened. She suspected, but could not be sure, that this was because she was a woman and married. The company has rarely managed dual transfers (her husband was in another division), and there were no systems in place to make it easier.

She began to wish she could leave, and explored ideas of what she might do next, perhaps twinning her business sense with older, scientific, interests.

'So I had this in the back of my mind and it began to fall into place.'

Her personal life was unsatisfying. Her early delight in being part of a dual earning couple with a busy social and sporting life had not been sustained. Both she and her husband were now very busy with their jobs and business travel.

'We had a nice house and garden in a small village, and life was work, work, work and garden, garden. There was no social life, it gradually disappeared altogether.'

They were drifting apart and did not work at their relationship.

'I was tired and stressed and just wanted to have some space and have a good time. I'd been working really hard since I'd left university. . . . I wanted some fun and some freedom and not to do anything anyone else expected of me.'

This tiredness resulted partly from working hard and consistently striving to be better than male colleagues.

Stevie had lost a centred sense of self. She thought this is something women are particularly likely to do.

'[Women] want to please people all the time and meet their expectations. So you develop your personality and the way you behave meets other people's expectations. I had a conflicting set of expectations. [At work] I was expected to behave like a man, [and I had] a husband who expected me to behave like a woman and wife, which I was never very good at anyway. I had a family who expected me to behave as a married women should. All sorts of. . . conflicts.'

Then, a particular incident brought Stevie's various senses of dissatisfaction together. Although she already had plenty of external reasons for leaving, an internal consolidation was needed before she would act.

She had taken up golf to compensate for the lack of other sports in her life.

'I'm very competitive as an individual and I think that's why I've survived. I want to be the best. . . golf. . . it's addictive for people with a personality like mine.'

Stevie entered her club's ladies' championship and reached the finals. They were scheduled for a weekday afternoon. She drove through heavy traffic to reach them, busy on her carphone trying to finish off things she had left at the office. She did not play well, finding it hard to switch into her game. She lost by a slim margin, believing that she was really the better player.

'I was furious at myself for not giving myself the time and space to concentrate, and furious because it mattered and that it was upsetting me. It was like a microcosm of all the frustrations, and I was powerless to do anything about anything, and it was my own responsibility.'

She drove to a friend's house and said she thought she would quit work and go away; at the time her friend did not believe she was serious. As she drove home she decided definitely to leave the company and go travelling for a year. She told her husband her decision that evening, but they never discussed it.

'Once I'd made the decision I never had any second thoughts about it. . . . I was definitely going and it was the best thing I ever did.'

Ironically, a month later, Stevie was offered promotion to UK sales manager – which she accepted. Again she had a dual response: she was pleased – 'it was a fairly heavyweight position' and the business needed restructuring, which excited her. But 'it was a job that caused no surprises. I was the obvious candidate and it really didn't challenge me at all.'

A further enticement was her new boss, who was a sensitive and caring individual, not aggressively competitive. He gave her the opportunity to manage differently, to leave behind the 'female man' approach. Instead she gave people enough space to do what they wanted and supported them, also setting high standards and being demanding. She developed in this way partly agreeing with 1980s views that women no longer needed to copy men's behaviours to succeed, partly enabled by the contemporary fashion for more relaxed, less confrontational, management styles, but also because she was becoming uncomfortable with herself.

'I realized that I was becoming a nasty piece of work. . . . I was becoming very opinionated and too sure of myself, probably not listening very well'.

Her family noticed this too, although she simultaneously received positive feedback from inside her organization, people there were comfortable with her 'being one of the boys'.

Stevie and her boss set about building a team that was different, one based on trust rather than fear. She worked hard, both doing the basic job and restructuring people's work and the way the team operated – 'it was such a joy'. So Stevie postponed her leaving date for six months, only later telling her boss that she was going. Having now experienced some of her vision of what organizational life could become did not deter her from leaving.

> 'Because there was still no future for me there. My card was already marked. I didn't fit and wasn't the [company] type. I had collected a couple of heavyweight enemies along the way and my potential was below what I felt it should be.'
> 'I just left because I was sick to death of the whole thing.'

Stevie told people that she did not think her future in the company would match her expectations, that she was more ambitious than they were encouraging her to be, and that she wanted to start her own business. Her immediate boss understood and congratulated her. Her leaving did, however, cause some controversy. Some senior managers expressed concern, having held high opinions of her calibre. Her peers and colleagues were sad to see her go, but shared her view that her treatment had been 'blatantly unfair'.

Stevie's leaving was celebrated at a sales meeting with a dinner and disco. People gave her gifts for her forthcoming travels. She felt appreciated. When we met, she still felt known within her company, even by people she had never met, because many documents carried her name. 'There still is that good feeling.'

Looking back at her ex-company Stevie had no regrets. Core values and caring were themes of the past; cost-cutting was the new priority. The senior manager she had crossed was very powerful. The boss she liked and respected had been moved abroad again against his wishes. A woman recruited at the same time as Stevie had reached the company's glass ceiling and was thoroughly demotivated. (She has since left.)

MOVING ON

Stevie spent a year travelling. She went to Asia and Australia, living on a slim budget, sometimes working to pay her way. She went to a meditation retreat in a Buddhist monastery, climbed volcanoes, scuba-dived and met a myriad of interesting and very fine people.

'I came back relaxed and happy with myself.'

'It was just a joy and I got back to who I really was in that year.'

She was welcomed back by her friends. She and her husband separated. She returned to no job and no money: she had spent all her funds travelling, and proceeds from her house remained unavailable and in dispute. A friend suggested that they go into business together, in a venture which would be commercial but also ecologically responsible. When I met Stevie, they had researched their markets and developed a business plan; they were trying to raise venture capital. They wanted to prove themselves and create their vision of organizational possibility.

'We're doing it to prove to ourselves we're capable of it... and it's not the system that's constraining us. We want to build the kind of company we want to work for, which is a lot of women, hopefully, but without hierarchical structures and the pissing in the corners and is allowing people to grow and having a good team.'

Stevie was drawing on the management style she had developed in her last six months with the chemical company:

'It's formed the basis of the thinking of how I want to run this company. It's about open communication and trust, and about seeing people as individuals who have a lot to give.

Maintaining her new sense of self was a challenge at times.

'My attitude is a lot different, but I revert to type under pressure – that is overworking and being aggressive and assertive and not listening.'

Dealing with the venture capitalists caused some tension: it was 'like moving back into what [organizational life] was at times.' For example, when they were told that the venture capitalists would prefer them to have 'a stronger management team', Stevie believed they would prefer there to be a man involved. Stevie and her partner must still play by the rules and negotiate sufficiently well with traditional systems to secure their freedom. Managing these relationships without becoming overtly angry or confrontational sometimes required self-control.

> 'I feel deep-down anger having come through the organizations and systems I have. I've got rid of a lot of it, but there's deep down anger about the unfairness of it all, and. . . it does get rekindled.'

Anita Roddick of the Body Shop was a model. She seemed to have rewritten the rules of organizational and business practice. Stevie believed that many men also appreciate that these are changing.

Stevie described herself as now 'quite a strong feminist'. She was willing to say when things were unfair for women, and when their company is successful will 'certainly broadcast the fact' that life in business is still difficult for women.

Stevie's life was much less comfortable and secure financially than it had been. I asked how this affected her.

> 'It's fine. It's uncomfortable sometimes, but money and the trappings of success are not necessary any more. I don't measure my success in terms of salary any more. I don't care what people think about me. That's what the travelling did for me, re-establish my sense of self. . . . That's a big release. I really feel like I'm into the next stage of my life and travelling was the transition point. . . . I don't know how many more times I'll change career.'

> 'It's not scary. It's exciting.'

She believed that she was still working at the need to prove herself set when she was a child – 'It's still the same little girl wanting to be the best.' She also described herself as very self-sufficient, an attitude learnt as the teenage daughter of parents working long hours in a small business.

If she can create a successful business she thinks she may aim less high next time, but she still has things to prove.

> 'But I think I'm coming to a point when I'll be satisfied once this is done. Then it gets rid of that question. It proves to me that I can do it and it's not the system that's holding me back.'

Then, when she is also financially independent, she can 'sign off' and use her skills 'more constructively for other people' rather than for herself.

222 Blocked promotion prospects

STEVIE'S FEEDBACK ON THE DRAFT STORY

Stevie suggested some amendments to the story to clarify details and enrich points. She said 'I was most impressed by the accuracy and interpretation of the taped interview material'.

ADDENDUM

Stevie sent me some press coverage of her company's products and a business update. Life for her and her business partner *is* the company for the moment. They have created a new marketing sector, and challenged traditional brands. They expect soon to face retaliatory competition. Their turnover reached £600,000 per annum after two years of trading. Publicity coverage has been extensive and enthusiastic. The company now employs four further people, all women. They started without venture capital input, and have funded growth from sales and cash flow, but now need additional funding. They have turned down one offer to buy them out.

Stevie is working long hours and travelling extensively. She and her partner encourage each other to take time off and unwind, but find doing so difficult because they are so committed to making the company work and there is so much to do.

'Each day is a mixture of exhaustion and tremendous job satisfaction and jubilation.'

They are doing what they set out to do. But life continues to be challenging. They are 'nearly famous but not even close to rich'.

Mentors, sponsors and powerful enemies

Stevie's account includes some compelling examples which led me to develop the notion of 'powerful enemies' introduced below.

The stories say less about mentors and sponsors than I had expected for a group of successful women managers. There are a few examples of such relationships. The stories also suggest that they can become more difficult at middle and senior management levels, especially if power relationships become more intense and confrontational.

The stories do also show clearly the dangers of acquiring powerful enemies. Some people fill this role because they are unwilling to accept women in business. Some chairmen or directors took this attitude. Some are new bosses moving into or taking over the organization who set out to replace the previous management regime. In such cases gender may or may not have anything to do with the subsequently difficult relationship.

Three people – Stevie, Teresa and Judith – found that powerful enemies developed during their time in the organization. These people took an aggressive stance towards the research participants, and in each case gender seemed to be at least an associated factor. All three women tried to challenge these people and reorient their relationships, but without ultimate success. The resulting tensions, and the feeling that they could not be remedied, contributed significantly to the women's decisions to leave.

Perhaps how to deal with powerful enemies needs as much attention at this stage in women's development as the more popular theme of establishing mentor relationships. And, of course, having the latter may unwittingly lead to the former as power alliances in an organization shift.

Incongruity of outer and inner images

Recurring issues in people's stories were their senses of self and whether these matched their public identities. The two stories just presented show major disjunctions in these terms, for example, which severely affected the women's internal senses of career while they were also managing external threats to their prospects.

A few people had lacked self-confidence and had not developed very positive self-images despite career successes and affirmative feedback. *Margaret* and Claire are strong examples of this. These incongruities had sometimes provided incentives to prove themselves, but had also been major drains on their energies. The majority of the group seemed, however, both confident, able to believe in their own competence, and open to self-questioning and doubt at times. Only three (Christina, Dorothy and *Pamela*) seemed to show little self-doubt.

The job situations which prompted them to leave or consider leaving had significantly undermined several people's confidence for a while. A few wondered if they would ever be able to work again. They had needed to re-establish their self-esteem, making a sense of the situation with which they could live.

Another facet to this theme was not liking the mismatch between who they felt they were and who they had become to survive and be successful. For example, Stevie described herself as 'a nasty piece of work' and Judith felt she had a tough outer shell at work because of defence strategies.

Some research participants talked about the tensions of living with other people's conflicting expectations. Some of the women's jobs heightened the difficulties of doing this successfully. For example, personnel and change agent roles exposed them to a wide array of potentially conflicting needs. Even in senior positions people could feel that they had lost their own voices and had to be what others expected of them.

Some research participants felt that they had lost sight of what was valuable in life or had lost a centred sense of self. It seems that many women control their presentations of self to make them acceptable in current organizational cultures. Such adaptive strategies are found widely in research on women managers (Marshall, 1984; Loden, 1985; Sheppard, 1989). They involve not only matching male styles of behaviour but also being careful not to fulfil negative or devaluing female stereotypes. The stories do suggest that many of the women were devoting energy to creating and maintaining viable public images, for example by concealing signs of stress. Trying to establish an affirmed identity as a lesbian manager is at the heart of *Ruth's* story.

A recurrent wish amongst research participants was to be themselves. They were seeking fit between their inner and outer self-images and between themselves and organizational cultures. Many reported their delight, and an associated release of energy, after leaving at achieving more sense of harmony. Christina and Patricia, for example, were both pleased to join companies that seemed perfect matches for them, with more integrated cultures in gender terms. Other people – especially those seeking promotion or development – wondered whether they could ever achieve this congruity in current organizational cultures.

This section reveals a theme which recurs throughout this book. People seemed to think in multiple frames, aware of various standards against which they would be judged by others and might judge themselves. They then had to reconcile these different expectations or to accept the disjunctions they created.

'I am not a feminist, but. . .'

(I have taken the title above from a phrase often heard in organizations. It is used by people who want to comment on gender-related issues but do not want to be branded 'feminist' because this label has so many disparaged associations.)

The research participants had very mixed views on feminism. (I had asked their opinions.) A few would describe themselves as feminist when they were in the jobs they left. Feminist viewpoints had informed their working approaches. (See 'Working strategies', p. 312.) Two, at least, had revised their views since and did not believe it was strategically effective to be so apparently confronting.

Two women believed they could not have adopted feminist perspectives earlier in their careers. Doing so would have meant seeing themselves as discriminated against, an awareness they could not have reconciled with working in male-dominated cultures. Stevie later felt 'deep down anger' and *Kim* a 'lot of resentment' at realizing the sexism they had previously encountered. Stevie would now identify herself as feminist.

Most people were sure that they would not call themselves feminist because of the label's derogatory associations, its sense of confrontation and the likely antagonism it would provoke (although some believed they would be seen as feminist, despite their reservations). Many did then explain that they held strong views on equality, using more neutral labels to describe them. Several acknowledged that their values were close to feminism, really. Some research participants had promoted more gender and racial diversity in their organizations through strategies designed not to provoke resistance or place them in the line of fire. Some would be willing to take a stand on women's issues and challenge sexist behaviour when they thought it appropriate.

The key preoccupations in these somewhat contradictory accounts were of seeking strategies which would influence the organizational culture but not brand the women concerned as militant or disruptive, and of creating identities which fitted their values but were viable in organizational contexts.

One potential disadvantage of this ambivalence about feminism is the lack of access to frameworks which might offer more external – social, political, structural or organizational – and affirmative explanations of their situations, and reduce the personal responsibility they felt and the stress they managed. One advantage was that they were not exposing themselves to critiques of the foundations of business organizations which might prove unsettling.

It seems difficult, then, to be both feminist and a senior manager. I greatly regret the covert pressures on women and men not to take feminist insights and analyses seriously as available perspectives in a wealth of possibilities.

No longer wanting to battle

The stories of: Kim and Margaret

I have grouped these two stories together because they share several themes. The women had previously had to battle to establish either their worth or that of the type of work they did. Eventually they were not greatly affirmed by their organizations, and both found the cultures inhospitable. I have placed these stories after those of Mercedes and Stevie because they seem to represent a possible later progression and state of disillusion.

Kim and Margaret were amongst the older age group in the research and there were hints of tiredness in their accounts. Both regained their sense of energy after leaving. Their decision-making processes were significantly different. Kim voiced her doubts and precipitated the decision to leave. Margaret was placed under pressure to take early retirement; she later felt grateful for the opportunity of change.

Kim

OVERVIEW

Kim was in her early fifties when we met. She had recently resigned her post as a senior trainer at a national staff college. Her decision had been motivated by several factors. Of central importance were her sense of losing vitality for work, and ageing. Her energy had partly been drained by changing organizational circumstances which meant both that her contribution seemed less valued in the college and that her immediate sources of support had gone. Also she was physically tired, and attributed some of her symptoms to the menopause.

Deciding that she needed a life change, Kim chose to give some research she was conducting priority over her paid employment. She resigned, but continued to work on a consultancy basis for the college and for other clients. She devoted more energy to her research and home life. She found this a more satisfying combination, despite its challenges. Five months after leaving she was feeling refreshed, more energetic, more in charge of her own life.

BACKGROUND AND EARLY LIFE HISTORY

Kim's early childhood was disrupted by the Second World War and her mother's death when Kim was 8. She was partly raised by 'a very loving' aunt and uncle, the former becoming her surrogate mother. She moved between homes several times, and remembers much criticism and few compliments; she grew up doubting her own competence and worth. She no longer feels these insecurities, but they have influenced her life, sometimes making her vulnerable to other people's critical comments. Like many women of her generation, she was raised to marry and have children, not to imagine other possible futures. In fact she was employed and responsible for herself financially from the age of 16.

Kim's career had been in education. She trained as a nursery nurse and later became a physical education teacher. During these early years she was also involved in international sport as a team member and coach. Later she added student counselling and welfare to her educational responsibilities, her interest fuelled by studying psychology.

Kim hardly paused in her career as she married and had a child. Her husband was also in education and pushed her to maintain her working life. Maternity arrangements were not generous at the time, and she returned to work six weeks after her son's birth. From then on she led a demanding life, taking most of the responsibility for child and home-care, and regularly taking on new challenges at work. Her husband was himself highly successful. His attitude to Kim's success was ambivalent. He sometimes complimented her on being bright and sometimes belittled her activities, even calling her a 'butterfly brain creeping vamp'. He consistently encouraged her to progress in her career, but she bore the guilt of being a working mother. Looking back, Kim is angry and resentful at the conflictual position she was encouraged to live in, and the great sense of loss she felt at being separated from her son, whom she adored.

In the early 1980s her husband was killed in a car accident. When we met, Kim had recently remarried.

MOVING INTO SENIOR MANAGEMENT

Kim moved up the hierarchy and into management. She also furthered her own education, gaining a Master's degree by doing research on counselling services. During her thirties and early forties she held various senior management posts. She ran a student counselling service, was head of an inner-city college, and later became head of a large department of health and site manager for a college campus. She became used to being the only woman in the senior management team, and learnt to cope with the consequences – typically by using humour and a direct style of engagement. Despite the rugged environments in which she worked, Kim enjoyed this phase of her career and looks back on her accomplishments with pride. But also, in retrospect, she recognized the anger she had accumulated by being a woman in a man's world, having to prove herself time after time, always needing to be better than male colleagues in order to survive, and needing to develop defence strategies for handling discrimination and negative stereotypes of women.

'I have become fed up with that male-dominated, belittling, patronizing, "you've done everso well for a girl" (not even a woman), and I've worked very hard not colluding with a lot of the stuff.'

During her career (including recently), she had often felt that men had taken over work she had produced or her ideas and labelled them as their own. She had not therefore always been able to take pride in what were initially her achievements.

Kim took a stand on women's issues and was challenging when she thought this appropriate. In one job, for example, she campaigned to have maternity leave extended to unmarried women. She was proud to have introduced women's toilets and sanitary towel machines in three institutions (there were none before because of the courses previously taught).

But Kim's success in management had disadvantages in terms of job satisfaction. She noticed how much she looked forward to the few direct teaching responsibilities she then had. She therefore redirected her career path, acting on her own evaluations rather than on other people's expectations of appropriate progression. She looked for a move which would give her more teaching contact. Through occasional consultancy Kim became associated with the national staff college. In the mid-1980s she took up a full-time post there. This, again, was a mainly male environment. For her first four years there she was the only woman staff tutor.

Her early years at the college were a satisfying phase in Kim's life, during which she exercised considerable influence. She was teaching human resources courses: counselling, interpersonal skills, team building, personal growth and associated programmes. Having senior management experience, which few other tutors did, helped her relate courses to participants' organizational situations. Her work with students was enjoyable and very highly regarded (based on course evaluations). She took initiatives in the college and felt that she was making a significant and valued contribution. But over time Kim's position began to be eroded.

BECOMING LESS VALUED

Kim began to feel that her areas of expertise were becoming devalued relative to more intellectual activities. She judged this from who gained promotions and resources in the college, who was in favour. She found this very disappointing, and speaks forcefully of the need for emotions and interpersonal dynamics to be appreciated as important aspects of organizational life. She spoke out for her programmes and their value, but 'the people stuff' was losing organizational priority, 'mainly because nobody was fighting on various committees to say that it was important'. Despite her seniority in expertise and grading she did not feel she was being attributed the influence she warranted. This feeling became more difficult to live with when she lost two close colleagues who had been her working team and particular allies.

'I suppose when I lost my bodyguards then I wasn't quite so prepared to carry the flag any more.'

New staff were appointed; most were young, and academic qualifications seemed to be given more priority in recruitment – to contribute to the college's perceived status – than were experience and expertise as teachers. Kim lacked respect for the training skills of some of her new colleagues and felt hesitant about having to co-train with them.

A year or so before she left, Kim applied for the assistant director post at the college, but was unsuccessful. She assessed the person who was appointed as less qualified than her academically and in training and senior management credentials. He had, instead, computing expertise. This experience contributed to Kim's growing perception that her skills as a competent trainer were not appreciated. It seemed profitability was superseding quality.

LOSING ENERGY

Kim described various ways in which she was losing emotional and physical energy for her work. The organizational pressures described above and the lack of like-minded colleagues undermined her vitality. Also, she was then going through the menopause. This added to her sense of tiredness and made her reluctant to travel for work assignments (a major requirement of her job), as she could not anticipate her physical symptoms. Later she found that she had also been suffering from acute anaemia for some time. Once appropriately treated, she improved rapidly. But initially she interpreted her physical tiredness as resulting more from psychological reasons, from her concern at lack of management appreciation for her work (although her 'excellent' evaluations from course participants exceeded those of all other, male, tutors). She therefore looked for solutions in this realm. Poor health prompted significant job decision-making, as it had for other women in the study.

Her growing awareness of ageing and her lack of role models for being an older woman in employment also played significant parts in undermining Kim's self-confidence.

'So there was a physical illness, emotional exhaustion, a loss of my secure group of people who I regarded very highly... and then my surrogate mother died.'

Her aunt's death left Kim feeling that she had now grown up, was old and would be next to die. (Her son was by that time her only living close relative.) She was then about 50. At around that time the college invited administrative staff over 50 to apply for redundancy. This initiative also impacted on Kim.

'I had this awful feeling of a kind of bag of rubbish being put on a rubbish heap. . . . There was this sadness about 50 which was a changing time.'

Kim had always been the energetic initiator of change, the person to speak out on behalf of students and potentially neglected issues. But she had become weary and did not see a place for herself. Her script for her life, her expectations developed in childhood, had run out.

'It was my turn next. I'd grown up and there were no more people to die before me, so I'd better put myself into the autumn of my life.'

Believing that she should 'grow old gracefully', Kim took the drastic step of having her hair cut. Since the 1960s she had worn it long and straight, initially red and later blonde. She could not imagine this as suitable for someone in her fifties:

'So, I had to change it because I was now old and old people don't have long, blonde, straight hair. They bun it and put knitting needles in it.'

Later she deeply regretted this decision, realizing that she had given up an image of her own vitality. At about the same time she began putting on more weight, another factor that made her feel out of connection with her external appearance.

STAGES OF DECISION-MAKING

The realizations and adjustments in attitude described above took some time to develop into decisions about employment. At two consecutive annual appraisal interviews Kim was forthright about her dissatisfactions with work and sought strategies to cope with them. She treated the meetings as 'opportunities to have some self-reflection', rather than putting up a false image. In this she was living up to her beliefs, purveyed in her training work, that good communication is based on 'openness, honesty and genuineness'. When I questioned her about the potential vulnerability of this approach, she said that whilst her appraiser was certainly power-ful, she did not have to give him power over her, and also she liked and respected him. Her agenda of articulating 'the truth' of her situation was more valuable as a base for learning and decision-making than maintaining a false organizational mask would have been.

In the first year's appraisal she concentrated on her concern that her area of expertise was becoming devalued in the college. She was assured that this was not the case, but believed that there was a 'kind of emotional abuse' in the way her work was being treated. She was assured of its importance, and yet 'was watching it being chipped away'. At the same time she was often asked to start off more general training programmes because her sessions were so warmly received by students.

As a result of this appraisal discussion, Kim enrolled on a PhD programme to serve several purposes. She wanted to address issues she was facing organizationally through research. She wanted to affirm emotions, intuition and empathizing, ways of being with which women are often stereotyped, and rescue them from being devalued relative to men's supposedly better – but no less narrowly stereotyped – rational ways of thinking. She also wanted to gain more qualifications (as these seemed to be valued in new appointments), and to develop new thinking skills to help her in her job (she had found doing a Master's degree beneficial in this way previously). Doing a PhD was:

'An escape route from it not happening at work. The job satisfaction at work had gone.'

'I thought it would improve my standing at work. It was a strategy for improving myself as a consultant and trainer.'

Studying for a PhD was, then, initially a strategy for staying more powerfully in her post, and 'being able to handle the criticism, the covert belittling of the area I still feel so passionately about'. Validation she could respect was no longer available since her close colleagues had left: 'I got it [validation] from my colleagues, and when they went it was a barren field'. Kim put on 'armour plating' to cope with working in a friendless environment. Doing the research also created an identified and defensible space in her home life for her interests.

But a year later, Kim's position had not significantly improved. This time at her appraisal, equally frankly, she said 'that I thought I was losing my bushy tail, which I prided myself on, and I was tired, and I thought one option might be to leave.' She was also explicit about her lack of respect for some of the staff with whom she had to work.

Various options were discussed. Her boss suggested that if the menopause were the main factor she could take time off. Alternatively she could explore retirement for reasons of sickness. Kim was unwilling to consider either option. She had been the strong woman for so long in her career and needed to maintain this stance. She decided to leave, but to work for the college part-time. Even when, shortly afterwards, her husband was made redundant she did not choose to revoke this decision. Instead she accepted more work to gain sufficient income.

AFTERWARDS

I met Kim about five months after she had officially left the college. She was very satisfied with her decision. She was then a trainer and consultant, partly independent and partly through the college. She had more work than she could handle, and was spending longer hours training than she had done while in full-time employment. She was travelling a great deal – which in her previous post she had become reluctant to do. She found returning home a better way to recharge her batteries after working than engaging with college politics and paperwork, which used to have the opposite effect.

Kim had had to take responsibility for herself financially and manage herself as a business. She had found it challenging to set a price on her services and ask people for money, but appreciated that she was attributing herself worth in doing so. Her life was, however, less financially secure, and she was aware of this as a pressure. Whilst her husband did contribute to the family finances, she was the main earner.

In some ways her health had improved. She attributed this partly to a homoeopathic equivalent to hormone replacement therapy (called FSH). She was feeling fitter and had lost some weight. She was no longer feeling heavy and sad facially, as she had prior to leaving the college. She was growing her hair into a longer style in which it could move and again provide an extension of herself which could express her vitality and sense of fun. She was planning to wear more of the 'way-out clothes' she loved, and had always worn as a complement to black suits as part of her professional image. But she had also had several minor physical ailments to contend with: 'so my health has been bad since I left work, but mentally I've been a lot better'. Her sense of enjoyment in life was coming both from her success as a consultant – which was no longer tainted by working in a hostile, devaluing atmosphere – and from her marriage, which she described as warm, loving and full of humour.

One irony was that once Kim was freer from employment her son no longer really needed her, having started at university. She felt some resentment and guilt about how her life priorities had been ordered.

ON REFLECTION

Kim welcomed the opportunity to talk through her experiences, setting aside her initial concern at being 'selfish'. It seemed that forging a new construction of her life in her fifties had both brought together her confirmed talents and required her to think through many past frustrations and denials of her own energy.

Our conversation wove back and forth between current circumstances and issues she was reconsidering. She was still in the process of developing a positive image for herself as an ageing woman. It was still unclear whether her hopes for the research study would be realized. But her consultancy work and home life were flourishing.

Kim's story is that of a woman's quest for a sense of value, internally and externally, and for authentic activities to express her energy in life. She is having to create her own images of possible womanhood as she reaches each new life phase. Before she joined the training college, she seems mainly to have proved herself tough against dominant, 'male', values. In her work at the college she was more openly exploring and speaking for 'female' values. But the organization became more hostile towards these qualities. Kim was no longer able or willing to defend herself in appropriate ways, especially once she lost her allies. After leaving, she was establishing her own working 'context', drawing on the nurturing base of her marriage to support her training and consultancy.

KIM'S FEEDBACK ON THE DRAFT STORY

Kim said that she enjoyed reading the draft story and that 'a lot of emotions and memories came flooding back'. She suggested some amendments as clarifications, particularly wanting to ensure appropriate details and tone in some comments about relationships.

ADDENDUM

Kim's work and home lives are now thriving. There have been difficulties in some relationships, unsettled times financially and she has so far failed to gain a PhD, but the overall picture is very positive. Her training for the college has been popular with clients. In this sense, and because she is a financial asset, she has felt valued by them. But few staff there support her area of expertise and this may limit work offers in the future. She now, however, has many other clients and feels highly appreciated by them. She has plans to develop her consulting work, and has positive physical images of herself in this role. She hopes to work fewer days to give more time for other activities and relaxation. Having increased her rates, she is currently working half the time she used to but earning four or five times as much money.

She and her husband have moved to a horticultural nursery, which they are developing. Kim is relishing the outdoor life and growing plants. Her marriage has developed into a strong, loving, supportive relationship and she is enjoying relationships with her son and other family members. Her health is good. She says she now feels in control of her health, body and mind.

Margaret

OVERVIEW

Margaret was a pioneer woman manager in banking. She talked about her career with little embellishment, little sense of drama, but she had been very successful. She was also very visible. Her story is one of battle and success, and some loneliness. Because of her isolated position she was largely cut off from feedback she could trust about her performance, so until recently she had harboured a relatively poor self-image. After times of stress because of recession, and an illness which influenced her attitudes, Margaret was offered early retirement. Since accepting she had re-appraised her career and credentials. When we met, she was vibrant, feeling free, and looking for new employment challenges.

ENTERING BANKING

Margaret left school at 16, having passed various examinations but with no career aspirations. She obtained a job in a bank, seeing this simply as a way of earning money; she expected to marry and have children.

Margaret joined a banking system in which men's and women's jobs were clearly segregated. Women, often called 'girls' whatever their age, were not offered career progression. When Margaret joined she was surprised at how mundane women's work seemed. She married but did not, after all, have children. After twelve years she became bored; she wanted more interesting work and was growing resentful at seeing men progress to more senior jobs. She asked to be allowed to do a particular task in the bank, working on the security box. She hardly knew what this involved, but could see that it was another step in responsibility, which no woman had been allowed to take. Her request was declined because she had not taken banking examinations.

This was the first explicit obstacle that was put in Margaret's way. She said: 'Since then I've found out that if somebody puts a hurdle in front of me I'll get over it.' She studied for her exams, passing all ten in four years, and was allowed to move on to security box work, the first woman to do so at her branch.

FIGHTING FOR PROMOTIONS

By the time she left the bank, after thirty-three years' service, Margaret had reached the grade of manager in a large branch. At every step she had had to fight to be allowed necessary training or progression. She had found the bank continually obstructive. For example, she was once offered a promotion they assumed she would refuse (her suspicion about this was later confirmed) because it would involve either moving or living away from home during the week. Margaret took the post, determined not to be intimidated in this way, and enjoyed the travelling.

After each progression Margaret would settle into her new job and enjoy the work involved. Only when she again became bored would she take an assertive line. This usually meant enlisting the help of a particular senior manager who had faith in her: 'He was really my friend all the way through. It was his encouragement that made me battle on.' Once she also wrote directly to the personnel director, bypassing the hierarchy, and enlisted the help of her union. Margaret later 'cringed' at the assertive attitude she had taken in her early career battles. At the time she did not mind what people thought of her.

Each time Margaret entered a new post some people were hesitant about working with or for her. For most it was their first experience of a senior woman: 'Obviously, wherever I went I was a peculiar animal.' But their qualms soon passed as she proved her banking and managerial skills. They only told her later about their initial reservations, once they were on good terms, so she was not aware of any significant discrimination or problems arising in day-to-day exchanges.

She seemed to have performed well. Some proof of her high standards of achievement came when she left jobs.

'Once I'd got the job as I liked it I always found that my workload was much more than my male counterparts' – it was a fact because often after I moved on the job was split between two people.'

CONTRADICTORY IMAGES

Reviewing her style, Margaret saw a marked difference between her outer image and her internal sense of herself. She thought those who knew her superficially saw her as aggressive, almost of necessity, given the rank she had achieved. But she was not authoritarian, she did not enjoy disciplining people, and would avoid confrontations whenever possible. Her immediate colleagues were more likely to appreciate her style, but also to judge her as 'cold'. This was partly because she preferred to get on with work, rather than talk 'chitchat', and so was not highly sociable. Also, despite her progress and success in exams and on courses, she always remained insecure about her own abilities.

'I always thought I got there because they thought "It's a woman, so we'll just keep her quiet and we can say we've got a woman here", not because of my ability. I never believed in my ability, and it's only since I've left the bank and seen people's reactions to me that I've begun to think maybe I wasn't so bad after all, and maybe I did get there on ability. But I never believed in myself during the job.'

Because Margaret felt that promotions had been given her on sufferance, to appease her and improve the bank's image, she could not take them as affirmation of her skills. That she was not approached with suggested posts supported her interpretation. She did not really believe the good appraisal reports she regularly received. One justification for not sending her on a particular training course had undermined her, and stayed with her. She had been told that it was not worthwhile for the bank to train junior managers, they wanted only to train potential senior managers: 'The seed had been sown that I was not good for anything beyond a [junior management] appointment.'

Margaret also discounted the positive feedback her husband tried to give her, thinking he was seeing her through 'rose-coloured spectacles'. He had throughout, however, played a vital role as a home-based mentor. He encouraged and pushed her, as her mother had done earlier, because he believed in her. Yet there was no one inside the bank she trusted sufficiently to disclose her insecurities to, and so she had no opportunities to dispel them: 'I couldn't let anyone else know that I didn't think I was good enough. It was something I kept inside.'

Margaret controlled herself, seldom losing her temper, keeping her feelings to herself.

'I don't think people who worked with me actually ever really knew me because I didn't know myself really.'

This inner lack of confidence, and her self-protective coping strategies, made Margaret feel lonely. She missed the possible companionship of having other women at her level, and yet was glad not to work with any, thinking their presence might somehow show that she was 'no good' by providing a comparison. Outside her immediate working environment she was on good terms with other women she met.

As usually the sole woman manager, Margaret did not identify fully with her male colleagues, although she had good relationships with them. For example, she wore clothes which she described as 'smart and professional', but in bright colours: 'I enjoyed being a woman and standing out in the managers' meetings, where they were all in their shirts and ties'. But neither did she identify herself primarily as a woman: 'I just did the job I was trained to do, how I thought it should be done.'

Margaret portrayed her sense of insecurity, and her need not to reveal this to others, as central features of her working identity. Given this, I was surprised and delighted to be told late in the interview of her confidence and openly recognized success in another professional arena. She had been an active and senior member of the Institute of Banking, locally and nationally, and had been the first woman to occupy several positions of responsibility. I asked why this recognition had not improved Margaret's self-image. She did feel affirmed by it, but it was too different to her experience as an employee of the bank to affect the latter.

'In the Institute I was treated as an individual banker, I think. I enjoyed being the first this and that and I revelled in it, and they knew I did. There was no pretence. I suppose it wasn't serious career-wise, it was light-hearted really.'

REACHING SENIOR MANAGEMENT

In her mid-forties, Margaret moved to her first full managerial-rank appointment. She was one of two assistant managers reporting to the manager in a large branch. Her job changed significantly several times in her four years there. Initially she was responsible for a portfolio of personal and business customers and the branch staff of fifty-five. Later she set up a small business centre serving 500 customers. She felt she had relaxed more than usual on gaining this job. She thought she had achieved her ultimate grade and was now weary of battling.

> 'I did think I would go another step up. But. . . . in the last couple of years I began to think "I'm not going to have all this fighting. If they don't want me, I'm quite happy, I'm earning enough money and enjoying myself.'

> 'I suppose I thought I'd got there because I'd battled for so long. . . . I think I began to switch off. I thought I'd proved my point and I was quite happy to stay there.'

She reported that her husband doubted this version of events. He thought that she would eventually become bored with the job, as she had each time in the past. But Margaret did not have the opportunity to become bored this time. Businesses were under pressure as recession bit, and bank managers generally were feeling the stress of trying to advise customers and having to stand by unable to help when the latter went bankrupt. Margaret was affected by this pressure. Within the bank she, and her boss, were appraised badly if their clients failed. Also she thinks she felt more responsible than was appropriate.

> 'Having got all this [promotion], I was always full of insecurity and never believed in myself in anything that I did. So when my customers did go downhill I thought it was my fault. Having now left the bank and having sat back and looked at it, I can see I can't be responsible for all my customers.'

Margaret was not alone in her feelings of pressure and in-security. Her male colleagues saw her as a sympathetic listener, and confided their very similar worries to her. She had seldom had such direct evidence to compare herself to. Her self-image began to change.

'It made it easier. . . . Until then I thought I was the only one [feeling under pressure] and all these male managers were good and did everything 100 per cent right 100 per cent of the time.'

ILLNESS AND RECOVERY

Suddenly Margaret became ill. She thought the pressure she had been experiencing was a contributory factor. At first she had 'flu symptoms, but soon seemed to be suffering from ME. She was completely physically incapacitated. Her doctor prescribed total rest. After two months she returned to work, having consulted an acupuncturist. But the recovery was only temporary: she had to stop work again. She finally returned nearly five months after her initial illness.

This episode unsettled Margaret and she wondered how she would cope. She returned to a stressful work situation. Client companies were still facing financial problems. Managers felt isolated and unfairly blamed by the bank for circumstances beyond their control. She was in charge of branch personnel again, and needed to arrange voluntary severance packages to reduce staffing levels. She found, however, that to her surprise she was enjoying the work itself, although recession made it difficult. She was welcomed back by many of her customers. Her secretary and assistant were supportive and at times protective of her. She continued working effectively, and in the main with satisfaction, for the next nine or ten months. Looking back she realized that she had become slightly marginal in the management team. Her boss and colleague had developed closer working relationships in her absence and she felt left out. But this did not greatly affect her at the time.

BEING INVITED TO LEAVE

It was then, and much to her surprise, that Margaret was offered early retirement. In this she felt selectively targeted; only one other manager was allowed to leave in this way. Managers who were experiencing stress were encouraged to resign.

Margaret was pressured in several ways to accept the generous terms offered. Managerial jobs were being cut back in a re-organization. She was offered an alternative post, as the sole manager in a branch, but senior management would not tell her where this would be; they threatened that it could be a long way away. She did not want to incur too much extra travelling and did not relish the loneliness of a solo manager post, particularly as a woman. She was also covertly threatened. Her appraisals had been poor because of business performance and she was warned that if they did not improve the next year she might be asked to leave without a financial package to cushion her.

Margaret found this decision very difficult to make. In her marriage she had been the one with the safe job, and was now losing this base of security and identity. She had few people she could consult. She felt angry at the senior manager who had identified her for possible retirement. But she also felt motivated to leave. To her relief, she had initially enjoyed returning to work. But after a while recession was biting again and the job had become tougher. She was no longer happy. She did not want to have to continue battling. The future of all managers in banking was anyway in doubt. Also she no longer had so much need to prove herself. She had achieved a great deal and she had recently found that some male managers experienced similar pressures and self-doubts to her own. Her image of being 'no good' had been challenged. These shifts in self-perception had perhaps freed her to take more charge of her career. She reasoned that she stood more chance of finding alternative employment in her late forties than if she stayed on, and now wanted to find something completely different. After a pause to reflect, she accepted the bank's offer.

LEAVING AND BEYOND

At her leaving there was little sense of ceremony to honour Margaret's thirty-three years of employment. She told colleagues that she did not want a presentation, but did not really want to be taken seriously. However, she was. Her own senior manager was away on the day of her departure so there was no public 'thank-you' or recognition of her contribution to the bank. She organized a buffet lunch for staff and walked out on the Friday afternoon feeling abandoned and flat.

In contrast, she attended Institute of Banking functions at about the same time and felt suitably honoured. There she 'went out in grand style'.

Margaret felt mixed emotions about this ending. She was bitter because her time in the bank had come to such a compromised end. She had found someone to blame in the senior manager who originally suggested she take early retirement, and who she therefore identified as having judged her expendable. She could not accept with any goodwill the flowers and letter he sent wishing 'good luck'. She also realized that she had left a stressful situation on good financial terms and with time to gain another job elsewhere: 'they did me a favour in the end'. This was especially apparent when she looked at her former colleagues. Most were experiencing great pressure, and some had left the bank with no financial help.

'Those that are left in are green with envy in the nicest possible way.'

Margaret's disillusion with her career and the harsh attitudes amongst management when she left made her ambivalent towards the ambitious young women she saw in banking. She realized that she had been a model for them, but was beginning to think, 'Foolish girls, if I were you. . . . '

Since leaving, Margaret had enjoyed herself. When she visited the bank she was told she looked so much better: 'I can't see it, but I suppose the stress is not there. It's bound to show.' She said she made a conscious decision not to regret what had happened, and so had not done so. She left the bank with sufficient money to live on for three years. Initially she thought she might take a mundane job to keep her occupied. She soon started making some applications.

When we first met, about five months after she had left, Margaret was enthusiastically pursuing new jobs. She was rested and her idea of finding 'a mundane clerical job' had disappeared: again she was looking for challenge and interest. Her husband was encouraging her in this, warning that she would 'degenerate and become lazy' if she had nothing to do – 'he knows me too well'. She had found several possibilities suited to her experience and was enjoying other people's reactions to her. She was being taken seriously and treated as highly competent. This feedback had further strengthened her growing self-confidence. There was little trace of the insecurity which had underpinned much of her time in the bank.

Margaret had left the security of the bank, leaving behind too its encouragement not to think for oneself, and its obstructive or merely uninterested attitude towards her, which seemed both to have challenged her to succeed and to have kept her from affirming herself. About leaving she said: 'It's done me a big favour in more ways than one.'

MARGARET'S FEEDBACK ON THE DRAFT STORY

Margaret thought that the draft story was 'still a very true picture'. It felt like reading a history chapter which had now closed. She made minor alterations to my draft to clarify and amend.

ADDENDUM

Margaret enjoyed her time off work, but she was then keen to return; she needs to be fully occupied and is not a house person. She soon accepted a job with a building society in their commercial recoveries department, where she has now worked for several years. Within six months she was promoted to assistant manager, and later to manager. Her role is very similar to the one she left. She feels extremely lucky to have found a job which she can enjoy so much but does not feel the same loyalty to her new employer as she did to the bank which she served for so long. This partly means she now has a more relaxed outlook on her career, although she is also a little wary of taking on too much. She enjoys work a lot, describing herself as 'fulfilled and happy'.

Tiredness, exhaustion, stress and illness

Tiredness, exhaustion, stress and illness appear repeatedly in the stories. Only *Pamela* had little to say on these themes.

TIREDNESS AND STRESS

People described extreme states of tiredness and stress. Many had little energy for any life outside their work. Over half described themselves as overworking and over-committed. Home, family and social lives were often kept to a minimum. Weekends were times to sleep, recover and prepare for the week ahead. Working long hours, cultures which involved evening working and business travel contributed to the sense of fatigue. Some people believed that they had come close to burnout. Many experienced a major depletion of their core life energy. They were still, however, pursuing outwardly busy lives, some taking on additional leisure activities to try to regain a sense of balance.

Many diverse factors contributed to the women's tiredness and stress.

Prime causes for many were the continual pressures of managing themselves and the images they presented as women in prevailing organizational cultures. For example, many had to find ways to operate effectively in the face of rejection or obstruction by male colleagues. Some had to maintain relationships with male bosses who would prefer not to work with women. Some had continually to establish their credibility as managers in order to be taken seriously. They also had to avoid the minefield of negative stereotypes of women available to them. Some felt their senses of self and integrity were threatened as a consequence.

Stress came for some women from the resulting incongruities between their outer and inner images and energies. Maintaining a public image which they thought inauthentic (sometimes because this is who they had become externally as they succeeded in their careers), or appearing confident when they lacked self-confidence was continually demanding (see 'Incongruity', p. 224ff.).

Some jobs the women did, such as personnel and boundary-spanning roles, seemed very emotionally demanding. They involved servicing other people's needs but often receiving little support in return.

Some research participants were reviewing their styles, lives and needs in midlife, and wanted to change and experiment. An additional pressure was not feeling that their organizations had room either for their change processes or for their potentially renewed selves. This lack of space and licence made them feel they would have to conform beyond their wishes. How honest, 'blunt' or outspoken they could be was a concern for several.

Other individual circumstances such as family pressures, home–work conflict (Sarah), dual-career lifestyles, bereavements and concerns about ageing (Kim) also contributed to stress.

Their sense of depleted life energy was a major factor prompting some people to leave employment. It was expressed as an immediate need for space or rest, partly justified by how hard they had worked for the preceding fifteen, twenty or so years. People wanted time for themselves and to put their own needs first. Some of the next steps after leaving were to gain the needed rest, let the sense of exhaustion work its way through, and recover a sense of vitality and life interest.

MAINTAINING SELF-CONTROL

In several stories people attached great importance to maintaining self-control despite their experiences of stress. Judith and Teresa particularly show this. They were being strong to help other people manage and as self-protection. Both were then greatly affected by crying at or about work. This revealed how significantly stress had affected them, and was taken as a sign that they should not continue with this way of living. In this attitude of control they were partly resisting stereotypes of women as weak or emotional. Paradoxically they were also modelling, and therefore reinforcing, cultural norms such as the repression of emotions which affect these stereotypes.

Making sure they avoid any behaviour that can be interpreted negatively is a further pressure on women. I wondered whether their ability to cope meant that some people had continued longer in difficult jobs than was healthy for them, pushing well past their stress limits but determined not to give in. Several women did not, however, like the tough people they 'had become through their use of defence strategies.

ILLNESS

Several women experienced illness prior to leaving their organizations. Some took this as a warning that all was not well in their lives. Some initially attributed their tiredness or other symptoms to psychological reactions to difficult work situations. They saw the 'cause' as within themselves rather than external and so took personal responsibility for coping with or resolving the difficulties. They were thus partly taking on structural or organizational factors as personal issues – a contentious attribution, but one research suggests women often make. It means that they are less likely to blame others or seek support. Taking on personal responsibility can also cause more stress. Some people were relieved to find that the incapacity they were feeling had some identifiable contributing factors other than their responses to work.

But this relief that the illness appeared 'physical' rather than 'psychological' does rely on a debatable distinction in Western medicine. In stress situations the divisions certainly seem much less clear-cut. Finding that their illness may have physical causes was however a relief for some people because it meant that it was more legitimate to take time off work and look after themselves.

I wonder whether women are cautious about admitting illness or tiredness because this invokes the negative stereotype of women being too 'weak' for employment and acknowledges that they are physical beings. Organizations are highly invested in overriding people's bodies and their needs, and this affects cultural norms. For example, it is unusual for menstruation to be publicly acknowledged in organizations, or in literature about them. Are women under covert pressure to ignore their bodies? Are they currently more likely to exert this bodily control than men are, because they apparently have more to lose – in terms of fitting devalued stereotypes – if they do not? At one workshop people confirmed that they had largely overridden attention to their health or tiredness until forced to take notice.

Once they did acknowledge their illness or stress symptoms as important several people made regaining or maintaining their health an important factor in decision-making. They judged the stress involved in potential future jobs and lifestyles. At least two (Judith and Kim) saw gaining weight as a sign of stress or disconnection from themselves and later weight loss as a sign of returning health. Christina and Margaret reported being told (after leaving) that they 'looked much better'. All four expressed these feelings as signifying greater congruity between their different self-images and energies.

Three people in the research found that once they had taken time off work with illness, their managers treated them unsympathetically and put them under some pressure to leave. There was a sense of threat in some cases; two people's previous work record was disparaged although this contradicted earlier appraisal evaluations. Male colleagues with stress illnesses seemed not to be placed under similar pressure. In marked contrast, Kim's manager offered constructive advice when she discussed her menopausal symptoms with him, and Mercedes' new boss was supportive (to her surprise) when she needed a hysterectomy. I wonder if some people are nervous about having ill women around in organizations. Do common women's illnesses linger more than men's, and therefore seem less easy to ignore? Or is illness generally confronting?

IN REFLECTION

You may wonder whether the research participants needed to work so hard, whether they were putting themselves under undue pressure. They described their behaviour as necessary. Much of their energy was used to create and maintain viable identities and sufficient power in cultures which did not accord them these of right. Some pressures are inherent in any senior management job. Such jobs do, however, often seem to present more complexity for women than for men at the moment.

Some people acknowledged that they put themselves under pressure. They recognized their needs to 'be perfect' or could not imagine working less hard because of their strong senses of commitment. These behaviours could be interpreted as personal patterns, but are also probably partly women's reactions to situations in which their credibility is in doubt and any 'mistakes' are highly visible.

Fighting for legitimacy

The story of: Ruth

This story stands alone for two reasons. It originally did so because of its content matter: it describes the efforts of a lesbian manager to establish a successful identity which other organizational members would find acceptable. It is now, also, presented in abbreviated form because the research participant eventually decided that her story was too exposing to tell fully.

Ruth

A story which cannot be fully told.

As the research drew to a close, one participant decided to withdraw the full version of her story. She, and I, had wanted it to be told because it reflects significant issues which are seldom addressed. She is a lesbian and has had to struggle to create a positive identity, acceptable to others, as a manager.

The proposed final draft of her story made Ruth feel too identifiable, vulnerable and exposed, however. She has just found her feet again after the events she had recounted to me, she has aspirations to develop her career, and she does not want to risk unsettling her life. She did not really know what terrible things she imagined might happen to her: her sense of unease was more diffuse than that. She then worried that in withdrawing she might have 'sold out', but also did not want to be a victim of feeling that she should take personal risks to be 'right on'.

We agreed that I would write a skeletal account of her experiences, presenting the main story line but omitting any details which might identify her. This has meant decontextualizing the original story. She has therefore become a typical case standing for some women's experience. In some ways this is an appropriate 'translation' of her story because it protects her in a world which does not offer her ready understanding or acceptance.

Also, in other analyses in the book I have generally omitted specific mention of Ruth.

CENTRAL THEMES

Being lesbian and feminist were central to Ruth's identity and to her story. Her account was both intensely political and personal.

She was harshly self-questioning at times, a flavour of which remains in what follows. In being interviewed she particularly wanted someone to hear and accept her telling of her experiences. Ruth believes that most organizations do not have room for her as a lesbian manager.

STARTING OUT

Ruth had trained to be a teacher, but teaching posts were scarce. She did various kinds of work before settling in one professional area. She was often unsure about whether she would be accepted as a lesbian and so did not know whether to present this overtly as part of her identity. She has had to operate in the face of some people's overt and covert rejection. She has had to manage her own internalized lack of self-worth and illegitimacy.

'YOU'VE GOT EVERY RIGHT TO BE HERE'

At one stage in her working life Ruth joined a new organization. At first she was challenged for her feminist views. People quickly stereotyped her as a lesbian: her sexuality was the subject of discussion. For several years Ruth had a hard time, living with the consequences of people's apparent disapproval, often opposing traditional aspects of the culture such as pornographic pictures on the walls. (Her preferred interpersonal style is straightforward and outspoken.)

Then two incidents helped her feel differently about her rights. As they did a task together a fellow worker commented: 'You know, you've got every right to be here.' On another occasion, Ruth answered the phone to a colleague's relative. When they were told Ruth's name, the latter said that she (Ruth) was being referred to as a lesbian. Ruth was taken by surprise and responded defensively. But the caller said 'It's all right, I'm one myself'.

These interventions gave Ruth a new sense of confidence.

'I suppose I stopped being so paranoid. . . repeating these stories it sounds like nothing, but at the time it was significant to me.'

She found that the environment was not quite as hostile as she had thought. For example, when she challenged colleagues for gossiping about her sexuality, she received apologies.

'It was as if, because I'd started to stand up for myself the tables turned, really. I'd been in a vulnerable frame of mind.'

In time Ruth was promoted to be departmental manager. She worked hard, felt on good terms with most colleagues and was proud of what she achieved.

'For the first time really I'd achieved success. . . . It was that turnaround from having felt so low about myself to being like the queen bee.'

After several years Ruth was looking for new challenges. She was rejected several times for promotion in her own organization.

ENTERING AS A MANAGER

As her career prospects seemed blocked, Ruth moved organizations. The department of which she became manager was unusual in that people were very overtly committed to issues of equality of all sorts. Most of the staff were female; some were lesbian, some were black. But the culture's working practices were dominated by attitudes of political correctness, making the atmosphere charged and often uncertain.

Ruth tried to blend concerns for effectiveness and social justice in her management approach. But her authority as a manager was often challenged in this egalitarian culture. Her staff were not very willing to be managed by someone new, and rebuffed her. She felt betrayed by their failure to accept her, because she saw herself as the same as them. But she also acknowledged that she did not wholly accept them because of the way the department operated. She therefore sometimes reverted to a more authoritarian style of management in order to make things she believed in happen. For example, she reorganized various administrative and finance systems which she felt were ineffective. Her style of action, and the repercussions of the tighter rules, were resented within her department. She later thought that she had been quite puritanical and self-righteous in her approach and so had done much to antagonize people.

Staffing was a very contentious issue in the department and Ruth was often in conflict with people about recruitment decisions. Attitudes of being 'right on' politically affected appointments. Ruth felt barred from using her senior organizational position as power, and under pressure to behave as if equal with her subordinates. She had to expose herself more personally in arguing her case and seeking to achieve agreement.

It seems Ruth had joined an organization which overtly accepted her as a lesbian manager. It was seeking to act responsibly in relation to issues of race, gender and sexuality. But a culture in which this is possible is highly unusual. In this case attitudes of equality were achieved largely by rejecting conventional norms of managing. But the department had not developed viable new practices to match its values, and so had to live with the consequent disruptions and uncertainties. Accountability and authority were particularly placed in doubt. The atmosphere was often highly charged emotionally as contentious issues were encountered, debated or handled in covert ways.

Another complication was the department's location in the organization as a whole. It operated largely independently. Whilst some senior managers were supportive, most were wary. Ruth received little support from this quarter: they were concerned about possible disruption if the department could not contain its tensions.

Ruth's ability to survive in this environment was further weakened by various incidents at work and by an upsetting experience in her personal life. She found that her vulnerability attracted people who had experiences of injustice or abuse to tell. Counselling them, and being unable to protect herself from feeling the issues they raised, was a further source of pressure. Looking back and referring to various dimensions of her experience, Ruth said 'It wasn't just them, I didn't help myself. I wasn't able to.' She believes she was very affected by having internalized devalued stereotypes of lesbians, undermining her feelings of competence and worth, and that she became too prickly and defensive.

The pressure accumulated and she became excessively tired. She became ill and needed some weeks off work. Senior managers pressured her to leave; she thinks this was partly because she was lesbian and therefore a potential source of tension and public exposure. Ruth took a proactive role in negotiating a generous settlement. She does not think she could have carried on in that situation.

'So it was a positive choice. I had to go to save myself.'

FINDING HER FEET

Initially Ruth spent time on 'rest, recovery, relaxation and finding out I'm a person in my own right'. She was out of work for some time. Finding her feet again was difficult. She did not feel that the incident would be closed until she had a worthwhile job again and had therefore recovered herself.

> 'I can't just burn out. I've got to carry on. . . . Now my own life is much more important. I've learned now that it is much more difficult to lead your own life, let alone sort all these other things out.'

Ruth has found the new job with a proper salary she was seeking. She is developing her management style in various ways. She would no longer describe herself as feminist, believing this too confrontational. She is particularly engaged in finding more playful ways to be in organizations, even when dealing with 'serious' issues such as gender and inequality.

She now wants to progress further, but does not feel like her image of successful women, who she thinks concede too readily to the male-dominated world. She might have to cover up her knowledge about women's devalued social position and put on a persona, a false self – and this she is reluctant to do. She is wondering how to reconcile these different aspirations.

I SHOULD NOT REALLY FEEL GRATEFUL

Ruth reported that many recent colleagues in different settings have encouraged her to worry less about her identity and accept-ability. Of one group she says: they 'could never understand what all the fuss was about and why on earth I couldn't just be myself'. These people have restored her faith in human nature through their acceptance of her. She has also taken personal risks to relax her previous guard with them, and benefited. She is suspicious, however, of feeling 'grateful' as a lesbian for being accepted, believing that this arises from her experiences and consciousness of being marginal. (Perhaps also her political appreciations of lesbianism cannot be easily accommodated within a more human-istic approach which respects her sexuality as a personal choice: see Kitzinger, 1987.)

262 Fighting for legitimacy

REFLECTIONS

It may not seem as easy to enter Ruth's world as some others portrayed in this book, especially in this cryptic account. Her voice was more raw than many in this volume because it spoke of social injustices which are not often openly acknowledged. The experiences of lesbian managers are seldom discussed (see Hall, 1989, for a notable exception). The organizations which are apparently willing to accept them undisguised are often experimenting with forms to live out their values, but have few models to draw on. Lesbians may encounter difficulties and become vulnerable. But Ruth's appreciation of the world is validated in her own experience and that of many other lesbians, and so deserves respect.

This story has two faces. It draws attention to political issues, showing what can happen to lesbians, feminists and women as social groups. It is also a personal account of one woman's attempt to create a viable identity as a manager while she maintains a stark awareness of this context. This world is not an established part of the management literature, even that about women. And yet it is woven into the backcloth of organizations and so, in some way, frames the experiences of many people.

Being forced or pressured to leave

The stories of: Pamela and Julia

These two stories are very different in many ways, but share an organizational dynamic. The women were forced or placed under intense pressure to leave by new top managers because they (the women) were members of the old regime. Both had already planned to move on, but wanted to do so in their own time.

Three other research participants were also forced or placed under pressure to leave – Patricia, Margaret and Ruth. Their stories were told earlier because they aligned thematically with other issues.

Pamela

OVERVIEW

Pamela did not set out to have a career. She worked to earn money to keep herself and her family. She chose jobs she enjoyed and her talents were recognized, opening up career opportunities. Her working life has been full of movement and achievement. She particularly liked the challenge of improving company fortunes in times of economic recession. About six years before we met she had moved to the service sector organization in which she had flourished. She had been its chief executive, and had developed the business and greatly increased its profitability.

Pamela was also very involved with her family and with an enterprise they run jointly. She had planned to leave her job in a few years' time – when she would no longer need the income – in order to enjoy other aspects of her life more fully. But organizational events overtook her.

Acrimonious buyouts and manoeuvrings left Pamela in a precarious position. Her company's future was threatened. Her new bosses seemed likely to remove her, she was too associated with the old management regime, and they were also unwilling to accept a woman with her own public image in a senior position. Her business sense and expertise were valued to the end, but she was forced to leave. She wanted to turn to her family and other interests, but expected to rejoin employment at some time for financial reasons.

BACKGROUND AND EARLY CAREER

Pamela left school without completing her final-year courses, although she was judged 'quite clever' (scoring 149 on Mensa intelligence tests), and expected to gain a place at Oxford University. She left because she was upset that a boyfriend left her for another pupil, and because of the quantity of work in the subject combination she had chosen. Pamela does not regret this choice. She takes pride in having achieved what she has without much starting help. Her grandfather, her hero, had his own business and was the only one to understand her decision. He took her in, and she worked for him for five years, gaining a wide range of secretarial, accounting and business skills.

Pamela married, moved away and had a child. She intended never to work again, following the 'long tradition' of women in her family. She had 'no ambitions or desires'. But she and her husband were short of money, and she found living on a housing estate lonely and boring. She took a part-time commission sales job, and was very successful. When the zone sales manager left she recommended Pamela as her replacement. The job paid well, provided a company car and its flexible hours fitted in with family responsibilities. Pamela enjoyed it and did well.

Pamela was head-hunted to a rival organization. She realized later that she had moved 'down market'; having started with the leader in that field, and thought this a mistake. She worked for various companies in similar jobs, but did not regain the organizational calibre of her first such employer. She decided to change direction and in the early 1970s found a job in the service industry within which she was to continue. It was largely female-dominated, so she did not have to prove herself in male-dominated cultures – 'it wasn't difficult to get on'.

Opportunities had occasionally been limited because she was a woman. In one company only men were allowed to deal directly with clients; these roles received the commission. In another the female company owner would not appoint another woman to the board, halting Pamela's progression. But Pamela had been relatively unaware of, and unconcerned about, gender issues. When faced with potential obstacles, she found other routes. Taking part in the research made her wonder whether being a woman had been more influential than she realized, but she saw no reasons to revise her attitude significantly. Also, in this female-dominated field, she had encountered some powerful women whose management practices were aggressive, manipulative or ethically dubious, and so she did not hold idealized images of women in business.

Pamela moved organization several times, seeking more money

and job challenges, and progressed steadily in management status. Many of her posts were starting up or revitalizing branch offices. She recounted repeated tales of success. Pamela's business area closely reflects general economic trends. She enjoyed working in difficult economic conditions because this was more of a challenge. Company statistics on performance made her achievements clear.

During this time she separated from her husband and it became more important to earn money – for basic income and to have 'quality of life'. She had also realized a childhood dream and bought a horse; this provided both a further incentive to earn and much enjoyment.

Pamela later moved to an organization with a relatively poor reputation, partly because the job was nearer home: 'I thought maybe I could make my name there'. She joined as the training manager, developing that function from scratch.

'It was good fun and interesting because I could set it up as I thought it should be and develop it the way I wanted.'

Wanting enough scope and freedom to implement ideas and demonstrate competence was a repeated theme in Pamela's story. Another was her active attitude when faced with circumstances she disliked – she either sought to improve them or moved on.

In this company, Pamela made it clear during an annual performance appraisal that she wanted to be appointed to the board. Her assessor replied that she stood no chance of doing so while she dressed as she did, and that she would have to spend more money on clothes, like some other women in the organization. Pamela resented this advice, and considered it impractical given other demands on her not excessive pay. She vowed not to change her comfortable, inexpensive style. (Only when she later joined the board and had a higher salary level did she enjoy spending more on clothes, but even then she remained relatively moderate.)

In the mid-1970s Pamela was thinking of leaving, objecting to what she saw as the owner's exploitative and manipulative management style. But the company was bought out, by a businessman who had great plans for its growth and development. She was 'very impressed and decided to stick it out'. She had an interview with the new owner, and bluntly asked what her prospects were.

'He was very patronizing. I said "I don't know you and you don't know me, but I get the impression that you're a male chauvinist", and he agreed. I said: "What future for me is there in this company?" And he said "If you're good enough I'll put you on the board."'

This he did, as a regional director, alongside another woman with whom Pamela became friends. Pamela thinks he appointed them to prove that he was not against women. She maintained this straightforward relationship with him, speaking her mind – 'everyone else used to be yes men'. She thinks she was permitted this behaviour as a woman.

'If I was a man perhaps he would have fired me, but as a woman I wasn't important enough to worry about.'

During her early years on the board, business was buoyant. But Pamela became dissatisfied. Her immediate boss had a style of putting his subordinates under pressure when he was worried, and she found this difficult. She had to work with poor business material, seeing better opportunities and rewards go to a (female) colleague. She was not feeling challenged, and was then refused a new role she requested.

'I stuck it out a bit longer, and things got more hairy and less enjoyable.'

She was considering what to do next when the group made a new acquisition, a company with considerable room for improvement, a great challenge. Pamela asked to be allowed to run it – 'and strangely they said "yes"'. It was a big job, managing far more branches than in her previous post – 'That's really where my career took off.'

A CHANCE TO PROVE HERSELF

Pamela was appointed chief executive. She knew that she had more capabilities than she had so far exercised; she just needed the opportunity to prove it.

'I think I did my best work there, and my brain expanded and I became a better person. The reason was that they let me do it.'

She had her own space and was given a free hand. The business was already profitable, and she greatly increased profitability. She attributed her success to being good at planning and at identifying the important issues, helping people re-focus and avoid potential trivia. She set in motion radical changes. She decentralized; paid staff better salaries and offered more incentives; and reformulated the corporate image. She personally selected these initiatives, and so felt highly affirmed by their success. She also said that she did well 'just to show them', because she had previously been denied chances to excel.

Pamela described her management style, learnt partly from one of her own early (male) managers; she thought it contrasted with the more aggressive way she saw many senior women operating.

'I manage by making people answer their own questions. I rarely give orders. Some people think I'm soft, but it works. People will do things because I make them talk it through. I instigate discussions, resulting in the fact that they'll take appropriate action.'

She had clear views on managing, on the importance of loyalty, honesty, treating people fairly, and on intelligence as a core prerequisite. She is very self-reliant. She has developed by working for different people and taking the best of everyone. She is highly confident in her own financial skills and organization – 'I think my advice is better than anyone else's'.

Despite her significant success, Pamela said, 'I never regarded myself as a career person'. Given her need to earn money, she took jobs she would enjoy. Her chief executive post was a delight, and its predecessors fitting preparation. Only when she joined this company, with which she still felt strongly identified, did she become 'properly hooked'.

DARK CLOUDS

But after several years, changes in the parent company began to threaten Pamela's position. The head of the company tried to take over a competitor. After several moves and counter-moves the initiative failed and he lost his position. Pamela critiqued what had happened; she felt he had been politically naive, she had seen the problems coming. His successor was far more control-oriented and politically ruthless. Pamela's company was the number one in its field. The new holding company head wanted their brand name, a close competitor, to take over this position. Pamela could not live with the prospect of deliberately moderating her own organization's fortunes to allow this to happen. She and her board could also see that they were too associated with the previous owner to survive easily. They launched a management buyout for their own organization. After protracted, aggressive, negotiations, their offer was unsuccessful, leaving them each with personal financial losses.

Pamela was effectively ensnared. She had added to her initial disfavour by attempting the buyout and thought she had also been unacceptable because she had a reputation for speaking her mind: the new top manager 'wanted someone he could boss around'. Gender played some part, but was not wholly determining; people generally were treated harshly.

> '[My immediate superior] came to see me and said he was now my boss, and he made it plain from day one that he didn't. . . want to deal with senior women in business. He liked talking about golf. He hated dogs and horses and women with families, etc. He made this very plain, whilst assuring me that they would give us every assistance to carry on.'

Pamela sought head office opinion on how she should be positioning her company. (Meetings only happened at her instigation.) She did not want to run it into the ground to satisfy their political interests. She was told: 'You just carry on as you are.'

She experienced many months of uncertainty. She felt under attack and apprehensive. She knew that she could not retain her post, but did not know how she would be treated. A fellow board member was asked secretly if he would be interested in her job. He had not been associated with the buyout initiative, so was considered a potentially loyal replacement. He told Pamela what was happening. Her company was accused by head office of gaining contracts unfairly when in competition with the other group enterprise. An investigation vindicated them.

It also seemed the group chief executive resented Pamela personally because she was well known in the business. If she received media attention she was sent 'rude letters', which implied that only he was 'allowed to be a public figure'. A rigorous internal audit was conducted of her business; later she was advised that the team had been sent to find something against her. They found nothing to criticize, congratulated her on 'running a very tight ship', but also warned her that someone did not like her.

WANTING TO LEAVE

Pamela's feelings at this time were mixed. She wanted to leave employment in a few years' time, when she would no longer need the income to pay family business loans. She also believes that senior people should not stay too long in companies and should make way for fresh ideas. But she had wanted to go at her choosing.

She was keen to be at home for various reasons. She could become involved in the family business, a riding stables. Her (second) husband works there and they enjoy doing things as a team. He is older than her and she did not want to work on and reduce their possible time together. She was already regretting how long she spent away.

'I loved the job, but I love being at home.'

'I used to hate going off in the morning knowing that [my husband] was here and doing what he likes. My daughter works here as well. My parents live here. And I'm very much a family person. If I had enough money I'd have a huge mansion with every member of my family living in it.'

Trying to summarize her feelings, Pamela said:

'So really I'm just as happy not working as working. There were lots of elements to the job. . . that I really loved. So I'm a bit mixed.'

WAITING

In Pamela's view it was not a matter of whether she would lose her job, but when and under what conditions. (She doubted whether the other directors involved would remain for long.) The months dragged on and she felt under a great deal of pressure, making her irritable at home. But she was glad that she was aware enough to know what would happen.

'I would much rather be prepared than not. I love the company and the job. It's the best job I've ever had. . . . [it] was the most prestigious job you could have in [that employment sector]. And I know I did a good job and was well respected. For it to finish like that was terrible, but to be caught on the hop would have been even worse. I might have cried and I couldn't have borne to have him see me being a woman, because he seems to despise women so much in business.'

Pamela was summoned to a meeting, and went prepared. Her boss told her he wanted her to leave and a formal offer was set before her. As she disagreed with some of its terms she was advised to see a lawyer immediately and was given until that evening to decide. Pamela did renegotiate some conditions, but was soon told, 'Either you sign now or you get nothing.' She did not feel she had much room for manoeuvre. She received a 'not ungenerous' cash settlement, but had to agree not to work in her industry again for a year. She thinks they were 'spiteful and vindictive', and has seen them treat other people similarly. In summary, Pamela said:

'So why I left was for two reasons. One, I was fired. And two, I always intended giving up as soon as I got rid of a few of the loans I've got.'

She had achieved what she wanted but 'in the wrong way and slightly at the wrong time'. She thus retained some ambivalence.

Her self-confidence had not, however, been undermined by the experience, she had not personalized it as failure. She was helped in this attitude by several factors. She was highly respected by people within and outside her company. When she was being dismissed she asked for a reason but her boss refused to give one – 'He could have said "Well we think you've done a lousy job".' But any such statement would have lacked credibility; she believed her competence was recognized, even by those who fired her. Also, she was allowed to implement ideas she had already developed.

'I had a load of new things to do, because you have to change with the times. And he made me implement every single one of them before I left. In a way that's a relief to me because if they'd thrown them all out they might have thought I was no good. But they took everything I had, so they must have thought I was good'.

(Pamela reported later that implementation of some of the ideas had been unsuccessful. She believes the originator needs to follow through change.)

ON LEAVING

Pamela was amused at the press coverage her leaving received. The company had tried to silence her, but the media were interested. She explained that she thought it was time for a change and needed to make it soon, before she reached 50. In the meantime she would spend time at home. Whatever other inter-pretations people made she wanted them to know that she 'really wanted to leave'.

Two things about the process of leaving did hurt her. One was that the other members of the board, people she had chosen and worked with, did not even send a card of acknowledgement or well-wishing. She had confided in another woman on the board who was usually the person to organize such things. There was a sense of special betrayal in her failure to do so or to contact Pamela at all. Pamela did have 'messages galore' from the rest of the staff.

Secondly, and in marked contrast to usual company practice, the memo circulated to announce her leaving was mostly devoted to praise of her successor. Mention of Pamela was cursory, which she saw as 'very insulting'. She believes in loyalty, rather than appeas-ing those in power, and paying due respect, and was hurt that she was not accorded these by her close colleagues and organization. She dislikes people making decisions for emotional and personal reasons, or acting vindictively: 'I hate people who don't run businesses like businesses.' Women are often accused of being too emotional at work, but Pamela believes this translation of emo-tional reaction into political conflict is common amongst men.

Immediately after leaving, Pamela experienced 'an enormous sense of relief' at losing the pressure of wondering what would happen to her. For six weeks she dreamt about her experiences every night, which she interpreted as sorting them out in her mind. For a few weeks she found it difficult to relax at home.

When I met her months later Pamela was thoroughly settled into her new life, and 'less inclined to think about jobs' with every passing day. She was enjoying spending time with her family, helping manage the stables, walking the dogs, having time to experiment with cooking (a new-found interest), and training at the local health club (and so losing weight).

'So I think the treatment was appalling, but at the end of the day they've done me a favour because I've never been so happy as since I've left'.

Pamela was left with some dilemmas. She was not yet able to pay off all her loans, and so might need to work again. She was 'not too worried' about her financial position; she likes taking risks and 'living slightly dangerously', and 'things have always worked out'. She had agreed not to take a related job within a year, and so had been unable to accept any of the several offers she initially received, one of which (a chief executive post) had particularly appealed to her.

She wondered what her value would be in a year's time. She was approaching 50 and so did not think that she would be welcomed in other industries, and certainly not in those which are more male-dominated because she is too outspoken. She was not keen to run a big company again; her previous organization was too special to replicate, and she did not want to move downmarket. These considerations limited her options.

One possibility was to develop a portfolio of non-executive directorships. Another was consultancy. She also wondered whether she should start up another business, to prove again that she can do so. If she needed to work for the money, she said:

'I will then do something worth doing, and that will be one in the eye for [her previous bosses]. That's the only thing that would give me any satisfaction. I rather think I won't have to bother anyway.'

Pamela also had ambitions to become more involved (unpaid) in the world of horse eventing and to bring sound management into some of its institutions. This would unite her business and personal interests, and provide activities which she could share with her husband and daughter.

I was impressed with Pamela's straightforward sense of self-confidence. She knew she had both succeeded commercially and done 'an honest job' in her company. She regretted little in her life, and thought that it had treated her well.

'I think I've been ever so lucky because everything I've really wanted I've got.'

She did feel sad about the probable fate of her former company.

She thought that those in power in the group would be happy to see it decline.

As we parted I wondered whether Pamela's comfort at home would outweigh her other potential agendas. Finances were the key determining factor. She noted that she was using her business surname less and less, perhaps a sign of a changing sense of identity.

PAMELA'S FEEDBACK ON THE DRAFT STORY

Pamela did not have 'any real criticisms' of the draft, and was surprised that her feelings about the experience had not changed much after two years. She made some additional comments to clarify points. She also said, however, that 'the overall story does not seem to depict me as I really am: i.e., I seem to come across as being very low key and a bit of a doormat'. She wondered if this was because it was a very factual telling.

I was concerned at this impression, because it did not match my feeling about Pamela, whom I had seen as active and forthright. I wondered if my attempts to compress her extensive experience and opinions had resulted in a somewhat terse style. She had told her story without much descriptive elaboration; perhaps this too had influenced my writing.

To revise the story I went through the interview transcript again, choosing some additional details to add as illustrations. Sometimes I found that I had originally incorporated the material in a more cryptic way, and so substituted the new text. I also added several quotations to give more flavour of Pamela herself speaking. Her opinion of the result was: 'it feels like me now'.

ADDENDUM

Pamela did return to employment for financial reasons. She also had other incentives. Family life brought its strains and additional expenses as well as pleasures, because of the elder care involved. She was, therefore, happy to have some outside interests.

She does not think, however, that she would have gone looking for another job. But she received many offers, big and small, and was able to pick and choose. She is now running three specialist companies in her field, one as its managing director, the others as a director through subcontracting arrangements. She has specified her own employment contracts so that she works only three days a week. She earns as much as she did in her previous full-time post. All the companies have shown outstanding results, so everyone is pleased with her. Her business life has been 'brilliant'.

She is a director for a charity and has taken on several unpaid roles in the horse eventing world. She is greatly enjoying these activities. Further job offers continue to arrive. Most she turns down, much to people's consternation. She has been approached by three companies to become a non-executive director. She was willing, but none of the boards involved could finally agree to appoint a woman. This part of her plan will have to wait.

But Pamela's home life has recently become 'terrible'. Her husband has been diagnosed as having leukaemia. This has changed their priorities. She is more ambivalent about working but their outstanding loans mean that it is still a necessity. She will also need to earn more money to pay for the many things they (he in particular) want to do – such as a cruise and flight on Concorde. She does not want to lose the long-term prospect of working as a potential diversion. But she would like to be at home more, and intends to reduce her working week to two and a half days, if possible.

Julia

OVERVIEW

Julia's story has many similarities to others in this study, but she did not decide to leave employment. Her account of the job which became untenable provides an interesting reference point. She held a senior post in public relations, geographically distant from supportive friends and family. The management team she joined was unsociable or hostile towards her. She performed well against her own professional standards, but received little affirmation within the organization. She disliked the culture of fear and rough interpersonal politicking.

Julia decided to leave, but secured another job before doing so. She does not believe in stepping out of employment without clear planning and financial security. When we met, she was feeling ambivalent. Her aspirations to progress in the organizational world remained strong, but her recent experiences had emphasized the potential stress involved. She was recuperating and weighing the different possibilities.

STARTING OUT WITH NO SUPPORT

When Julia left university in the early 1970s she received little career advice from her parents. Neither had been to university themselves; they wanted her to have 'a good education', but expected her soon to marry and have children. Her academic department also seemed unhelpful. Julia had generated her own dream, of doing postgraduate research. Unfortunately her father died just as she took her final exams so she did not obtain the grades needed to register for research, and no one spoke up for her at the examiners' meeting – which she resents. She saw only two choices: to teach or to become a secretary.

Julia regrets this unsupported start to her working life. Despite her success, it is still significant that she did not choose what she would do, that circumstances have shaped her career, and that her own volition has at times been silenced. An associated factor is having felt under pressure as a child to conform to her parents' ideal image of her, rather than being encouraged to become her own person.

'In retrospect I wish I'd had a clearer development path from earlier on.'

A CAREER BREAKTHROUGH

Julia did a postgraduate secretarial course and took a job as personal assistant to a publicity manager. Within eighteen months she became a public relations executive in her own right. Her career continued in this field, taking her into several major blue chip companies. Moves were offered to her or came through company amalgamations; she did not need actively to seek them.

FROM MARRIAGE TO INDEPENDENT PARTNERSHIP

Early on Julia was married twice, each time relatively briefly. She decided after her second marriage to concentrate on her career rather than on relationships. She later met a more suitable partner. He is older than her, is willing to be supportive and has not objected to her living elsewhere to take on job opportunities. His own career aspirations have moderated; having been made re-dundant he has taken less demanding and time-consuming jobs. Julia finds his advice helpful. Their relationship maintains each person's independence, including financially.

TAKING ON A CHALLENGE

In the late 1980s Julia was feeling dissatisfied. She had enjoyed her management role in public relations and communications for a major UK organization, but it had lost its sense of challenge. She was on the junior rungs of senior management, but saw no prospect of moving further because of political factors and the need to wait for 'dead men's shoes'. She wanted a much larger job, and contacted some job search agencies. From these contacts come an invitation to become a senior manager in corporate communications to take a substantial consumer-based organization through flotation on the London Stock Exchange. Julia could not resist. The main attraction was the value of the experience to her career profile, it was 'a plum job'.

She moved to take the position. Very soon her situation became difficult. There were several aspects to this. Most prominent in her account were personality clashes amongst senior managers and a male-dominated organizational culture.

She had been appointed by the outgoing chief executive and had expected him to be there for her first few months. In the event he stayed for only a very few weeks, leaving her somewhat abandoned. She had to work directly with the chairman, whom she found difficult, but felt that she managed this relationship satisfactorily by being professional.

The organizational culture at her level did not seem very accepting of women.

> 'I've never come across such a chauvinistic environment in my life.'

Julia was the only woman on the top management team, which consisted of directors and heads of department, she being one of the latter. She had the privileges of rank, including the right to use the executive dining room, but did not feel that she was accepted.

> 'The men didn't want to know. They're all long-serving and didn't want their cosy "club" disturbed. The only person who was halfway decent to me was a fellow countryman. . . . Basically they just couldn't cope with a woman in senior management at all.'

The culture had no place for her.

> 'There was a definite "She's a woman, she can't compete with us." You could tell when you walked into the dining room. The conversation would immediately change and be stilted for the rest of the lunch. That's why I ended up having lunch in my office. There was a fair amount of animosity. They just didn't know how to handle me at all, because they couldn't treat a

woman in a management role as they could a secretary. They knew that much, but they had no other role models to go by.'

Looking back she is 'baffled' that a woman was appointed. She wonders if she was expected to be public relations material in her own right. Unfortunately her selectors did not support her in this inhospitable climate.

Julia had not previously felt different or disadvantaged as a woman. This was not an expectation she took with her to the organization, and it therefore seems unlikely that she contributed much to the initial tensions. In response, her strategy was to be professional and not try to play politics.

'I just think in terms of the job to be done and of setting objectives and understanding what it is you're trying to do and trotting off to do it. And you use the best people, be they internal or external. . . to get the job done. . . I don't think of myself as political.'

No-one was available to negotiate politically even had she wanted to, as no one treated her as a colleague in this way. Other management team members had no expertise in corporate affairs, and the organization itself had no track record of such activity, so attempts to undermine her publicly were unsuccessful. But people tended to step back and see how she would cope, rather than engage in debates with her as an equal.

'They could see that basically I was talking some fair sense. But they weren't going to help me.'

As the company prepared for flotation, Julia had plenty of opportunities to show her expertise and value. She introduced basic public relations systems and more sophisticated processes for the launch itself. Whilst she was overtly necessary in this way she felt that she was tolerated. Once she had built up the function and the immediate pressure was removed, she became dispensable, and indifference and animosity towards her could be more freely expressed. She did not, for example, believe that a senior colleague would have shouted 'Shut up' at a man in a public meeting, as he felt free to do to her. She did not, however, think the 'personality friction and unpleasantness', which she found so wearing, were only directed at her as a woman. She saw them as common features of senior team dynamics in many organizations.

Within her own department Julia was also faced with pressures, resulting from senior management's failure to establish a viable organizational structure. The person who had previously been running a related department was still in post. She challenged this situation, but people thought any reorganization might create resentment and disruption. She was advised to manage as best she could, as he would be leaving in the foreseeable future. Julia tried to co-operate with him for a while but eventually gave up, finding her only solution in isolating him. Also, some of her staff were insufficiently skilled to manage the new level of work so she did more herself to compensate for shortages of expertise. With hindsight, she believed she should have insisted on reviewing staffing, roles and the departmental structure. But the timescales for flotation were short, given the amount to be done, and she 'took the line of least resistance'.

FEELING ISOLATED

Julia soon felt under pressure. She was isolated, with hardly anyone in the company seeming open to being friendly, and with no peer group to talk to. There were no other women at her level with whom to discuss her experiences. She was also working long hours, into the evenings, and at weekends. Her potential sources of support – her partner and mother – lived a lengthy journey away. Her social life was limited. The region she moved to seemed unfriendly, and she did not settle to life there. Julia soon became aware that the move did not suit her.

'I think I realized that I'd made a severe mistake in terms of my own personal happiness within the first month.'

As the pressure continued, Julia began to experience signs of stress. Her health was affected. She started drinking far more than she would normally. Living away from family and friends proved a strain. Dealing with the interpersonal difficulties and managing demanding tasks simultaneously and for so long was stressful and wearing. She began to feel physically sick every day she went into the office, dreading being there. She felt these were unacceptable costs.

After a year she decided that she had achieved a lot for her function, but that she should leave. She had initially imagined staying two or three years, but it was not worth the struggle.

'I'd had enough, and wasn't happy. I wasn't going to fit in the environment. I'd actually done quite well by my own professional standards, but it was such an organization that you were basically lining yourself up to be hit with a big stick every day, no matter what you did.'

This atmosphere of potential punishment and fear was not only a feature of senior management, but affected the whole organization.

'It was like living in the middle of an inquisition. It was all going on underneath, not on the surface. And you could tell the way middle management wandered around hunched over – they were frightened. It was fear throughout the place, and it was pervasive.'

Julia did not believe in jumping out of employment. She did not want to rely on anyone else financially, and had not done so since she was dependent on her father: 'It wouldn't seem morally right. There's only me to look after me.' She cited a female friend who left her job with no immediate career plans as a salutary example. This person was then unemployed and lacked confidence to go to job interviews. Julia preferred to have more control. Any move, she said, should be done in a planned fashion, not as an emotional response. She felt it was necessary to 'stick it out' in a difficult situation, and thought that many men would adopt a similar approach.

Julia said she would have moved out of management had she had enough money to do so. But in deciding what to do next, re-establishing her personal and professional self-confidence seemed her main concerns. She contacted several agencies, signalling her desire to move. Ironically her post did provide the additional credentials she had hoped for. She soon received encouraging replies.

BEING BOUNCED AROUND

The political climate of her organization had deteriorated for Julia, and several other senior managers, when a new chief executive was appointed, nearly a year after she had joined.

'His view was that the way to manage a company was to create fear and have people bounce around.'

Having been in the organization for only a few months, he decided to remove six senior managers, including Julia. She was, by then, already looking for a new post.

'The new chief executive. . . decided that my face didn't fit. . . . Forget job descriptions and objectives and measuring any of that. He didn't like me in the role. He liked me, but not in the role. He told me that.'

The chief executive invited Julia to a meeting, at very short notice. He asked her to stand aside and let someone else take over her position. She felt that at first she did not cope particularly well with this situation; she decided not to respond and stayed quiet about the matter for several weeks. At this point her one internal ally was helpful (he was also being forced to leave). He advised Julia that the chief executive's behaviour amounted to constructive dismissal, which she could fight, should she want to. He suggested that she point this out to the personnel director and agree suitable terms on which to leave. Julia especially valued this advice because she would not have thought of such tactics herself. (The male managers involved were told to leave in similar ways, and negotiated financial deals commensurate with their seniority.)

Her suggestion that she be paid to leave and not make a fuss was accepted. She and the company agreed that the overt reason would be her wish to return home for domestic reasons. She stayed to see the organization successfully through its first annual general meeting. The chairman instigated a special farewell lunch for her. Some people were, by then, sorry to see her go. The public messages were positive and friendly: 'but politically it was very nasty'.

Julia noted with interest that her successor, a man and older than her, who might therefore have been expected to fit the organizational culture more readily, was said by her informants to be having a worse time than she had done.

FINDING ANOTHER POST

Julia had little trouble finding another job. She continued in public relations. Her new position was a sideways move, but another 'plum job' in the corporate affairs world. The company culture was more positive, 'very pleasant': 'you're not worked into the ground, although you're expected to work hard'. There were also a few other women at her level; this indicated the openness of the culture, but did not mean they were instant allies. The potential of her role, and forthcoming organizational developments, meant that she foresaw plenty of opportunities for interest.

Julia had been determined to find another post as soon as possible, and so chose one of two immediately available. She felt she had to accept, given the high salary and benefits offered. It was also important to her self-confidence not to wait. She would have liked more time off work before taking up her new appointment, but the company insisted that she join them after only two months' leave. She was still exhausted for her first two months in post. Her previous job had 'knocked the stuffing out of [her] workwise'. The experience had also undermined her confidence. She thought that many senior jobs are like this.

Only in retrospect did Julia believe that the new chief executive's behaviour was not directed at her personally. He wanted to appoint his own team, to build his own power-base.

> 'I suddenly sat up one day and realized "It had nothing to do with me at all. I was the wrong face at the wrong time and it was political".'

POSSIBLE FUTURES

Julia reviewed her visions of possible futures. Her debates about what she would like to do showed conflicts between different types of ambition. Despite her reservations about senior corporate life, it seemed she was preparing herself to pursue this path, in time. One tentative dream, which Julia never felt she had the chance to think through, was

> 'At some stage, to take a year or two off to just enjoy myself. I'd love to do a lot more travelling. . . . I'd like to better my golf and get fitter generally and relax. But then after a while I'd want to do something that in some ways gives back. Probably to do with the environment. . . . work. . . but on an unpaid basis. . . . I want to look back and think I've contributed somehow to the development of society.'

But this possibility was not one she dwelt on at any length. As she needed to earn a living, it was not realistic to dream. Instead she debated the complex and conflicting issues, which she expected men face too, about whether she wanted to progress further in management and what the costs of doing so would be.

Her recent experiences had given her a harsh view of senior management. She debated whether it was appropriate to generalize from this example. She thought that the hostile culture, of 'jostling for topdog position', might be more common than she had realized. Her image of leadership had become 'a little bit seedy'. She suspected that people she respects are too 'nice' to be promoted further and that only those who are 'ruthless' reach top positions. These characteristics do not fit her self-image.

'You begin to think, "If this is how the big boys play, do I really want to be a big girl and join them?"'

She also believed that 'only a very few people have the real power'. So far Julia had trusted in merit as the key to success, and thought that she 'could play just as well as the boys'. She now wondered whether this strategy was sufficiently powerful in the type of management culture she had experienced. Weighing all these factors, she was not sure if the rewards of advancement would actually be worth it.

One possible answer was to be satisfied with her achievements, with the increased competence that more experience had brought, and with the prospect that she could take early retirement due to anticipatory pension planning. This answer fitted with asking herself questions about her quality of life as she came to middle age. She did not think she could 'yet' choose a less stressful life by taking a job with less pay. This would be 'compromise', and although she described herself as 'lazy', she would get bored. She also recognized her own ambition, driven by 'the need to be one of the best'. Viewing herself against her own peer group of women friends she was highly successful.

Julia felt she should rest on her laurels before making up her mind. She was still 'pretty bruised round the edges'. But there was a contradictory voice on this issue: 'The fact that I'm getting bored is a healthy sign.' She might be ready to take on new job challenges and she also had an ideal image for this possible path.

'If I decide to go up to the next level, I'll tell you what I'll be looking for. It's a few years away yet. I'm looking for a small company, industry irrelevant as long as it's not immoral or environmentally unfriendly, who think they might well be

going to the Stock Exchange for flotation within a two to three
year period. . . and who actually need a perfect communications
director.'

From this experience she could make money (via stock options),
and retire early. She was already mentioning this objective to
people who might know suitable organizations, 'keeping options
open'. Despite all her hesitations about the nature of top management, she also admitted: 'If I was offered the job tomorrow, I
would take it.' Her willingness to move company is one strategy
for surviving as a senior woman manager and not becoming
blocked by limited opportunities or sexist attitudes.

From the attention she gave different possibilities, Julia seemed
willing to take on a more senior position within the next few years.
No other options had presented themselves sufficiently robustly
to her. She noted her mild annoyance that when she consulted a
careers advisory service a few years previously she had been told
she was in the right job. She had been hoping to discover an
unexpected talent. It also seemed that Julia was not allowing
herself space to let other life choices emerge, although she did, at
one point, say she would like a break to 'find out what other things
are important'.

As she weighed quality of life, becoming older and the rewards
of work, Julia felt clear that she had little choice.

'You take all these things together and wonder where you're
going and what you're doing and why you are putting yourself
out. And when you have the financial and prestige rewards, or
a reasonable dose of them, why carry on beyond that? And
that's what's been in my mind. I know I have to go on working.
If I could I would definitely stop and do other things, but I need
to work for financial reasons. . . . It's also nice to give yourself
prestige, but I think you can take yourself out of that loop
because you're older and have achieved. . . . '

The balance of Julia's lifestyle supported her career involvement. She had little energy for socializing: her work role involved
too much of this. Nonetheless, her network of friends, mostly
female, were an important feature of her life. With one woman
friend she had developed a possible plan for their old age. As both
are childless and self-reliant, when they reach their sixties they
will buy a rambling house somewhere, and run it as a limited

company with staff to look after them. They will allow other people in on a fee-paying basis.

'MOST OF THE TIME I WASN'T ENTIRELY HAPPY'

Given her obvious career commitment, I was surprised, towards the end of our conversation, that Julia described her working life as not especially meaningful. Because of the products she had worked with she did not feel that she was 'making a contribution to the overall prosperity and well-being of the community'. Only one early job was highly satisfying, although she had enjoyed running departments and helping teams work well together.

> 'I've never had a job where I could say 90 per cent I love this, this is me. It's usually been 50/50.'

> 'There have been good spells, but most of the time I wasn't entirely happy. It just didn't fulfil something somewhere and I'm not sure what it is. If you expect to get it all from one source, such as work, you're always going to be disappointed.'

This background dissatisfaction was partly because she was never sure she wanted to stay in her discipline, but did not find it easy to move out. Also she would like to be able to create something and say it is hers.

IN REFLECTION

By the end of our conversation I felt both clear and unsure about Julia's motives. She was committed to employment, but hinted that other interests might develop if she gave herself space. She was maintaining sufficient control over her life not to let this happen, for the time being. It was interesting, therefore, that she shared questions about quality of life and disillusion with the nature of senior management with other research participants.

Julia seemed poised to pursue further management success. She was motivated by prestige, proving her talents and the need to maintain a satisfactory income.

JULIA'S FEEDBACK ON THE DRAFT STORY

Julia made some minor alterations to the draft. She also responded to questions about her motivations. She affirmed that financial security is important 'to pay for a mortgage, pensions and savings', and to maintain a desirable lifestyle. Even if the option were available she would find it 'very difficult' to rely on someone else economically. Maintaining control and being responsible for herself are core life attitudes, developed during childhood.

ADDENDUM

Julia's company move has been successful. She is respected and valued. She is 'much more phlegmatic' about big company politics – although still not political enough herself – and probably therefore more resilient. She has done well, although not well enough by her own standards. She would like to take the next step into 'the top quartile' in her field – and have the resulting prestige. This would provide a sense of belonging in her own right, and avoid any implication that she is the 'little woman', a stereotype she strongly resents. However, she recognizes that she has secured a worthwhile role, and is not planning to seek another.

Julia is not sure whether her motivations match her aspirations. Only if a job really takes her imagination will the drive slip into place and the 'big stresses' seem worthwhile. She maintains her image of unpaid, environmentally contributing work as a possibility, perhaps part-time and related to early retirement.

Domestically she is much more settled. Her partner's involvement in employment has decreased again, and Julia is the main breadwinner. She has a much nicer home, and more time for leisure.

As a postscript, Julia reported her impressions of young women she has recently mentored. They want careers, marriages, children and comfortable lives. In her view they lack the vital quality of endurance, and despite their talents and more focused initial expectations, she doubts any will really 'go places'. She imagines that in middle age they too will feel frustrated, and wonders if this is just a natural part of maturing.

Collecting together strands

Decision-making, moving on and next steps

The purpose of this chapter is to review the study's data on why women leave or contemplate leaving management jobs and what happens to them next.

The sixteen stories do not reveal a short, coherent list of reasons for leaving or a similar dynamic form in people's decision processes. I am aware, above all, of their diversity. This is a key conclusion of the study. Whilst it is possible to suggest shared themes, each decision is individual and multi-stranded; some are complexly so. Looking for simple summaries of why women leave organizations is futile and inappropriate.

The stories of people who stayed in employment or were forced to leave show many similarities to those of people who left with more sense of choice. This suggests that these are not discrete groups, and that the experiences of organizational life described in this book may be more widely shared. Leaving is one of a range of possible responses.

DECISION PROCESSES

The stories show a range of decision processes. A commitment to leave often emerged from an accumulation of dissatisfactions, pressures and/or other life aspirations. Sometimes one final trigger crystallized the person's growing resolve, for example when a critical incident made them realize how constrained or stressed they felt (especially Judith, Teresa and Stevie). In other cases the decision was made more gradually. Some people prepared other activities to move to. Some were reluctant to leave despite the difficulties of their situations, staying out of a sense of commitment to the organization, a change initiative or because of people who might be unprotected should they go. Once they had decided to leave, some people became relaxed about time-scales. Six stayed to see through organizational changes as 'leaving presents'. For Julia and Judith it was very important to their self-esteem to secure other jobs before moving.

Several married women made the decision to leave largely alone, consulting their husbands only briefly or presenting them with formed decisions.

A MATTER OF CHOICE?

Whether leaving was a free choice is not a straightforward classification. In many cases a combination of factors blurs whose initiative it was, and in whose interest. Pamela and Patricia were actually dismissed, although Pamela had wanted to go in her own time. Julia was pressured to leave, but was already very unhappy and planning to move. Ruth was encouraged to leave, but also took action to ensure she escaped an intolerable situation. Margaret was strongly invited to take early retirement, but thinks that the company did her a favour.

In other cases, there is both a sense of choice – of willingness to take radical decisions and risks – and a sense of necessity. Even many of those who apparently more freely chose to move at that time felt that their organizational lives had become highly un-satisfactory, stressful or untenable in some way, and so felt an urgent need to leave. Jane's decision was forged during such an experience. Mercedes was close to defining her job as un-tenable, but found a way to live with the situation, at least temporarily.

REASONS FOR WANTING TO LEAVE

Most people gave several reasons for wanting to move. Summar-izing these in Table 7, and allowing multiple counting, shows the variety involved. Table 7 incorporates the views of all sixteen women, as those who stayed in employment (Mercedes, Julia and Judith) and those who were forced or encouraged to leave (Patricia, Pamela, Julia, Margaret and Ruth) held opinions closely similar to the rest of the group. (Table 7 provides a guide to which themes appear in which stories.) Only two women in this study left for family-associated reasons: Sarah to achieve a better balance

Table 7 Reasons *given* for wanting to leave

Did not leave: employment	Julia, Judith
that job	Mercedes
Forced or encouraged to leave	Patricia, Pamela, Julia, Margaret, Ruth

Organizational cultures

Dynamics of male-dominated cultures	Julia, Judith, Jane, Stevie, Kathy, Kim, Mercedes, Teresa, Patricia, Margaret
Repressive organizational situation	Christina
Hostile organizational culture	Ruth

Job became untenable or lacked opportunities

Change agent roles became untenable	Patricia, Dorothy, Judith, Teresa
Narrowed organizational opportunities	Pamela, Kathy
Job had become unrewarding	Margaret, Kim
Having achieved what they could in role	Christina

Organizational conflicts and lack of recognition

Difficult relationship with boss/senior colleagues	Judith, Mercedes, Teresa, Jane
Forced out by new CE or chairman	Pamela, Julia
Feeling unappreciated	Margaret, Kim
Blocked promotion prospects	Mercedes, Stevie

Stress and tiredness

Stress	Christina, Julia, Judith, Teresa, Kathy, Claire
Difficultly maintaining viable sense of self	Judith, Ruth, Kathy, Dorothy, Teresa
Wanting to stop/ have space	Sarah, Claire, Kathy, Stevie, Jane
Wanting a different lifestyle	Pamela, Jane, Christina, Kathy, Claire
Illness contributed to decision-making	Margaret, Ruth, Jane, Kim
Excessive tiredness	Kathy, Claire, Teresa
Unbalanced/overloaded life	Sarah
Ageing and losing vitality for work	Kim

Identity development factors

Incongruity of inner and outer images	Kathy, Claire, Margaret
Not liking what they had become	Stevie, Teresa
Wanting to explore other aspects of identity	Kathy, Christina
Major life change	Christina

Fostering relationships

Wanting more time with husband and family	Pamela, Sarah
Move suited husband's career as well	Dorothy
Time running out to have children	Claire

between home and work lives and Claire (partly) because time was running out for her to have children. This research therefore contradicts a common stereotype of women's reasons for leaving employment. Instead, dominant themes in the decision-making are leaving 'male-dominated' organizational cultures (which were associated with tense relationships, isolation and stress), seeking new lifestyles with more balance and sense of personal energy, and moving out of roles which had become impossible or demotivating. These women were not, as a group, highly concerned about financial security.

This is not a full or enduring array of possible factors. It does not acknowledge issues of race or elder-care, for example. Also, in this study, the dynamics of tokenism seem to be operating at senior management team and board levels (see 'Organizational cultures', p. 300); this is perhaps a generational phenomenon which will decline.

NO LONGER FEELING DRIVEN

Leaving was sometimes associated with the lessening of a driving force which had previously significantly shaped a person's life. This shift in emphasis took different forms. Most common were no longer feeling driven to prove themselves, being satisfied that they had established their competence, and no longer wanting to give up so many other aspects of their lives for employment (although doing so had been acceptable earlier). These themes are associated with midlife reviews in which the women took more control over how and why they worked, and what they considered worthwhile. The organizational world had previously been a significant value system for some. Several talked about no longer using its markers, such as salary, as measures of self-worth. They now felt more independent; their motivations were more internal.

AMBITIONS

A few people were still clearly achievement-oriented when we first met. Mercedes wanted to become a director, Stevie to establish a business, Julia to 'be one of the best' and Pamela to prove to her previous bosses that she could develop a successful business again. (Is it significant here, I wonder, that both Mercedes and Julia judge themselves in relation to peer groups of successful women?)

For others, 'ambition' was taking different forms, such as seeking positions of influence.

WHAT DID LEAVING MEAN IN THEIR LIVES?

As I worked with each story I developed a sense of what leaving might mean in that person's life progression. These are impressionistic assessments only. Some people were acting from a feeling of major change, a deliberate opening to new *life* possibilities (Jane, Christina, Claire, Kathy and Stevie). All reported relaxation, satisfaction and continuing self-development immediately following their moves. Some people's ways of seeing their world or acting effectively in it would not hold together any more (Dorothy, Judith, Ruth, Kim, Sarah and Teresa). Moving on meant accepting this situation and opening up space for change to occur. They varied in their immediate satisfaction with the consequences. Mercedes' situation was similar, but she made adjustments in attitude to obviate the need to move immediately. Some people were not seeking change but later took the opportunities it presented, varying in how radically they changed their lives (Margaret, Julia, Patricia and Pamela). There is a sense of significant development in many people's lives.

LEAVING AS A MORE WIDESPREAD PATTERN

This group of research participants may be especially willing to be leavers and joiners. Some have moved on before, in employment and personal relationships. Kim and Christina, for example, had significantly redirected their careers. Three women left marriages at about the same time as they made the job moves explored in detail here. A further seven are not now with their initial partners.

THE LEAVING PROCESS

People varied in how much they told others about why they were leaving. A few disguised their reasons, a few told a full version of the truth; many were in between, giving simplified accounts which they thought would be understood but not too confronting. This finding may help to explain why other organizational members are often later somehow unclear about why women managers have left.

Several people enjoyed their leave-taking. It was a time of mutual recognition: they gave special messages to their allies and friends; either they or the organization provided celebrations; and they were pleased – if sometimes surprised – that people were sorry to see them go. Other people had tainted memories. Two had been hurried out of the building, at short notice. (Pamela felt some satisfaction at anticipating this situation.) A few people had felt unrecognized and unappreciated – their leaving ceremonies had been low-key, perfunctory affairs.

Financially, six women felt that they had achieved good terms on which to leave. Two did so through redundancy and early retirement schemes. The others negotiated, three with more than a hint of threat that they should be well compensated for poor treatment. Achieving satisfactory conditions for leaving contributed to their feelings of self-worth about the move.

NEXT STEPS

In this sample, three people did not leave employment even temporarily: Mercedes stayed in her post and later moved for promotion, Julia moved to another full-time job, and Judith found a career-developing part-time post.

In other people's stories there is a mixture of next steps and timescales. These trajectories are not easy to summarize. They show a great deal of both variety and movement.

Many people next rested, giving themselves time to recuperate and regain a sense of vitality. Another woman leaver I met called this process re-membering: collecting herself back together. Some people mentioned the release of energy they had experienced on leaving. Stevie and Christina talked about becoming the people they had once been and about their delight at finding that this sense of enjoyment in life was still possible.

In contrast, some people felt very exhausted immediately afterwards. They had not resolved their sense of pressure prior to leaving and so had 'unfinished business'. (Julia and Teresa also soon went into other jobs, limiting their time to rest.)

Many enjoyed the opportunities they had to reconnect with home, family, relaxation or leisure activities, and vowed to build these more prominently into revised – healthier and more balanced – lifestyles in the future. Some people travelled. Some pursued training or academic study related to new career directions. At least three have been involved in personal growth work, partly reviewing their previous life experiences.

At different speeds most people moved back towards employment or towards self-employment in some form. Only two of those who left felt immediately under pressure to find work again. Teresa needed to for financial reasons. (But her new post proved unsatisfactory; within two years she had moved again.)

Several people received offers of consultancy or employment. Three (Patricia, Christina and Pamela) were invited or head-hunted into managing director or chief executive positions. (Two years further on two had left these posts to work independently.) Dorothy and Margaret initially looked for mundane jobs, as planned. They soon became involved in demanding, satisfying work again and were promoted. Sarah took part-time work to fit with her family. Stevie set up a company with a partner. (Becoming entrepreneurs is a common route for women wishing to place employment on a different footing in their lives: Still, 1993.)

Many women have combined satisfying developments in their lives generally with enjoyment and success in employment terms. Others have found the transitions more difficult and stressful. Some people are now very busy again, returning to lifestyle patterns they had hoped to change.

A RECENT UPDATE

By the time I contacted people for feedback on their draft stories, most were either in employment or self-employed (see Table 8).

Table 8 Research participants' life situations at the close of research

Consultants	Kim, Patricia, Kathy, Teresa
Directors	Dorothy, Mercedes
Senior managers	Julia, Margaret
Managing director (and other roles)	Pamela
Non-executive director and public speaker	Christina
Academic and trainer	Judith
Middle manager	Ruth
Parent at home	Claire
Part-time employment and consultancy	Sarah
Entrepreneur	Stevie
Setting up own business	Jane

Although most of those who had left appeared to have 'returned' to employment, this is a superficial evaluation. Many had very different perceptions of their working lives. Pamela, Christina and Kim, for example, were pleased that they were earning either as much or more than they had previously for working less busily. They were enjoying the discretion to spend time on unpaid organizational activities of their choice, on their own development and with family and friends. Many people held similarly revised perspectives. For example, work was both immensely satisfying and less important in Margaret's life, and Ruth was enjoying more sense of play and experimentation. Several people emphasized that they were being true to themselves, doing things for themselves or putting themselves first. Many seemed to have achieved what they said they wanted two years before. Most experienced more alignment of energy and activity than they had in the jobs they left several years ago. Some were achieving this sense of congruence within organizations.

Several noted that they had been or were repeating some patterns of behaviour they had hoped to escape, such as overworking and taking on too much responsibility for others.

Few people now needed to achieve a daily fit with cultures they found inhospitable or to rely on organizations to promote them. Whilst there were exceptions, many people had moved to positions of more choice. Their lives were on different terms, ones over which they felt they had more discretion. Most were both involved with organizations and enjoying the influence they had, and not wholly committed to employment. Participants at a research workshop explored these issues and seeming contradictions. They would not necessarily choose to be employed, but as they were they would do their jobs with commitment and seeking to promote necessary organizational change. They also thought it important to be able, and willing, to judge situations that are not amenable to influence, and then exit.

This material suggests that people had paused in their careers and placed them on different, and varied, footings. There are echoes here of what had happened to Hennig and Jardim's (1978) 'successful' women managers, although this book's research participants seem to have a broader array of notions of 'success', grounded in life as much as career concerns.

A FURTHER INSTALMENT?

I contacted people to approve the proposed final drafts of their accounts only a few months after the 'updates' summarized above. The tone of several people's comments about their jobs or lives had subtly moved on yet again. It was interesting to see how much their life stories were evolving, shifting, changing. I have chosen not to present any of this material. Whilst some of its themes seem enticing, it also seems especially ephemeral given the brevity of our conversations. Also, it is time to move on in my own life, by completing this book.

Working in 'male-dominated' organizational cultures

COMMON CONCERNS

I shall now explore the dissatisfactions and pressures eleven of the sixteen research participants reported about working in what they termed 'male-dominated cultures'. Those involved are: Kathy, Claire, Jane, Teresa, Judith, Patricia, Mercedes, Stevie, Kim, Margaret and Julia. These experiences were central in making their working lives demanding and in prompting them to leave. This finding is consistent with those of quantitative studies. For example, lack of promotion opportunities, organizational politics and male-dominated corporate cultures are identified as primary reasons for women leaving organizations in Rosin and Korabik (1991) and Stroh and Senner (1994). It seems likely that similar issues were faced at times by Sarah, Dorothy and Christina, but were not used as major explanatory themes in their stories. Pamela and Ruth described their working environments as female-dominated, these could also hold their tensions.

Labelling cultural patterns as 'male-dominated' is contentious and risks unhelpful stereotyping. I have chosen to persist in doing so here, however. It is faithful to the women's stories. It also expresses undisguised *a* (not *the*) current 'truth' about senior organizational life, in order to make this available for review and development (see 'Reflecting', pp. 330–1).

Working in 'male-dominated cultures' affected most aspects of the eleven women's working lives, often rendering their organizational environments hostile. Many of the themes covered in other sections – such as tiredness, relationships with other women and isolation – take their shape largely as a result.

The issues explored below were discussed at great length and with relatively widespread consistency. The qualities of what 'male-dominated' meant are, however, different in nature and severity of impact in different stories. The accounts of Jane, Teresa, Julia, Judith, Mercedes and Stevie show more extreme examples. What follows is an amalgamated picture of the issues raised. The phenomena described are more often collective, group, processes. The women's relationships with men individually could be very different. Some subsections also portray people's contrasting experiences as appropriate. My discussions with other women during the course of the research frequently confirmed the picture below as recognizable and a matter for concern.

AGGRESSION AND ISOLATION

Most of the managers had become more aware of organizations as 'male-dominated' when they entered senior management. By this they meant descriptively that there were few women at these levels, but also that interactions tended to fit negative stereotypes of men's behaviour and that there was considerable evidence of men banding together in reacting to individual women.

Interpersonal behaviour at senior levels was described as often very aggressive, rude, territorial, status-conscious and hostile, with conflict, power struggles and politicking as common features. Research participants (variously) disliked the atmosphere of potential punishment and fear, 'the rough play of big boys', the 'hostile environment' and people running businesses on emotions and vindictiveness. They were shocked at these ways of operating, and thought them ineffective and energy-wasting. Some women were disappointed that senior managers seemed inadequate, ordinary men in big jobs, or childish (acting like young teenage boys). These disillusioning and rather seedy images had undermined some women's aspirations to progress further.

In these environments the women often felt isolated, excluded and/or placed under attack. Several research participants seemed different in too many ways to their colleagues (for example being a woman *and* nurse, or in personnel, a woman, young *and* from head office) to build strong relationships. Most were pioneers for women in their organizations. Male bosses and colleagues therefore were unused to working with senior women and seemed to have no positive or suitably powerful images of women to draw on. They could not treat fellow directors or senior managers as secretaries. Teresa said that she had been the one management woman they could not recognize, because she was not 'a flirty tart, bitter spinster' and so on. Claire felt that people appreciated her as much, if not more, for her physical attractiveness as for her competence. These ambiguities about image could undermine the women's organizational status and personal confidence.

Several research participants spoke about the 'sense of kin' men seemed to maintain even when they were fighting each other. (The men involved may not have felt this kinship; but their legitimacy did not seem to be contested in the same ways that women's was.) Several women reported how entering executive dining rooms, which until their appearance had been men-only, had seemed a testing out of the culture. They felt they had interrupted 'normal life' for the men involved, and that there was no willingness to develop a culture in which they could be more equally included.

Many women were 'out of place', perhaps because they held more power than women were expected to in their organizations or because their specific expertise intimidated male colleagues. Some came to assume that they should cope alone, and were in some ways proud of their ability to do so.

Many of the issues discussed above seem to be about inclusion: about whether the women were allowed to, or could, establish operating membership of the management groups to which they had been appointed. Also at stake were their abilities to exercise power effectively, as the next sections show. 'Male-dominated' referred also to the processes by which cultural norms were actively reinforced by members of the prevailing power elite, and outsiders were repelled.

BEING TESTED OUT AND HOLDING BACK

Some women felt that men had banded together, bypassed them in communication, publicly blocked initiatives to which they had agreed in private and protected each other. Performing effectively was thus made more difficult. In a few cases sponsors or mentors had either drawn back or left the organization at this stage in the woman's career, accentuating the latter's sense of isolation. Relating to women in cultures which contained many habits of male bonding seemed a challenge for individual men, who risked becoming marginalized or suspect themselves. (As an exception Claire noted that a particular senior male manager *had* managed to favour women *without* endangering himself.) Many research participants gave the impression that most senior men kept communication with them at a relatively superficial level, that very few reached out to form relationships or to support initiatives when requested.

The women reported often being challenged and tested out; their behaviour was closely scrutinized. Some felt judged against gender stereotypes. People seemed to step back, try to trip them up or set traps, and see how (or if) they could manage without support. Sometimes issues became personalized and the manager would feel under attack. For example, Teresa described meetings she chaired as opportunities for people to 'bait' her rather than as debates. Jane was sexually harassed by her immediate boss, undermining her credibility with colleagues and subordinates.

In this climate, research participants had to take care not to offend, undermine or appear to threaten men, lest this provoke retaliation. They would sometimes hold themselves back, modify their behaviour or try to control their presentations of self. But they might then feel inauthentic (see 'Incongruity', p. 224).

Exerting power in such contexts can become a double challenge, because it potentially involves both organizational and gender dynamics. Claire explained how she had tried to realize the power in a somewhat elusive personnel role and at the same time not be seen to be threatening men (who in her experience then became defensive). The managers faced the dilemma of how 'outspoken' they could be, especially if they risked offending against gender stereotypes. How they resolved this dilemma seemed likely to affect both their further career opportunities and their satisfaction with their own self-image.

Some roles were more readily available to women. Some research participants became confidantes or counsellors to senior men. But such roles have their complications. The men involved can be wary of the women's subsequent power to make them vulnerable; the women can feel used. People may think that they are having an affair. Women who worked closely with more senior men might be seen as good assistants, not as potential leaders in their own rights.

Some participants found that strong relationships of collaboration and respect within their own departments countered the more hostile attitudes outside. Several worked with supportive and protective secretaries. Others now felt separated from people below them, losing the sense of team they had enjoyed at earlier career stages.

THIS ALL SEEMS VERY FAMILIAR

The patterns of interaction described above are very similar to the classic dynamics of tokenism portrayed in Kanter (1977). It took me some time to realize this and I did so with a sense of shock; the rawness of some of the reported encounters seems surprising, outdated.

Kanter argues that these dynamics are the result of relative number rather than gender, and are likely to occur when groups contain one or a few people who are apparently different from the dominant cultural type. These are called 'tokens' because they are seen as symbols of their social category.

Kanter identifies three core perceptual processes which tend to reinforce dynamics of difference and inequality. *Visibility* draws attention to the person(s) of token status and to their behaviour. *Contrast* effects make majority group members self-conscious because tokens appear to interrupt 'normal life'. The former may exaggerate their similarities and the enforcement of cultural norms, thus heightening supposed differences. *Assimilation* means that tokens' behaviours (which may well be ways of coping with the other processes) are judged against stereotypes – in this case of gender attributes. 'Exceptions' are treated as unusual for their social category, rather than evidence that the available array of stereotypes is inadequate. These processes pose many dilemmas of identity and effectiveness for the tokens.

The material in this book suggests that these dynamics have risen up some organizations as women pioneers have reached successively higher management levels. They are now likely to be experienced at board and senior management levels (as well as more generally, depending on organizational circumstances). This may be a generational phenomenon. It may decline as more women reach such positions. Or these organizational levels may be more resistant to incorporating different sorts of people, because cultural meaning is made at them and bonding between people of like kind, who think they can trust each other, becomes very important. These dynamics may therefore be characteristic of such levels whether or not gender differences are present. They could be enacted around other kinds of difference such as functional area, background or non-conformity to cultural norms of (alcoholic) drinking behaviour. Many research participants suspected that this was the case, but believed that they became targets for the dynamics because, as women, they were more readily identified as different.

Many of the women who found working in male-dominated cultures difficult were at first very surprised at their experiences. They had not encountered or been aware of gender discrimination in earlier posts or other companies and so felt unprepared and undefended. Their surprise suggests that these were not expectations they brought with them or initially contributed to creating. Their resulting disillusion with senior management was a major reason for leaving.

Some research participants did not initially know how to cope with the behaviour they encountered. But these are high-risk, high-visibility environments in which to learn new strategies. As they developed ways to survive and work effectively the women reported becoming tougher, more astute, better able to protect themselves. But some also regretted the hardening of self this involved. This data suggests that some people stayed in hostile environments longer than seemed healthy for them because their coping strategies became so robust.

ORGANIZATIONAL REALITY OR CHOSEN CONVENTION?

Some management writers advise women to realize that the behaviours they might describe as 'male', such as those above, are the 'rules of the game' and that they must learn to play them to be successful. This 'reality' is sometimes given the label 'organizational politics' as its legitimation. Doing so appreciates that power needs to be exercised, that different interest groups will operate. It is a persuasive argument. But is this all there is to the behaviours? Are they any more than the conventions of an elite group? And are there other processes through which such needs and interests could be expressed and reconciled? (See 'Working strategies', p. 312.)

Some of the behaviour women disliked seems to be about negotiating membership and relative power using male cultural forms of association. See, for example, Tannen's (1990) research summary on the potentially different relationship patterns amongst boys and girls at play. Using such analyses, Teresa's chief opponent could be interpreted as using aggression to test her boundaries as a step in trying to establish friendship.

Another possibility is that the dynamics reflect a backlash against women, which involves granting formal inclusion but denying it at a more fundamental level of colleagueship. If this interpretation is sometimes plausible the reaction may be conscious, awarely enacted, or an unconscious reaction to threat (Vince, 1991).

It seems likely that women and men (as social groups) are placed differently in this context. Many men may feel uncomfortable about and limited by such patterns of interaction, but they may also be more used to them and may have been socialized to judge themselves by their abilities to survive such dynamics. Cultures typically incorporate gender rules about appropriate behaviours (Mills and Murgatroyd, 1991). Men are more likely to be operating within expectations, whilst women are likely to face conflicting expectations of them as female and as managers. Also, partly through organizational status, men traditionally have more access to the social powers to interpret, name and value (Spender, 1982; Marshall, 1993a). These provide potential influence over how their behaviour is viewed by others.

If women do not want to play by these rules, what other choices do they have, especially if inclusion is being negotiated? If they adopt 'unconventional' styles their behaviour may be interpreted and responded to from within dominant cultural frames. Judith reported this happening. Similarly, Teresa's attempts to help the directors develop local human resource strategies seemed to be misunderstood. Perhaps communication styles were partly significant here. Open-ended, inquiring styles – which women use more frequently than men – can often be interpreted as weak or indecisive, and so raise anxiety for those with more immediate, solution-focused styles – more characteristic of men (Tannen, 1990).

DIVERSITY AND POTENTIAL RELATIONSHIPS

A few managers did report experiences of senior management which were different from the dominant picture above. Julia moved to a company where there was a pleasant atmosphere amongst senior managers (in a culture with more women). Christina found that diversity amongst senior men meant potential interests in common and a freer building of alliances. Many people had good relationships with individual men who were kindred spirits, allies, good colleagues or bosses, which helped create sound working relationships to counter wider cultural dynamics. For example, her one friendly peer gave Julia advice on striking a good financial settlement, and a male colleague helped Stevie feel befriended at the sauna.

CONFLICTS, BULLYING AND BEING PATRONIZED

The stories show how important relationships with senior people are, especially those with immediate superiors. Research particip-ants preferred to work with people they could respect, whose values they shared, whom they saw as competent and who did not doubt their abilities simply because they were women. They discussed their relationships with other powerful people, par-ticularly chairmen and chief executives, almost all of whom were men, in some detail. Much of the women's energy went into building relationships in which they could be both powerful and effective. They felt they were usually successful in this, despite the challenges involved. (The research workshops I held showed that this attention to relationships and deliberate development of their strategies was continuing.)

Many of these powerful people (including a few women) were reported as difficult to work with, aggressive, manipulative, and engaging in power-plays and interpersonal conflicts. Some be-haved in bullying ways to men and women alike. Several women believed that they had felt more disabled by this behaviour than their male colleagues had seemed to. Julia realized in retrospect, for example, that the attacks she thought were personal were more because her 'face didn't fit' – the new chief executive wanted to put his own team in place.

Sometimes, however, the hostility seemed to be directed at women, by men who were seen as unable to cope with female senior managers, who openly stated that women are unsuited to the business world or who preferred working with men. Several research participants felt that because they had stood out as different in the culture they had become the focus for aggressive behaviour, blame or attack. A few felt placed in especially difficult circumstances early in their time with their organizations. They were recruited by people who soon departed, leaving them feeling 'orphaned'. This put their right to position in potential doubt; their new seniors may not have chosen to work with women. Some clearly did not, and were willing to state this openly. In the cases of Julia and Teresa it is particularly puzzling that women were recruited, given the cultures' lack of readiness to accept them.

Often these underlying tensions made research participants' relationships with their superiors and colleagues difficult. Some women felt silenced, on guard or forced into positions of continual fight. One, at least, thought there were unspoken hints of sexuality involved.

An alternative pattern of interaction was more amicable on the surface, but equally undermining. Some people felt patronized by their managers. Their achievements were variously ignored, rendered invisible, devalued, belittled or marvelled at.

GENERATIVE RELATIONSHIPS

In contrast to the above picture some women talked about managers or chief executives encountered during their careers who were 'great', 'on the same wavelength', or held no prejudices against women. The research participants enjoyed working with such people, felt both at ease and stretched to perform well. Three particularly developed a sense of loyalty, which they maintained when tested by shifts in organizational power alignments. Established sound relationships could be put in jeopardy, however, if the organization was bought by another company. Three had lost their bases of credibility and power when this happened.

EXCLUSION: RECRUITING IN LIKE IMAGE

A further strand of concern in the stories was how women, and members of other social groups, can be excluded or marginalized through recruitment and career development processes. Cultures can be replicated by recruiting in the image of those with power, in this case certain types of white men. In a large-scale UK Institute of Management study the operation of the 'old boy network' was still the major factor women identified as holding back their careers (Coe, 1992).

Several organizations' career development processes had contributed to slow movement by failing to offer the women promotion, even when the latter had pushed for this. One potential consequence was that the women might then have to work for men they considered incompetent. This was especially disappointing if the former had applied for the posts themselves.

The study does also show networks of recruitment working for women, particularly after their experiences of leaving. But several cases were also reported of senior men saying 'no' to women as board members and therefore blocking appointments that other men advocated.

MEANINGS OF 'MALE-DOMINATED'

Three main meanings of 'male-dominated cultures' appear clearly in this data. Firstly, men were heavily in the majority numerically. Secondly, and most importantly, many cultures were marked by dynamics of collective and interpersonal interaction which fitted stereotyped and/or degenerative images of men's behaviour. These made the women feel excluded, under attack, less than effective, marginalized and isolated. Thirdly, some recruitment and career development practices seemed not to offer women opportunities equal to those experienced by men. Although these dynamics were common and shaped most cultures discussed, there were also organizations or departments which operated differently.

DIFFERENTIATING NOTIONS OF GENDERED CULTURES

Researchers have now begun to offer differentiated accounts of potential organizational cultural patterns which incorporate gender inequalities in some form. Maddox and Parkin (1993), for example, identify six common 'gender cultures' from their work in local government. They emphasize that these are actively created by both men and women, but typically have differential impacts. 'All women operate strategically, to combat resistance to them as women in order to be effective. Women manage gender cultures as well as their work' (p. 3). The six are:

the gentleman's club;
the barrack yard;
the locker room;

the gender-blind (based on arguments of no differences between
   women and men);
paying lip-service and the feminist pretenders (these have equal
   opportunities policies and language, but ignore them);
the smart macho

Collinson and Hearn (1994) offer a complementary analysis. They
describe five ideal-typical masculinities which shape organizational life and, they believe, 'in practice. . . are likely to overlap
and co-exist within specific processes'. These are:

authoritarianism
paternalism
entrepreneurialism
informalism
careerism

Both analyses show how cultural patterns which appear gender
neutral may still position women and men differently through
their practices of work and through incorporating management
ideals which are transforms of (male) gender stereotypes. For
example, success in a careerist culture tends to require commitment to working long hours, putting organizational needs before
other life interests and being geographically mobile. These requirements favour people with few domestic demands and interests.

The research participants generally used the label 'male-
dominated' for patterns of culture which they could identify and
'prove' clearly. They portrayed some of the more overt and harsh
expressions of potential dynamics. A few pointed to other factors
which placed them differently from men or covertly disadvantaged them. Their experiences ranged across many of the
cultural types identified above. Their stories suggest that they
have, at times, been affected by more subtle gender-typings of
cultural assumptions, such as those associated with commitment,
extensive working hours and maintaining impressions of control.

AND WHAT WERE THE RESEARCH
PARTICIPANTS DOING MEANTIME?

The chapter so far has explicated the women's experiences of
organizational cultures, concentrating on tensions and boundaries
of acceptability they faced. The fuller picture of how much
they were also achieving in their jobs should be emphasized.

The women's, often negative, views about the patterns of interactions they encountered have been noted. They were also both
actively creating themselves as managers in images they did
approve and developing strategies for managing in the environments described above.

The stories show women seeking to create viable operating
identities, which fitted their values, within organizational cultures. This was generally an active, choiceful process: they
resisted attributions they disliked, continued to revise strategies
to seek more effectiveness, and circumvented or reframed potential boundaries.

The data includes various examples of the discussions they held
with themselves about how much to accommodate to prevailing
norms and how much to risk being overtly different. Often they
pushed against cultural constraints – either deliberately or unawarely – and lived with the consequences. Sometimes they were
able to reframe difficult situations: for example Christina enhanced her internal credibility by developing a public image.
Sometimes roles they attempted were rejected, or there were limits
to the cultural redefinition they were individually able to achieve.
Stevie could not change her management potential rating, for
example. But people typically and repeatedly sought alternatives
if they found one approach limited. Teresa is a particularly
persistent example. Margaret showed determination in creating
her career despite lack of encouragement. Thus even when
'adapting' might be an appropriate label for their behaviour, this
was not a passive acceptance, but an active managing of self to be
effective, realize the potential power in a given role and survive.

This is demanding work and can be personally costly. It caused
stress and tiredness, and some people felt they had become less
than themselves in the process (see 'Incongruity' and 'Tiredness',
pp. 224, 250). One choice is to leave.

In the workshops people seemed to feel better able than
previously to shape organizational cultures; as a group they had
become less dependent on organizational systems for acceptance.
They exchanged stories about ingenious ways of operating which
anticipated and circumvented some of the cultural dynamics they
thought ineffective or unfair. They also recognized that there are
limits, that not all situations can be changed.

I shall next map the women's general working strategies in
more detail.

Working strategies

I shall now briefly review the working strategies research participants talked about adopting. At issue throughout is the extent to which their styles were adaptive to current cultures, the result of limited available options or active choices to which they were committed even if these might set them apart in the organizational contexts they inhabited. There is some evidence for all these possible interpretations, with (as I indicated in 'Organizational cultures') an emphasis on feeling a sense of choice within a context of potential constraints.

The approaches reported are not mutually exclusive. Most people seemed to use a range; some had changed their styles significantly during their careers.

PROFESSIONALISM AND EFFECTIVENESS

The dominant preferred working strategy was that of professional competence twinned with concern about organizational effectiveness. Most research participants believed in doing their jobs well in these terms. This framework allowed them to judge, and accredit, their own performance even when no one else was affirming them.

Their maintenance of a professional stance could mean that the women were perceived by colleagues as 'cold'. Margaret, Teresa and Julia believed that this was the case. This designation may indicate, simply, that they were contradicting stereotypes of nurturing female behaviour. It could also mean that some colleagues were genuinely puzzled about how to build relationships with them. Several people who adopted this approach also seemed vulnerable to personalizing difficulties, either as attacks or as reflections on their competence. This was draining and contributed to their tiredness.

Some commentators would question whether the women are overemphasizing the value of competence in establishing organizational inclusion and credibility. Others might wonder if expertise was a power-base to which they had access whilst others were effectively denied them. This working strategy was, however, seen as a matter of choice and conviction by the women concerned.

BEING BLUNT AND HONEST

Over half the women liked to be honest, straightforward and possibly 'blunt' in their communications. They thought this effective, sometimes a matter of living up to one's values, and likely to contribute to a healthy working culture, despite being challenging. Some had a reputation for such behaviour. They are likely to persist in it, but the stories reveal potential negative consequences, as this style does not appear to be common practice in organizations. Research participants found that speaking honestly was sometimes disliked or experienced as confusing by people who preferred to play politics; it was also dangerous because it could lead to confrontation or make them vulnerable. How to judge when to be direct and honest, and the need sometimes to take the consequences, were topics of discussion at the workshops.

Most research participants placed great value on 'truth speaking' when possible. They preferred to decribe their own lives and dilemmas clearly, believing that they would learn more by doing so and be more likely to open up opportunities for development. Kim, for example, was very straightforward about her dissatisfactions and concerns in her annual appraisals. This was a deliberate personal power strategy, clarifying her issues to herself as much as to her 'assessor'. Some people might think this preoccupation with honesty naive. For the women concerned it was a matter of commitment to an alternative style of managing, which they appreciated was demanding and risky in many organizational environments.

STANCES ON POLITICS

Some people deliberately did not play politics. This was usually because they held a vision of a different organizational possibility, a culture of openness, empowerment, decentralization and mutual respect. It was also sometimes because their isolation meant that they did not feel men were available for them to build political alliances with, they were not colleagues in this way (see 'Organizational cultures', p. 300).

In contrast, three people – Dorothy, Christina and Mercedes – held overtly political models of organization, deliberately building alliances and networking. There were differences in how they deployed this approach, partly reflecting their organizational contexts. All seemed, however, to seek maximum influence without placing themselves in the direct line of fire. They believed that change requires readiness which they could enhance but not wholly control. They seemed unlikely to take personal responsibility for disappointing outcomes. They had ways to explain these which reduced the potential for hurt or loss of self-confidence. It was a change attempt that failed, not them personally.

A repeated debate in the literature about women managers is whether 'organizational politics' is a 'reality' of life to which women should adjust. More is obscured than revealed in this simple label. Invoking 'organizational politics' can be a technique for branding women 'naive' and unsuitable for senior management, or for expressing women's disgust at or ambivalence about certain aspects of organizational life. Issues of valuing and interpretation are at stake rather than those of normality and deviation. Certainly many women in this group resisted joining in what they felt were empty, ritualized, often aggressive, games. They favoured alternative visions of effectiveness. And most also saw some forms of political activity as inherent in current cultures. Some research participants, therefore, debated whether to become more political. For example, Mercedes and Julia wanted to make their strengths and ambitions known to people with influence. Again it seems that the women were living between different possibilities, creating their individual resolutions to the dilemmas they faced.

RELATIONAL STYLES OF MANAGEMENT

Some people described their styles as open, collaborative, person-oriented, empowering, based on consensus and equality. Similar themes are implicit in other stories, for example in the ways that Judith and Teresa developed their departments. Such relational

management styles – which incorporate high performance expectations – have recently been identified with women (Rosener,
1990).

Some people had adopted 'male' styles of managing earlier in
their careers, by which they meant being more directive and
assertive. They had variously enjoyed, thrived on, or coped with
what they called 'male' characteristics of organizational cultures
such as aggressive territoriality or late-night drinking. Some had
later deliberately adopted more 'female' approaches, partly because they had become dissatisfied with their previous selves and
partly because more flexibility of style seemed to become acceptable in organizations.

FEMINIST THEMES

Two people – Judith and Ruth – were strongly influenced in the
jobs we discussed by feminist theories. They interpreted their
work situations in terms of power-holding groups and the dynamics of exclusion. These views sometimes brought them into
confrontation, as their actions challenged established cultural
norms and they eschewed 'compromise'. These theories could
reduce their sense of personal blame when their initiatives were
resisted. But their sense of mission also made them feel highly
responsible for persisting in difficult change attempts and exploring issues which other organization members preferred to
ignore. Both are now less likely to align with an overtly feminist
stance, believing this too contentious and likely to evoke unnecessary resistance. They now hold broader views, incorporating
other ways of appreciating organizational dynamics and offering
a more diverse array of operating strategies. One consequence is
less likelihood of experiencing guilt at being unable to live up to
ideals of action.

FIGHTING

A few women came to see their situations as those of fighting the
dominant culture. The stories of Judith, Teresa, Ruth and Patricia
show this trend, for different reasons. Isolation was a likely
consequence; the manager therefore relied heavily on sources of
support external to the organization.

LEARNING

The stories show that many people were frequently reappraising their styles, devising and testing out new strategies and revising their theories of action. Mercedes is a good example of such a review in process. Judith did this in an especially developed way (both in order to survive and be effective in her role and in retrospect), and radically changed her perspectives on organizations and herself as a manager.

The workshops showed that this preoccupation with learning was continuing. Much of the conversation was about strategies for effective action, taking for granted working in male-dominated cultures alongside powerful, politically minded, colleagues, most of whom were men. The participants traded and explored stories of change initiatives, difficult encounters and everyday managing. They debated, for example, whether they *really* acted with integrity – as they aspired to do – if they shaped situations to have the outcomes they thought appropriate. Whilst there were differences in emphasis, they focused on how to build productive relationships with men and how to maintain power. Several now had more senior women colleagues than at previous times in their careers and so were paying attention to these relationships too.

ON REFLECTION

The research participants portrayed their working strategies as mainly active choices. They were both adapting to their environments and often aware that their approach would set them apart. Lack of respect for established organizational practices such as politics was a major cause of many women's disillusion with employment. They quoted this as a primary reason for wanting to leave: not because they could not cope but because these were cultures they did not want to be part of.

Reflecting and moving on

Given the form of this book it would be inappropriate to attempt a neat final chapter, collecting together conclusions or summary statements. Through the text I have hoped to open issues and debate, to explore, and to share the complexities of making sense of this material with you as reader. In this chapter I offer some closing impressions and reflections. The motif of *moving on* is strong for me, but I must necessarily and appropriately leave many avenues for reflection open.

A MAP OF POSSIBILITIES

The stories told here depict a rich, but certainly incomplete, map of possibilities which can be used as a resource. They offer many glimpses of life to ponder, identify with, reject and learn from. During the last six months, for example, I have found key phrases and themes from the research echoing through my own life, particularly when I applied for promotion in my organization. It was helpful to have this diverse realm of voices to inform me. The experiences portrayed and the issues raised are not only relevant to leaving a job or employment, but also to staying and returning. The processes of decision, and those of enduring impasses or testing times, are varied, thought-provoking.

One cycle of renewing energy in relation to employment appeared in the data, and was discussed and affirmed by participants at the research workshops. It is not an inevitable or necessary sequence, but one possibility. The cycle started with a person encountering an organizational culture or job situation which they found both exciting and challenging. They developed their effectiveness and coping abilities, some passing through several phases as they tried different strategies. They typically experienced achievement and satisfaction. But they also became bruised and tired. Some temporarily became habituated to this situation, until a critical incident or insight revealed how unacceptable or stressful it was. Through various processes they left. They then renewed their life energy and sense of their own purposes. The respite and re-membering made them ready to find or encounter new life and career opportunities, and to develop their working strategies and attitudes further.

For various reasons, such as excessive stress or isolation, renewal did not – perhaps could not – usually happen while they were in employment or in a specific job. This raises questions about whether organizations can accommodate, and benefit from, members' development. It could be argued that organizations have other purposes, and that the processes involved might be disruptive. But there is currently much rhetoric about learning companies and transformation. The claims to these descriptions seem shallow unless professional/personal change can be acknowledged, facilitated, or at least allowed.

CONTRIBUTING TO CAREER THEORY ABOUT WOMEN

As the material in this book is from a small and perhaps distinctive sample it can be used as a base for reflection but should not be over-interpreted. It supports suggestions that many women have more open senses of career than do many men (Gutek and Larwood, 1987; Nicholson and West, 1988) and that women may make decisions as life choices rather than simply as career choices (Marshall, 1989). Based on a study of members of the British Institute of Management, for example, Nicholson and West (1988) suggest that two (of five) trends in women's career development are 'their more spontaneous and "existentialist" value-driven career orientations' (p. 216) and their 'retention of high levels of upward and radical career moves much later into their careers than men' (p. 216). But the implications that can be drawn from these apparently consistent findings are far from clear. Nicholson and West suggest that 'important differences in career paths and patterns of men and women' mean that, in these terms, 'men represent the past and women the future of organizational society' (p. 216). This seems a bold and hopeful statement. I remain somewhat wary. Women's flexible career paths could be another way for them to become marginalized organizationally (Still, 1993), unless current organizational changes do radically affect men's career patterns and expectations too.

THE WORK WOMEN DO

One of the striking impressions made by this data, and other studies, is the 'extra' work many women currently do because of gender-related aspects of their roles and of organizational processes. Women are often working simultaneously on several levels. In dealing with tasks and roles there is the continual possibility that, overtly or covertly, gender expectations or associated power differentials may become salient. Operating with these possibilities in mind requires awareness, and care in behaviour. For example, some research participants faced the dilemma of wanting to establish themselves as having organizational status in other people's eyes – to avoid the disadvantages of being misperceived as secretaries or assistants – and yet of not believing in or wanting to reinforce notions of hierarchic power. It seems that many women are trying to transform the received world as they operate, unwilling to adapt fully to current norms and values. They are creating meanings of being senior managers as women as they do so, with few models to draw on. Their behaviours may be active, chosen and seeking to redefine, *and* are still performed within systems of possible constraints whose boundaries are sometimes flexible and contestable and sometimes not (Apter and Garnsey, 1994; Devine, 1994). This adds another dimension of uncertainty to people's lives. Any extra work women do can contribute to tiredness and stress, as the stories show graphically.

A remedy which is often suggested is for women to try less hard, expect less, care less and become more self-protective and distanced. This advice seems potentially sensible; in some measure, learning to become less engaged, or perhaps more selectively engaged, is wise. The stories give examples of people doing this, and show the mixed consequences. But resorting to this remedy may also make people forget the purposes of some sorts of 'trying', and forget the visions of possibility on which they were based. Adopting a more distanced approach to workplace issues reduces the opportunities for organizations to become places of fuller being, where diverse needs, concerns and aspects of self can be acknowledged and expressed rather than having to be controlled, denied and hidden. More engaged organizational cultures would at times facilitate greater congruity of selves, and at others require more openly living with discord. They would probably mean members doing less self-presentational work to achieve acceptance from others, but allowing more in-the-minute vulnerability which would require different forms of awareness, competence and management. Such possibilities might not be easy to live, but are worth exploring. One benefit, if people were less constrained in narrowed role selves, might be more openness to ethical concerns and debate.

ISSUES OF IDENTITY

Much research on women managers explores issues of identity and self, and this has been no exception. Is this preoccupation an indulgence, as Still (1993) believes? She advises women, instead, to focus on achievement, on gaining power in current organizational structures and on identifying common agendas for change. There certainly is the significant danger of individualizing societal or organizational phenomena if identity is the only focus of sense-making. *And*, at this stage in women's development in the organizational world, identity issues are vitally important for several reasons and deserve attention. As the stories illustrate, the women's senses of self were challenged, questioned, cast into doubt or made contentious by the ambiguous social positions they found themselves in. People were often rendered invisible, lacked affirmation or were judged against gender stereotypes. Many lived with incongruities between outer and inner self-images. Many sought ways to judge themselves and their effectiveness, because readily available frameworks devalued them. Many felt that their senses of personal power were undermined by people's reactions to them or by the general dearth of positive models for women on which they and colleagues could draw. So they were often seeking to maintain viable senses of self amidst discordant images and in the face of challenges. Often, it seems, they were experiencing broader social and political pressures translated into their lives. Managing these processes represented a significant further source of demand on their adaptive energies.

Too strongly identifying with and internalizing other people's perceptions of oneself or negative stereotypes of one's social group can have harmful consequences for individual identity. Such identification can cause conflict and disorientation, often leading the person to devalue or lose touch with their own direct experiences (Fanon, 1970; Esterson, 1972). In their extreme these are the processes of 'spoiled identity' (Goffman, 1963). Social roles may subsequently be enacted in a relatively conformist way, as one seeks to please or be accepted by others, whose perceptions are, however, generally unsympathetic projections. In some measure such processes are currently available to women managers to live out. Their force may be accentuated because of mystique about the nature of senior management, making newcomers feel initially that they have much to learn.

Many research participants wanted to feel more authentic and less defined by other people. They especially wanted senses of self which – however multiple and relational these might be – they could validate internally, and which could then provide firm, alive, bases for knowing and acting. Are their wishes naive or a glimpse at an alternative vision of organizing? Who we are can become mirrored in organizations. And organizational practices can become mirrored in how we experience ourselves and act towards others. In these terms the stories reveal potential processes of distortion through which individual lives and organizational cultures were degraded. Are these inevitable in management generally, particularly at these levels? Are organizations with more person-appropriate shapes and healthful fit at their hearts possible (Marshall, 1994)? I believe that they are, but that enacting the authenticity and resonance many research participants were seeking is complex and challenging, and means engaging actively with the opposites of these possibilities.

PATTERNS OF ORGANIZATIONAL CULTURE

Dissatisfaction with 'male-dominated' characteristics of organizational cultures is now frequently identified as a key reason that women managers leave jobs (Rosin and Korabik, 1991; Brett and Stroh, 1994). The data in this book confirms and elaborates this theme. Several women emphasized that it was their disapproval of these behaviour patterns, rather than ultimately feeling unable to cope, which led them to leave. Are some reactions partly because women are relatively 'untrained' as participants (rather than as observers) in these aspects of organizational life? If so, now may be a valuable time to explore alternative ways of relating, while these 'newcomer' perceptions are still fresh and before more women accept current conventions and accommodate their own behaviour.

It is worth wondering what functions behaviours, such as interpersonal aggressiveness, (described in 'Organizational cultures', p. 300), serve, and how amenable they are to change. There are no ready answers to these questions, although they are now receiving attention. Recent analyses suggest, for example, that management can, at least partly, be understood as an arena in which men negotiate the satisfactions and discontents of masculinity (Roper, 1994). Sinclair (1994), studying male chief executives of Australian companies, comes to such a conclusion and argues that the exclusion of women has served to preserve the heroic notion of senior management. Amongst her sample group she found ambivalence about the associated behaviour patterns, a sense of achievement in surviving them and a genuine desire to move beyond them.

How readily, then, can women become involved in shaping organizational cultures? Do covert processes of power undermine their abilities to do so? How much change is already afoot in these terms? Can processes of inclusion–exclusion generally, which affect all sorts of differences, be more openly addressed at senior management levels?

'OVER-SENSITIVE' OR SEEING THE WORLD DIFFERENTLY?

One of the repeated impressions I had in working with the stories was of the women thinking in multiple frameworks, juxtaposing several ways of seeing the world and either reconciling different expectations or living with the disjunctions they faced. (See, for example, 'Judging', p. 157, 'Incongruity', p. 224 and 'Working strategies', p. 312.) They often enriched their appreciations as a result, but simultaneously encountered potential contradictions and difficulties. I was also aware that some women's interpretations of their experiences, such as those of being undermined, could be judged 'over-sensitive'. Late in the study I put these discordant impressions together in the interpretation dilemma: 'Are the research participants "over-sensitive" or seeing the world differently, using multiple frameworks simultaneously?' This is a question research participants often had to live with, but could not easily resolve. In retrospect its either/or form is probably unhelpful, but I was partly addressing the fantasy critical reader, and my need to make such evaluations in my own life. I favoured the latter possibility; the story data and the participants' ways of engaging in the research process supported this. I decided to test the question in a limited form. (There is a parallel with how women managers sought ways to judge themselves, looking for reference points outside their situations: see 'Judging', p. 157.) To do so I asked the research participants to fill in a version of the Washington Sentence Completion Test, which is being used in association with a framework of ego development explicated by Torbert (1991). This was scored professionally and independently. The resulting material generally supported the possibility that the women were seeing the world from multiple frames, allowing them choices of interpretation but also challenging them. I shall report this strand of analysis briefly here. I must emphasize that I am not treating the questionnaire assessments as definitive categorizations, nor the theoretical ideas below as true. They are both used to explore possibilities.

Torbert (1987) develops a framework of ego development stages to study leadership skills and phases of corporate growth. He outlines eight successive stages, each of which can be seen as an implicit frame from which a person views the world and shapes their action in it. Torbet labels the stages: impulsive, opportunist, diplomat, technician, achiever, strategist, magician and ironist (Fisher and Torbert, 1995). In relation to this research I was particularly interested in the transition between *Achiever* and *Strategist*. I shall next outline its key characteristics, and some associated concepts, as a context for placing the research participants.

The Achiever is highly focused on goal accomplishment. They are interested in how to be effective in their wider environment rather than concentrating only on the internal parameters of their tasks. They appreciate complexity and attend to differences between their views and those of other people, valuing teamwork, mutuality and consensus. They are primarily concerned with implementing pre-established strategies and goals rather than questioning these. The Achiever is open to feedback as long as it fits with their existing schemas.

The Achiever views the framework of assumptions he or she 'inhabits', not as a framework at all, but rather as 'the way the world really is'.

(Torbert, 1987: 11)

The transition from Achiever to Strategist is pivotal in Torbert's developmental schema. (It has associations with Bateson's Level III Learning, 1973, and Argyris and Schön's double loop learning, 1978.) It involves:

> becoming aware that different persons, organizations, and cultures are not just different from one another in visible ways but also in terms of the frames through which they interpret events. The evolving *Strategist* begins to realize that all frames, including his or her own, are relative. No frame is easily demonstrable as superior to another because there are no objective criteria outside all frames. Frames are constructed through human interaction, not given by nature. These sorts of realization, experienced not just as intellectual statements but as emotional truths, attune the evolving *Strategist* more deeply than managers at any prior stage to the uniqueness of persons and situations. But they also leave... [them] radically un-anchored in any particular, taken-for-granted frame.

(Torbert, 1987: 143–4)

The Strategist appreciates other people's frames as valid and relevant. The realization that all frames are relative opens up new behavioural possibilities. Unlike the Achiever, the Strategist is able, at times, to 'reframe' their viewpoint and purposes in a situation, and to help others do so. They can consciously seek new frames that accommodate the conflicts and paradoxes of multiple perspectives.

The Strategist position represents a development of competence, but can at times prove highly uncomfortable. Seeing multiple frames and being able to choose new frames of meaning creates life as turbulent and fluid. 'This person can feel virtually paralyzed at moments in terms of taking action' (Torbert, 1987: 144). The Strategist's abilities to see many meanings simultaneously can, however, prompt them to develop encompassing frames that reconcile apparent conflicts and bring order out of seeming chaos. Engaging with the world in this way can mean that the person is both vulnerable and open to transformation.

The above descriptions of the Strategist have many similarities to those of *constructed knowing* developed in research about how 'women view reality and draw conclusions about truth, knowledge, and authority' (pp. 201–2) by Goldberger *et al.* (1987). Their framework contains four other perspectives: silence, received knowledge, subjective knowledge and procedural knowledge; the last is the voice of reason. They describe constructed knowledge (used by 18 per cent of their sample) as integrating the voices.

> Women at this position overcome the notion that there is One Right Answer or a Right Procedure in the search for truth. They see that there are various ways of knowing and methods of analysis. They feel responsible for examining, choosing, questioning, and developing the systems that they will use for constructing knowledge.
>
> (ibid. p. 217)

This knowing is a thoroughly grounded, personal process, not one of the intellect alone.

> For these women, intimate knowledge of the self not only precedes but always accompanies understanding. They are intensely aware of how perceptions are processed through the complex web of personal meanings and values; they resist excluding the self from the process of knowing for the sake of simplicity or 'objectivity'. They strive to find a way of weaving their passions and their intellectual life into some meaningful whole. All the polarities – self and others, thought and feeling, subjective and objective, public and private, personal and impersonal, love and work – lose their saliency. The constructivist mode of thought, in women at least, stresses integration and balance and inclusion rather than exclusion and parsimony.
>
> (ibid.)

The descriptions of the Strategist and of constructed knowledge seem a little idealized, but they represent a significant theme in discussions of competence in postmodern Western society. In this view, which I support in outline, people are advantaged by appreciating that truth is constructed and multiple.

In this sample of research participants, eleven of the sixteen scored at later ego development stages in Torbert's schema. Four scored at the Strategist stage and seven at the transition moving to this stage from Achiever (i.e. they were demonstrating qualities of both frames). This makes them an unusual group (as the professional scorer spontaneously commented). In two studies of senior managers (reported in Torbert, 1991), for example, 14 per cent of participants were classified as Strategists (with none beyond this stage), and 33 per cent and 40 per cent as Achievers. The stories suggest that development can be associated (causality cannot be inferred) either with leaving or with finding ways to stay in employment (as Julia and Mercedes did). The specific details and workings through are likely to be more important than these broad classifications of experience.

Women managers are often depicted as speaking multiple languages because the worlds around them offer discordant expectations and require various processes of translation between available codes of meaning (Marshall, 1984, 1993a). This can be a burden, and has often been portrayed as such. It can also be a base for living in complex worlds, holding multiple perspectives and leaving behind notions that there is one dominant, 'right' form. I believe that organizations need people who have access to a range of frameworks in this way, and are aware of the personal, social and power-political processes through which frames are created, maintained and resisted (Belenky *et al.*, 1986; Torbert, 1991; Marshall, 1993b). Such talents may not, however, be readily welcomed in many current organizational cultures, and may prove disruptive.

It is likely that women who have succeeded organizationally have encountered sufficient 'challenges' of conflicting expectations (perhaps less available to male colleagues), to prompt their development towards appreciating multiple frameworks. This development may, ironically, lead them to question organizational cultures and goals, and therefore make career movement more likely.

Living with multiple frames is no easy or comfortable matter, as the stories show and the descriptions of the Strategist affirm. Key challenges are choosing sufficient truths to live by, realizing that things will unravel, managing to avoid undue anxiety and adopting an ever-inquiring attitude to encounter change as it occurs. In complex situations where gender themes are interwoven with other dynamics, I think that people also need to send multiple messages – for example being willing to be apparently self-contradictory or showing both strength and vulnerability – to avoid becoming trapped in any one frame of other people's (or their own) perceptions. (They cannot, however, control how such behaviour will be perceived.) Multiple signalling may help to create more play in organizations (see p. 330), and to open the field for change.

Applying the themes explored above to theoretical sense-making, I believe that entertaining multiple possibilities is generally valuable. I, therefore, particularly regret that there is so little acceptance of feminist analyses as available (but not necessarily exclusive) interpretive frames in mainstream organization theory literatures. This reduces the richness of interpretation, choice and action for academics and managers alike.

WOMEN'S REPRESENTATION IN MANAGEMENT

The stories reveal some of the organizational and individual processes through which women may be displaced or may disappear from senior jobs. In some cases the wider operation of these processes was noted. For example, Mercedes identified how restructuring management can remove the level which women have only recently reached in significant numbers. They may be considered insufficiently qualified for the enhanced-status posts created as a result, and find themselves effectively demoted. This is happening in various occupational sectors.

Whilst leaving may mean individuals taking power in their lives, more generally it may also appear to involve women 'leaving' management and senior decision-making posts to men (Still, 1993). If this is the case, and no other processes counteract this trend or its effects, it is truly troubling. Change could be no change after all.

I do not interpret these stories and the research of people like Rosin and Korabik (1991) and Brett and Stroh (1994) as indicative of a major withdrawal from employment by women. Looking at where the research participants were at the close of the study is interesting in this regard (see Table 8, p. 297). Most are in either employment or self-employment. Their job positions suggest slightly less organizational seniority overall than previously. Some are, however, experiencing increased influence from independent positions, and consultants are enjoying being able to shape their own working contexts and conditions. Those who are at senior management and board levels are now more likely to have a few female peers. Most research participants have a greater sense of choice and fit about their lives. Some are exploring ways to stay in jobs – despite encountering new challenges – wanting to do so without paying such a high price in terms of their energies.

I believe that, for the moment, many women have to live with their potential marginality in organizations. This places their inclusion and potential influence, especially informally, in doubt (see 'Inclusion', p. 154). Seeking full membership of the senior management community they have 'joined' may well be a false trail. It is worth questioning what kinds of inclusion are valuable in times of increasing diversity. Conformity or recognition of colleagues as 'of like kind' is no longer an appropriate model. In these circumstances people who perceive themselves as potentially different, whether women or men, may be able to develop alternative strategies. One possibility is to award oneself inclusion, or to challenge oneself about why it feels in doubt. Another is to live with aware and chosen marginality, being both a member and suitably detached. This may involve calculating how to achieve sufficient inclusion to exercise influence. These strategies will be facilitated by having allies, sources of grounding and support, and friends willing both to support and challenge. It is also worth women doubting whether men's apparent sense of kin is that solid or stable, finding ways to inquire about this, and treating male colleagues as if they are diverse. There will be other alternatives.

The stories *do* signal significant dissatisfaction (which I believe is widespread), with employment and organizational cultures in their current dominant forms, which would be best heeded. In the longer term, this could and should be a powerful force for revision. Change will not be significant unless the organizational world in which women join is transformed. A sense that women's expressions of discontent are not signs of their inadequacy but a generally relevant warning is gaining some currency. Barrentine (1993), for example, collects together (United States) women executives' and consultants' ideas for incorporating more interdependence, balance, authenticity, openness, intuition and sense of community into the workplace. She explains why the book is entitled *When the Canary Stops Singing*:

> Carol Frenier and three female business associates. . . were trying to understand the frustrations each of them felt working

in the corporate environment. Many of their friends and co-workers were experiencing similar difficulties. It occurred to them that perhaps women were to business what the canary once was to the coal miners – when the canary stopped singing, it was a warning that the environment was too toxic for living creatures. Perhaps women in business are harbingers of a needed transformation. . . . The challenge for business is to create more humane and nurturing workplaces for everyone.

(pp. 9–10)

The basic tenets of organizational life, career development and employment do now seem to be opening for review. Women's voices can and should be strong in debates. I would particularly like to see a questioning of the primacy employment and organizations take in many people's lives, and of extended working hours, which often seem to be surrogate measures of commitment but do severely curtail people's life and health choices.

HOW 'CLEVER' DO WOMEN HAVE TO BE?

In later conversations several research participants told me either that they would do things differently *and better* next time or that this is already happening. They were reporting processes of learning which delighted me. One such account is at the heart of Judith's story, for example. *And* I became wary. By developing greater skills to handle confronting organizational contexts, women can (again) take responsibility, set themselves to become superwomen who are able to survive and facilitate change. Recognizing that – and how – they may sometimes contribute to sustaining unequal power relationships or gendered expectations is valuable. So is appreciating that some people's aggressive behaviour may result from defensiveness in the face of potential change rather than from gender bias. But portraying women as able to be wholly responsible and skilled seems as inappropriate as portraying them as wholly victims. This route could lead solo women to try to do change work for the whole organization. (They will sometimes succeed. I do not mean to dismiss this as a viable possibility.) This agenda is likely to be ineffective unless other people, including men if they hold positions of power, are actively and reflectively involved.

And there is a tension, which some people discussed at the research workshops. Exploring issues of gender, navigating through organizational life and creating an alive career can all become such serious and earnest endeavours. People wanted more sense of experimentation, fun and play. Some reported how they were achieving this. Ruth, for example, was being playful and provocative about gender stereotypes in ways which contributed to organizational fun – as well as probably puzzlement – and had the potential to prompt developing awareness without malicious or defensive combat. Several people justified their changed attitudes by seeing them as the outcome of midlife reviews, quoting 'you only have one life'. They perhaps have some choices *because* they have proved themselves successful in a major evaluative framework of current Western societies, that of employment.

'THANK YOU FOR TELLING MY STORY' – 'DO YOU THINK REPORTING THIS RESEARCH IS REALLY WISE?'

As I was completing this book, I had an opportunity to discuss the research at a Women in Leadership conference at Edith Cowan University, Perth, Western Australia. In question-time I received the two comments above, which summarized divergent feedback from elsewhere. Several people were glad that stories akin to theirs were being told, and/or wanted to hear of other women's experiences to inform their own lives. One questioner was more doubtful. She said that as so many gains have now been made by and for women, it might not be the right time to express any doubts or report negative experiences. These might unnecessarily complicate the situation or lose hard-won support and acceptance. This dilemma has been at the heart of this project.

Writing this book has felt like breaking silence, particularly because I have not tried strictly to control the sense-making implied, but have acknowledged it as contentious. This feels like a voicing of experiences and views which are seldom heard, alongside those which are more familiar. I hope that the women's accounts will be respected and believed as sense-making they lived, and will not be dismissed. I expect that I have made women, and myself, vulnerable, but I/we have done so with longer-term purposes in mind. I hope that this book will raise questions, prompt debate which will prove excitingly inconclusive and encourage people to entertain different possibilities. Patrolling silence or seeking to tell only palatable truths requires a lot of energy, inhibits creative expression, and may paradoxically reinforce constraints the speaker overtly opposes. Seeking to maintain control is often futile; what is being denied can lurk, barely disguised, just below the surface.

I doubt if we (women or men) can engage in significant change if we remain comfortable, adjusting within dominant perspectives and assumptions of the world, answering questions and challenges set by others. People hoping for change must be willing to be disturbing and disturbed (see 'Change agent roles' p. 188); their intent does not, however, have to be adversarial or combative. I also realize that there must be some appropriate protection in these processes. Many environments are still hostile to women's meanings; the paths to rejection and martyrdom can be surprisingly short.

EXPLORING THROUGH SENSE-MAKING

Moving sense-making about women managers and organizational practices on requires, I believe, wholehearted expressions of what appears to be. These are not bids for ultimate truth, but expressions in the moment, open to review, 'truths' to be held lightly. I believe that engaging in debate and action in such forms opens the way for radical change to emerge. I have used three images to guide my processes of inquiry in this study. Each has been a way of seeking to hold interpretations open or not to push viable sense-making beyond its limits. My images have been in the following realms:

Vision – I have been turning things in the light, taking different views, wondering about interpretations (See 'Introduction', p. 3 and 'Making sense', p. 9);
Touch – I have been pulling the strands of wool (in the tangle) just so far so that they remain pliable and do not become too tense (See 'Inquiring in practice', p. 23);
Voice and hearing – I have read the stories and other sections aloud, listening for the note to ring 'true' and noticing and adjusting when it does not (See 'Inquiring in practice', p. 23).

These practices have been my ways to judge authenticity, the 'truth' appropriate to this telling of the stories and accompanying narrative. I have also always realized that not far away there could be another possible view, feeling or voice which could enhance, deconstruct or shift the meaning. I offer this book as an exploration in form, a way of speaking and inquiring whilst appreciating these shifting processes of sense-making.

Appendix

The initial invitation for people to participate in the research

**RESEARCH WITH SENIOR WOMEN MANAGERS
WHO LEAVE EMPLOYMENT: AN INVITATION
TO PARTICIPATE**

Over the last few years I have been intrigued by stories of women who have reached senior management jobs and then decided to leave employment, usually with no immediate plans for the next steps in their lives. Such stories are told as 'test cases' by different groups of people to prove different points. Sometimes they are used to prove that women are not suited to senior positions after all, sometimes that organizations are still essentially hostile to women's abilities, and so on. Research in North America is picking up similar cases and puzzling over them. Some surveys suggest that there are a mix of reasons which prompt women out of employment, and that having children (one very ready explanation) is only one.

Having spoken to some women who have made this move, and sometimes wanted to leave myself, I decided I would like to tell the stories of leaving from some women's points of view. I am embarking on a research project in which I shall work with about a dozen women to produce their case studies. These will then form a book, to be published by Routledge (who have given me a small Research Prize to contribute to expenses) in 1993. [The research and writing took longer than anticipated; publication is therefore in 1995.] My idea is to tell appropriately individual stories, rather than put people in boxes.

I am looking for suitable participants. I want to find people who have left or are leaving senior organization positions without other immediate career plans. This is, however, an inevitably hazy

distinction, the haziness reflecting important issues. I shall therefore include in the sample a range of situations: people who clearly
meet the specification above, and others who have left for a mix
of motives, have been forced to leave, want to leave but have not
yet decided to, and so on.

The people involved will have been in middle or senior
management, and shown considerable commitment to employment. I want the sample to provide valuable contrasts, given what
we know about women's access to senior jobs. Local government,
health services, banking and industry will probably be included.
The study will be small scale and qualitative. Its validity, in
research method terms, will come from taking a depth approach
and working collaboratively with participants to arrive at interpretations.

And who am I? I am a Senior Lecturer in Organizational
Behaviour in the School of Management, University of Bath. I am
married with two children, aged 9 and 11. I have been researching
and writing about women managers since 1977 (before that I was
into job stress). My best known publication is *Women Managers:
Travellers in a Male World* (Wiley, 1984). In that book I questioned
whether women should be expected to adapt to organizations and
models of management which are largely derived from men's
experiences and styles. I think this is a limited meaning of 'equal
opportunities', and have suggested alternative strategies. I have
also looked at organizational cultures and how they change or
remain the same. For example, I jointly produced a Workbook for
people in local government to use to analyse culture. I do describe
myself as a feminist, but warily. I do not blame 'everything' on
men, or on women. Rather, I am interested in achieving organizations and work practices that value women and men equally,
and allow everyone flexibility in their identity and life pattern.

If you are interested, please read below for details of the kind
of participation I am looking for. If you know someone you think
suitable, please pass this invitation on.

PROPOSED RESEARCH APPROACH

Please note: The 'full' participation outlined in this invitation may
not be appropriate to you. If, instead, you would like to write or
phone with ideas, suggestions or experiences, I shall be glad to

hear from you. I would like to hear from a wider network than the few people I can contact by interview.

With this invitation I am particularly looking for the twelve women whose case studies will be the core of the project. I want to work with each participant to produce an agreed profile of their situation and decision-making, which will then form one chapter of the book. I want to portray how the woman concerned would tell and interpret her story, not fit it into other people's boxes. I propose the following possible process, but am open to other suggestions.

We would meet for an initial conversation (of approx. one and a half to two hours), in which we agree the ground-rules of our 'contract' and the manager tells her story, facilitated by me interviewing if appropriate. I am happy to discuss my own views and experiences if relevant. I would prefer to tape-record this meeting as this leaves me free to concentrate on the discussion.

Following this I will take responsibility for having the tape (if used) transcribed and writing an initial draft of the case study. At the first meeting we will have decided how best to proceed to develop the case to our mutual satisfaction. This may involve meeting again or exchanges of letters and telephone calls. Should it become necessary, the woman manager will have right of veto over what appears in 'her' chapter.

Later, I plan to invite all participants to a one-day, collaborative inquiry workshop. The agenda would be to review together their experiences of employment and of 'leaving' (in whatever form this has taken), and to discuss issues of mutual interest. I would want to be able to use this material in publications, and would negotiate a specific 'contract' at the time.

MY IDEAS FOR THE BOOK

I expect the book to contain approximately fifteen chapters:

- the twelve case studies;
- an introductory chapter outlining the topic and reviewing popular and academic coverage;
- a chapter on research methodology; and
- a closing chapter reviewing the cases as a whole and reflecting on them theoretically – for example, their relevance to understanding organizational culture, careers and so on.

I would like to circulate the three non-case-study chapters and receive feedback on them. I see them as a place to put my views, and to pursue my more academic concerns. I do not expect to criticize individual participants in this, but can imagine including them as examples of some theoretical or applications point or other. I do not want to give away right of veto in respect of these chapters. If there are conflicts about this material, which I doubt, they will need to be discussed and resolved to the satisfaction of both parties. (As a final resort, any participant has the right to withdraw her chapter from the book, should that become necessary.) [I did not eventually circulate non-story chapters, for several reasons. I developed the form of the book differently, as explained in the text. Consulting about the detailed drafts therefore seemed inappropriate and would have been over-whelming – for research participants and me. Instead, people who attended research workships discussed emerging themes with me. Non-attendees were sent schematic notes for information and comment. These changes in arrangements were discussed and agreed with participants.]

I do not expect the people involved to be named in the book, or identifiable from their profile. Some participants may choose to be.

OTHER PUBLICATIONS

I shall want to draw on the material for other publications, and for research presentations. This can be done in full consultation with participants.

I do not expect to have answered all possible queries at this stage. We shall need to discuss further issues as the research progresses.

If this invitation is of interest, please do get in touch with me.

Dr Judi Marshall

Bibliography

Apter, T. and Garnsey, E. (1994) 'Enacting inequality: structure, agency and gender', *Women's Studies International Forum*, 17 (1) 19–31.

Argyris, C. and Schön, D. A. (1978) *Organizational Learning: A Theory of Action Perspective*, Reading, Mass.: Addison Wesley.

Bakan, D. (1966) *The Duality of Human Existence*, Boston: Beacon Press.

Barrentine, P. (ed.) (1993) *When the Canary Stops Singing: Women's Perspectives on Transforming Business*, San Francisco: Barrett-Koehler.

Bateson, G. (1973) *Steps to an Ecology of Mind*, London: Paladin Books.

Bateson, M. C. (1989) *Composing a Life*, New York: Plume.

Belenky, M.F., Clinchy, B.McV., Goldberger, N.R. and Tarule, J.M. (1986) *Women's Ways of Knowing: the Development of Self, Voice and Mind*, New York: Basic Books.

Brett, J. M. and Stroh, L.K. (1994) 'Turnover of female managers', in M.J. Davidson (ed.) *Women in Management: Current Research Issues*, London: Paul Chapman, 55–64.

Brown, R. (1989) *Being Brown: A Very Public Life*, Toronto: Random House.

Calas, M. and Smircich, L . (1992) 'Using the F-word: feminist theories and the social consequences of organizational research', in A. Mills and P. Tancred (eds) *Gendering Organizational Analysis*, Newbury Park, Calif.: Sage Publications, 222–234.

—— (1993) 'Dangerous liaisons: the "Feminine in Management" meets "Globalization"', *Business Horizons*, March-April, 71–81.

Coe, T. (1992) *The Keys to the Men's Club: Opening the Doors to Women in Management*, Corby, Northants: British Institute of Management.

Collinson, D. and Hearn, J. (1994) 'Naming men as men: implications for work, organization and management', *Gender, Work and Organization*, 1 (1) 2–22.

Cooper, C.L. and Marshall, J. (1979) *Executives under Pressure*, London: Macmillan.

Denzin, N.K. (1989), *Interpretive Biography*, Newbury Park, Calif.: Sage Publications.

—— (1992) *Symbolic Interactionism and Cultural Studies: the Politics of Interaction*, Oxford: Blackwell.

Devine, F. (1994) 'Segregation and supply: preferences and plans among 'self-made' women', *Gender, Work and Organization*, 1 (2) 94–109.

Dix, C. (1990) *A Chance for the Top: The Lives of Women Business Graduates*, London: Bantam Press.

Esterson, A. (1972) *The Leaves of Spring: Schizophrenia, Family and Sacrifice*, Harmondsworth, Middx: Pelican.

Fanon, F. (1970) *Black Skin, White Masks*, London: Paladin.

Fisher, D. and Torbert, W. R. (1995) *Personal and Organizational Transformation: Continual Quality Improvement and Beyond*, London: McGraw-Hill.

Freeman, S. J.M. (1990) *Managing Lives: Corporate Women and Social Change*, Amherst, Mass.: University of Massachusetts Press.

Gallese, L.R. (1985) *Women Like Us*, New York: William Morrow.

Gallos, J.V. (1989) 'Exploring women's development: implications for career theory, practice and research', in M.B. Arthur, D.T. Hall and B.S. Lawrence (eds) *Handbook of Career Theory*, Cambridge: Cambridge University Press, 110–132.

Gilligan, C. (1982) *In a Different Voice: Psychological Theory and Women's Development*, Cambridge, Mass.: Harvard University Press.

Goffman, E. (1963) *Stigma: Notes on the Management of Spoiled Identity*, Englewood Cliffs, New Jersey: Prentice-Hall.

Goldberger, N. R., Clinchy, B. McV., Belenky, M. F. and Tarule, J. M. (1987) 'Women's ways of knowing: on gaining a voice', in P. Shaver and C. Hendrick (eds) *Sex and Gender*, Newbury Park, Calif.: Sage Publications.

Gordon, S. (1991) *Prisoners of Men's Dreams: Striking Out for a New Feminine Future*, Boston: Little, Brown.

Gutek, B. A. (1993) 'Changing the status of women in management', *Applied Psychology: An International Review*, 42 (4) 301–312.

Gutek, B. A. and Larwood, L. (eds) (1987) *Women's Career Development*, Newbury Park, Calif.: Sage Publications.

Hall, M. (1989) 'Private experiences in the public domain: lesbians in organizations', in J. Hearn, D.L. Sheppard, P. Tancred-Sheriff and G. Burrell (eds) *The Sexuality of Organization*, London: Sage Publications, 125–138.

Hammond, V. (1992) 'Opportunity 2000: a culture change approach to equal opportunity', *Women in Management Review*, 7 (7) 3–10.

Handy, C. (1989) *The Age of Unreason*, London: Business Books.

Hennig, M. and Jardim, A. (1978) *The Managerial Woman*, London: Marion Boyars.

Hewlett, S.A. (1986) *A Lesser Life: the Myth of Women's Liberation in America*, New York: William Morrow.

Hollway, W. (1989) *Subjectivity and Method in Psychology: Gender, Meaning and Science*, London: Sage Publications.

hooks, b. (1984) *Feminist Theory: from Margin to Center*, Boston, Mass.: South End Press.

—— (1989) *Talking Back: Thinking Feminist, Thinking Black*, Boston, Mass.: South End Press.

Institute of Management (1994) 'Fewer women managers: the number of women managers in Britain's top organizations is falling', press release, 3 May.

Kanter, R.M. (1977) *Men and Women of the Corporation*, New York: Basic Books.

Kitzinger, C. (1987) *The Social Construction of Lesbianism*, London: Sage Publications.

Lee, M. (1994) 'The isolated manager: walking the boundaries of the microculture', *British Academy of Management Annual Conference Proceedings*, 111–128.

Lincoln, Y.S. and Guba, E.G. (1985) *Naturalistic Inquiry*, Beverly Hills, Calif.: Sage Publications.

Loden, M. (1985), *Feminine Leadership, or How to Succeed in Business without Being One of the Boys*, London: Times Books.

Maddox, S. and Parkin, D. (1993) 'Gender cultures: women's choices and strategies at work', *Women in Management Review*, 8 (2) 3–9.

Mann, S. (1992) 'Telling a life story: implications for research', *Management Education and Development*, 23 (3) 271–280.

Marshall, J. (1981) 'Making sense as a personal process', in P. Reason and J. Rowan (eds.) *Human Inquiry*, Chichester: John Wiley, 395–399.

—— (1984) *Women Managers: Travellers in a Male World*, Chichester: John Wiley.

—— (1989) 'Re-visioning career concepts: a feminist invitation', in M. B. Arthurs, D.T. Hall and B. S. Lawrence (eds) *A Handbook of Career Theory*, Cambridge: Cambridge University Press, 275–291.

—— (1991) 'Senior women managers who leave employment', *Women in Management Review and Abstracts*, 6 (3), 4–10.

—— (1992) 'Researching women in management as a way of life', *Journal of Management Education and Development*, Autumn, 23 (3), 279–287.

—— (1993a) 'Viewing organizational communication from a feminist perspective: a critique and some offerings', in S. Deetz (ed.) *Communication Yearbook, Volume 16*, Newbury Park, Calif.: Sage Publications, 122–143.

—— (1993b) 'Patterns of cultural awareness as coping strategies for women managers', in S. E. Kahn and B. C. Long (eds) *Work, Women and Coping: A Multidisciplinary Approach to Workplace Stress*, Montreal: McGill-Queen's University Press, 90–110.

—— (1993c) 'Organizational cultures and women managers: exploring the dynamics of resilience', *Applied Psychology: An International Review*, 42 (4), 313–322.

—— (1994) 'Re-visioning organizations by developing female values', in R. Boot, J. Lawrence and J. Morris (eds) *Managing the Unknown: By Creating New Futures*, London: McGraw-Hill, 165–183.

—— (1995) 'Feminism' (extended glossary entry), in N. Nicholson (ed.) *Blackwell Dictionary of Organizational Behaviour*, Oxford: Blackwell.

Marshall, J. and McLean, A.J. (1985) 'Exploring organisational culture as a route to organisational change', in V. Hammond (ed.) *Current Research in Management*, London: Frances Pinter, 2–20.

—— (1988) *Cultures at Work: How to Identify and Understand Them*, Luton: Local Government Training Board.

Marshall, J. and Reason, P. (1987) 'Research as personal process', in D.

Boud and V. Griffin (eds) *Appreciating Adult Learning: From the Learner's Perspective*, London: Kogan Page, 112–126.

—— (1993) 'Adult learning in collaborative action research: reflections on the supervision process', *Studies in Continuing Education*, 15 (2), 117–132.

Martin, J. (1990) 'Deconstructing organizational taboos: the suppression of gender conflict in organizations', *Organization Science*, 1 (4), 339–359.

—— (1994) 'The organization of exclusion: institutionalization of sex inequality, gendered faculty jobs and gendered knowledge in organizational theory and research', *Organization*, 1 (2) 401–431.

Mills, A.J. (1991) 'Organization as gendered communication act', *Canadian Journal of Communication*, 16, 381–398.

Mills, A. J. and Murgatroyd, S. J. (1991) *Organizational Rules: A Framework for Understanding Organizational Action*, Milton Keynes: Open University Press.

Morgan, G. (1983) *Beyond Method*, Beverly Hills, Calif.: Sage Publications.

Nicholson, N. and West, M. (1988) *Managerial Job Change: Men and Women in Transition*, Cambridge: Cambridge University Press.

Piercy, M. (1973) *To Be of Use*, Garden City, NY: Doubleday.

Pringle, R. (1989) 'Bureaucracy, rationality and sexuality: the case of secretaries', in J. Hearn, D.L. Sheppard, P. Tancred-Sheriff and G. Burrell, *The Sexuality of Organization*, London: Sage Publications.

Rakow, L.F. (1986) 'Rethinking gender research in communication', *Journal of Communication*, 36, 11–26.

Reason, R. and Rowan, J. (eds) (1981) *Human Inquiry*, Chichester: John Wiley.

Roper, M. (1994) *Masculinity and the British Organization Man since 1945*, Oxford: Oxford University Press.

Rosener, J.B. (1990) 'Ways women lead', *Harvard Business Review*, Nov-Dec, 119–125.

Rosin, H.M. and Korabik, K. (1991) 'Workplace variables, affective responses, and intention to leave among women managers', *Journal of Occupational Psychology*, 64, 317–330.

—— (1992) 'Corporate flight of women managers: moving from fiction to fact', *Women in Management Review*, 7 (3), 31–35.

—— (1995), 'Organizational experiences and propensity to leave: a multivariate investigation of men and women managers', *Journal of Vocational Behaviour*, 46 (1), 1–16.

Schein, E. (1985) *Organizational Culture and Leadership: a Dynamic View*, San Francisco: Jossey-Bass.

Schein, V.E. (1976) 'Think manager – think male', *The Atlanta Economic Review*, March-April, 21–24.

Sheppard, D.L. (1989) 'Organizations, power and sexuality: the image and self-image of women managers', in J. Hearn, D.L. Sheppard, P. Tancred-Sheriff and G. Burrell (eds) *The Sexuality of Organization*, London: Sage Publications, 139–157.

Sinclair, A. (1994) *Trials at the Top: Chief Executives Talk about Men, Women and the Australian Executive Culture*, Melbourne: University of Melbourne: Australian Centre.

Spender, D. (1980) *Man Made Language*, London: Routledge & Kegan Paul.

—— (1982) *Women of Ideas (and What Men Have Done to Them)*, London: Ark Paperbacks.

—— (1984) 'Defining reality: a powerful tool', in C. Kramarae, M. Schulz and W.M. O'Barr (eds) *Language and Power*, Beverly Hills, Calif.: Sage Publications, 194–205.

Srivastva, S., Obert, S.L. and Neilsen, E.H. (1977) 'Organizational analysis through group processes: a theoretical perspective for organization development', in C.L. Cooper (ed.) *OD in the UK and USA: A Joint Evaluation*, London: Macmillan Press.

Stanley, L. and Wise, S. (1993) *Breaking Out Again: Feminist Ontology and Epistemology*, London: Routledge.

Statham, A. (1987) 'The gender model revisited: differences in the management styles of men and women', *Sex Roles*, 16 (7/8), 409–429.

Still, L. (1993) *Where to from Here? The Managerial Woman in Transition*, Sydney, NSW: Business and Professional Publishing.

Stroh, L.K. and Senner, J.T. (1994) 'Female top level executives: turnover, career limitations, and attitudes towards the work place', *Industrial Relations Research Association Proceedings*, December.

Tannen, D. (1990) *You Just Don't Understand: Women and Men in Conversation*, New York: Ballantine Books.

Taylor, A. (1986) 'Why women managers are bailing out', *Fortune*, 18 August, 16–23.

Torbert, W. R. (1976) *Creating a Community of Inquiry: Conflict, Collaboration, Transformation*, New York: Wiley.

—— (1987) *Managing the Corporate Dream: Restructuring for Long-term Success*, Homewood, Illinois: Dow Jones-Irwin.

—— (1991) *The Power of Balance: Transforming Self, Society and Scientific Inquiry*, Newbury Park, Calif.: Sage Publications.

Trost, C. (1990) 'Women managers quit not for family but to advance their corporate climb', *The Wall Street Journal*, 2 May, B1 and B4.

Vince, R. (1991) 'Management by avoidance: male power in local government', *Management Education and Development*, 22 (1) 50–59.

Watzlawick, P., Weakland, J. and Fisch, R. (1974) *Change: Principles of Problem Formulation and Problem Resolution*, New York: W.W. Norton.

West, C. and Zimmerman, D.H. (1991) 'Doing gender', in J. Lorber and S.A. Farrell (eds) *The Social Construction of Gender*, London: Sage Publications, 13–37.

Index